The SEWA Movement
and Rural Development

The SEWA Movement and Rural Development

The Banaskantha and Kutch Experience

Daniel W. Crowell

SAGE Publications
New Delhi   Thousand Oaks   London

First published in 2003 by

Second Printing 2003   **Sage Publications India Pvt Ltd**
B-42, Panchsheel Enclave
New Delhi 110 017

<table>
<tr><td>Sage Publications Inc
2455 Teller Road
Thousand Oaks, California 91320</td><td></td><td>Sage Publications Ltd
6 Bonhill Street
London EC2A 4PU</td></tr>
</table>

Published by Tejeshwar Singh for Sage Publications India Pvt Ltd, typeset by C&M Digitals (P) Ltd., Chennai in 10/12 Elegant Garamond and printed at Chaman Enterprises, New Delhi.

Library of Congress Cataloging-in-Publication Data

Crowell, Daniel W., 1975–
The SEWA movement and rural development: the Banaskantha and Kutch experience/Daniel W. Crowell.
      p. cm.
Includes index.
    1. Self-Employed Women's Association (Ahmedâbâd, India)–History. 2. Women in economic development–India–Banâs Kântha. 3. Women in economic development–India–Kutch. 4. Women in rural development–Indian–Banâs Kântha. 5. Women in rural development–Indian–Kutch. 6. Economic development–Citizen participation–Indian–Kutch. 7. Economic development–Citizen participation–Indian–Banâs Kântha. 8. Banâs Kântha (India)–Social conditions. 9. Kutch (India)–Social conditions. 10. Banâs Kântha (India)–Economic conditions. 11. Kutch (India)–Economic conditions. I. Title

HQ1240.5.I4 C76   305.42′0954′75–dc21   2003   2002190893

ISBN: 0–7619–9581–1 (US-Hb)   81-7829-189-4 (India-Hb)
      0–7619–9582–X (US-Pb)   81-7829-190-8 (India-Pb)

Sage Production: J. Sri Raman, Abhirami Sriram, Rajib Chatterjee, Sushanta Gayen and Santosh Rawat

To my parents, Helen and Greg Crowell,

whose optimism and hard work are
my inspiration

and

to Rameshbhai,

who laid out the foundation in Banaskantha
on which most of SEWA's rural organizing has grown.

CONTENTS

List of Abbreviations and Acronyms

ASAG	Ahmedabad Study Action Group
BDMSA	Banaskantha DWCRA Mahila SEWA Association
BPL	Below Poverty Line
CHC	Community Health Center
DMI	Disaster Mitigation Institute
DRDA	District Rural Development Agency
DWCRA	Development of Women and Children in Rural Areas
FPI	Foundation for Public Interest
FPS	Fair Price Shop
GSFDC	Gujarat State Forestry Development Corporation
GSRDC	Gujarat State Rural Development Corporation
GWSSB	Gujarat Water, Sewerage and Supply Board
GSWDC	Gujarat State Women's Development Corporation
IIM	Indian Institute of Management
IPCL	Indian Petro-Chemicals Limited
KDRDA	Kutch District Rural Development Association
NABARD	National Bank for Agriculture and Rural Development
PHC	Primary Health Center
SEWA	Self-Employed Women's Association
TLA	Textile Labor Association
TRYSEM	Training of Rural Youth for Self-Employment

Foreword

This book describes and analyzes SEWA's rural organizing process, beginning with its early efforts in the semi-arid area of Banaskantha, using water as an entry point. Young and new to the field, I was assigned the post of District Coordinator of Banaskantha. The area of Banaskantha was completely new to SEWA, as was the task of organizing indigent rural women on the basis of their work. SEWA had no blueprint to work from, and no experience in a place so far away from Ahmedabad. Therefore, it became a formidable as well as an exciting challenge to initiate the entire process with a new approach.

Until then, I had neither lived nor worked in a rural area, let alone a drought-prone, resource-poor area such as I found myself in. However, I made the town of Radhanpur my home and my headquarters, and commenced the work. Out of my newfound commitment to SEWA, and out of SEWA's commitment to the rural development, came the realization that unless I shared the life experiences and living standards of our members and organizers, I would not be able to understand their issues. Therefore, the shift for me was not only one of geography but also one of lifestyle.

In my efforts, I was continuously guided, motivated, supported and encouraged by the late Shri Rameshbhai Bhatt, founder and director of the Foundation for Public Interest. He was a true mentor. His guidance deepened my understanding of poverty and rural development, and I also learned from him the meaning of mentorship, which would become essential to my future efforts in building a team and decentralizing the organizing process.

The early days were challenging in many ways. At times, I would be mentally and physically exhausted after a long day in the villages. On returning to the Radhanpur office, I would crave for cool air and cold water. But the reality was that there was not even electricity! I would feel agitated by the multitude of inconveniences and absence of comforts, only to be reminded the next minute that this was how the thousands of women I worked with lived everyday. In so questioning my own frustrations, I came to understand my mission, its means and its ends better.

Such experiences also taught me to imbibe the true values of simplicity, and gave me the strength to try to make my own life a reflection of those principles. Through these early challenges that I had to face for the first time, a personal journey began to acquire the structure and meaning described in this book.

My immediate task was to build a rapport with the local rural women and their communities, and to identify and build a local team of organizers. There was no schedule, as work became all-consuming. Very often, the rural women, along with their husbands, would visit the office at night or early in the morning. In one instance, my first encounter of the day took place at 6 A.M.!

One day, a resolute woman named Puriben arrived with a group of women from her village. It was only 6 A.M. and I expressed my surprise at seeing them so early. "Our first bus leaves the village at 5 A.M.," they explained to me. We sat down together, had tea and breakfast, discussed the needs of the village and, to this day, have continued to work according to our plans. Now, however, we usually meet a little later in the day!

In fact, Puriben has become a very dynamic leader within the district federation and within SEWA. It was in this capacity, two years later, that Puriben narrated a story in a meeting, harking back to our first encounter: "We really wanted to check. We villagers wondered why an outsider, a city-dweller, should take all this trouble to come and work here. So we went early in the morning to see what she was doing, how she would respond. We found that it was all true, what we were told about SEWA and its office!"

The fact of my being based in Radhanpur, and being available day and night on working days and holidays alike, helped tremendously in building a rapport and confidence among SEWA's future members. There were also several occasions such as Janmashtami (Lord Krishna's birthday) or Id, which I celebrated with our members and organizers. These occasions also offered local families the opportunity to learn about the work of SEWA members and organizers. The understanding and familiarity so established helped consolidate the support we needed, and thereafter build a team as we identified local organizers of the required capacity and energy. This was the heart of the initial phase of launching SEWA and its work in Banaskantha.

The next logical step, after building a core team, was to organize the rural workers, utilizing their status as water-users as an entry point. This process also proved quite slow, lengthy, and trying. In the village Madhutra, when our team went to meet the Rabari women, we were literally pushed, shoved, and chased away. We left, nervous, humiliated, and irritated. At that point, we had to control our emotions and, as people determined to do our work as best we could, also had to ask ourselves: why were we treated like this?

After two hours of discussion, we could still not find any reason for the treatment we had received. So, I suggested another visit to the village. Two days later, we went again, mentally prepared for even worse treatment. But, this time, it was different. We were welcomed. The same women said: "We once asked for a lift in your vehicle. You did not even bother to stop. Then you come and talk to us about development. We thought that since we had chased you away, you would return only if you believed genuinely in what you preached. You have returned, so we will trust you now." We discussed the events and then moved on. Since then, Madhutra has become a very active village in the district federation. It had also taught us a significant lesson: that if you want to lead a process of organizing, you have to learn to swallow bitterness, anger, and humiliation, put your ego last, and listen to your members.

Gradually, the women were organized — in particular, artisans around their embroidery work. The work was gaining momentum. Soon, however, we learned that a caste panchayat had put a ban on women doing our work, especially if it involved moving out of the villages. I discussed the predicament with the women, and all of us tried to figure a way out. "You come and meet our caste panchayat," they all said. But why would the caste panchayat listen to me? Would it really help? Puriben and Bhachiben, another leader in the village, said: "Let us first go and talk to them. You stay in the village. If the need arises, we will also request the panchayat to meet you." This was my first encounter with an issue of social change at such a level.

The women handled the situation with strength and unity. Upon the initial refusal of the panchayat, the women protested by opting not to do the cooking and serving for the meeting. Eventually, their voices were heard, and their reasoning and the income they were earning prevailed. Two years later, the same caste panchayat felicitated five women artisans for bringing respect and recognition to their community. Participating in the function, I realized what a major step had been taken. Considering the social forces they were up against, it was nothing short of a peaceful revolution by the women.

Ten years later, the women artisans have established a model of economic self-reliance leading to social change. In May 1999, while this book was being written, the women continued their revolution on an enhanced scale. Banas Craft, the district craft federation's sales and marketing outlet, organized its first international solo exhibition in France, at the invitation of the French association, Quilt en Sud. The production schedule for the exhibition, however, clashed with the wedding season, an auspicious time in the social calendar. It was a centuries-old tradition that, in the entire caste, all weddings took place in March.

But the women, including some of the brides, who were the artisans, owners and managers of Banascraft, made an unprecedented decision. In order to complete the production for the French exhibition, they postponed the weddings. In all, 216 weddings in the entire region were postponed by eight months, signifying not only the importance of the work to the women, but also the level of acceptance it had won within the community. It proved that economic/livelihood security did, indeed, lead to empowerment.

The leadership of women like these, and others with different skills and occupations, blossomed because of SEWA's integrated approach. SEWA began organizing women as water-users through an action research approach. This action research identified the existing local skills and resources available. The information gathered through this process then formed the basis for identifying a diverse range of economic activities that would integrate women, water and work. We organized women as water-users and as workers, uniting them in groups and collectives around productive activities. Simultaneously, women were organized into village water committees, or pani samitis, to help improve access to a resource that was key to their work and the lives.

Through the integrated approach of women organized around water and work, SEWA's strategy was to fight poverty. In the process, women have become the leaders of their own regional development programs. They now have a more assured water supply and a significantly improved access to work, capital, markets, and social security. Each and every program was and is full of struggles and challenges. But the progress has been steady.

Among those challenges, operationalizing the pani panchayats and strengthening the regional water supply scheme were major. SEWA's strategy was to augment the existing, traditional sources of water, such as village ponds and tanks, build up democratically functioning water-user groups or cooperatives, and thereby influence and facilitate the functioning of the pani panchayats. By 1991–92, SEWA started mobilizing the local communities for taking up the revival of the traditional water sources and building local resources by way of contributions from the people themselves and some funds from the government. It was a long struggle to cross the final obstacle: lack of technical expertise for upgrading and constructing village ponds. First, the people were not ready to go for such expertise. Then, when they were ready, the experts were not available.

A series of meetings were conducted with the Gujarat Water, Sewerage and Supply Board (GWSSB) for technical assistance. However, the

GWSSB was reluctant to help, as it was apprehensive if safe drinking water would result from such open structures. However, the villagers were familiar with their needs and persisted in their efforts to find support. The Minor Irrigation Department offered expertise in designing and constructing small check dams and the like, but village ponds were too small for the department. The Ground Water Corporation, when consulted, felt it could not offer expertise regarding the pond, as it was not a ground water source.

Meanwhile, it became difficult for SEWA to maintain the morale and the momentum of community participation. Also, with monsoons approaching fast, everyone was worried that the pond would not be ready in time. Finally, SEWA hired private engineers for providing the needed technical assistance. But, this strategy, too, failed as the engineers collected the money but produced no work.

Ultimately, the issue was resolved with the help of Indian Petro-Chemicals Limited, the GWSSB, and the Foundation for Public Interest, in the form of a unique, agrifilm-lined pond that exceeded the initial expectations of the project by minimizing the seepage of salt into the water.

Several lessons were learned along the way in this early experience, and these were useful in other non-water activities as well. Whether it was revival of dairy cooperatives or the launch of a fodder security scheme or the formation of a group for salt farming, the process necessarily involved technical issues and working in tandem with the government and other organizations. As a community organizer that was not equipped with the technical expertise to match the diverse needs of the community, how did you plan, design and implement highly technical programs? The answer often lay in building relationships with other groups and in building the capacity of the members, leaders and organizers from the bottom up.

The process of learning by doing has increased the confidence and strength of the team. It eventually came to form its own local organization, the Banaskantha DWCRA Mahila SEWA Association (BDMSA), that continues to build upon increasingly complex situations and programs. Today, the BDMSA is a vibrant, dynamic, self-reliant local organization with a membership of 35,000 members. Not only does it now implement the programs, but it also takes up newer challenges, be it drought-proofing, earthquake mitigation, or water resources management. It is an example of how a trade union can organize rural workers through the joint action of unionism and cooperatives. We established a joint working relationship with local people's organizations, mutually engaging ourselves in the task of fostering the improvement of the lives of the people by increasing their work opportunities and income security. Perhaps, the most significant indicator of the progress made is the decrease in the migration of the members and their families. When SEWA began work in Banaskantha in 1988, the migration was of 3,245 families from 110 villages. In 1999, the migration was of 236 families only from 110 villages. The villagers now had work, stability, and their own organization.

Along the way, these experiences have helped SEWA learn some important lessons. We have now developed a model of people-centered, integrated rural development based upon the process initiated in Banaskantha. With the strength of this approach, I was eventually able to assume the lead in expanding rural organizing to the point where SEWA is now active in 11 districts of Gujarat. Confident in the strength of the Banaskantha team, I no longer have Radhanpur as a home. Instead, it has become the headquarters for an organization that has exceeded the expectations with which I arrived there over a decade ago.

I am grateful to Daniel Crowell for his success in documenting 10 crucial years in SEWA's experience. Danielbhai, as he is now known, has spent several months in the field in both Banaskantha and Kutch, and has met our members, leaders, organizers and managers. His is a first-hand account of the ground realities of the region. Bravely, he has borne the scorching heat and drought of the area, and tried to bear with poor translation as well at times. I really appreciate his patience in sharing the drafts and going through them several times, adding and deleting, unmindful of the long wait, due to our preoccupations, at times.

Danielbhai has not only documented the process, but also tried to analyze it. I hope the story told in this book, which has a great personal meaning for me, can contribute to the achievement of similar goals elsewhere.

Reema Nanavaty
Date: July 2001   General Secretary,
Place: Ahmedabad   SEWA

Preface

This volume describes the efforts of the Self-Employed Women's Association (SEWA) in the field of rural development. Many readers are likely to be aware of SEWA's work in urban Ahmedabad. What is less known is that, since the late 1980s, SEWA has significantly expanded its activities to include over 200,000 rural members. Commensurate with this expansion, has been an expanded base of experiences, lessons, and philosophy. Ultimately, SEWA has had as much of an effect on the lives of its newest rural members as those members have had on SEWA. This book will attempt to describe that process, in a 'readable' manner, dealing with the ideas and events within a framework that incorporates lessons that could be useful to the broad range of people interested in human development.

The story of SEWA's efforts in rural development is primarily told through what has taken place in the districts of Banaskantha and Kutch in the state of Gujarat. Banaskantha is not only where SEWA first became deeply involved with a rural membership, but also where the environment is especially averse to human habitation: isolated, drought-prone and resource-poor. Kutch shares these harsh conditions, and also represents an instance where SEWA has been able to take the lessons learnt through experience and apply them in a new place, continuing to evolve ideas and actions. Furthermore, Kutch has presented its own distinct challenges, unique to SEWA's experience, perhaps, but certainly prevalent elsewhere in India and beyond.

The rural economy described in the pages that follow is labor-intensive, driven by the workers in the fields, forests, roads, and homes. Most of these workers are part of what is called the informal sector and, as such, are often underestimated and misunderstood. The informal sector is often perceived to be a syndrome connected to underdevelopment. Many feel that in order to make the economy healthy, the informal sector needs to be quarantined and ultimately eliminated, so that those people can become part of the formal sector, where they can be more productive and achieve income security.

SEWA has taken a different approach, recognizing the legitimacy of the informal workers and endeavoring to build the capacity of the people working in this vulnerable sector. The vast majority of rural households in India are productive in a multitude of activities. One woman may be an agricultural laborer or a gum collector or a salt farmer or an artisan, depending on the season, or even the time of day. In some cases, she may work for a contractor and, in others, may work on her own, selling the fruits of her labor to traders. In any case, she lives in an isolated area, has very little income security, and has largely been neglected by social investment policy. Particularly if she is a rural woman, she has not had an education and has little access to healthcare, childcare, capital resources or financial services, and limited access to information in general.

The SEWA strategy described in this book recognizes the informal sector as a legitimate, dynamic part of the economy. Rather than forcibly cutting the informal sector off from social investment, SEWA seeks to integrate it into the national economy. By providing linkages in training, technology, marketing, capital, and social services, SEWA builds the capacity of its members to take control of their own lives. As it is, the informal sector contributes 92 percent of the national employment, 65 percent of the national income, and 67 percent of the national savings (Jhabvala and Subrahmanya 2000). The SEWA strategy embraces this productivity, and seeks to enhance rather than erase it. The informal sector is not part of the problem. It is part of the solution.

In addition to integrating the informal sector into the mainstream economy, the SEWA strategy seeks to incorporate the diversity of productive activities into a multidimensional, employment-based approach. In the interests of clarity, this book is mainly organized into chapters based upon occupations or support activities. However, it should be kept in mind that this is only a convenient break-up of what is in reality a fluid, coherent, and integrated approach.

With the belief that the best methodology is a balance between thought and action, equal attention has been given to SEWA's deeds and its philosophy. In describing events over the past decade, inevitably certain things may have been overlooked. Hopefully, these gaps will be at least partially filled by the reader's own faculties of reason and imagination, taking into account the philosophy that motivates the actors. Similarly, the SEWA philosophy has a subtlety and spirit that admittedly defy the author's powers of description. It is hoped that the actions described will help compensate for this limitation.

Throughout the book, the challenges that SEWA faces are put in the context of circumstances that are not endemic to India alone. For example, many of the obstacles faced here are based in gender discrimination, from which no corner of the world is immune. Most issues of such discrimination in work, at home, and in politics are shared across cultures. The compounded responsibilities of an income-earner and a housekeeper, the problem of lower pay for comparable work, or the lack of ownership of assets are not the exclusive burden of the women of Banaskantha and Kutch. Therefore, perhaps their efforts in overcoming these prejudices can be of direct use to others.

Similarly, few of the issues here, from state government policies to problems of a specific occupation, should be perceived as limited to the circumstances under which the author's description places them. However, there are also issues dealt with in this book with a broad applicability that is not difficult to recognize as such. In particular, the issue of globalization is very much on the minds of many people, and is the subject of the concluding chapter. The SEWA experience also has a great deal to offer in this debate: much more than has been captured here. But the hope is that these pages can contribute SEWA's unique way of thinking and acting, to the globalization debate as well as to the multitude of other debates with a bearing on human development, which is achieving more than words can convey.

The shortcomings of this book are hopefully few, and remain the sole responsibility of the author. They can perhaps serve, however, to generate productive discussion and encourage the reader to look further into the issues and institutions described in the following pages.

Acknowledgements

First, I would like to express my gratitude to the Fulbright Fellowship Program for supporting work that I could not have otherwise undertaken. My thanks also to the United States Educational Foundation in India, to Mr. Subhash Chawla and others who make the India Fulbright program so special. Their gracious hospitality went well beyond the call of their duties.

I thank Dr. Jan Powers, of Gettysburg College, who was quick to embrace my desire to learn about the NGO movement in India. She is the one who gave life to my plans by introducing me to SEWA, in a city whose name she had to repeat several times before I could pronounce it correctly. She also gave this manuscript a thorough reading, with valuable suggestions that have been incorporated without exception and that are greatly appreciated.

To the members, leaders, and organizers of SEWA, some of whom are mentioned in the pages that follow, a 'thank you' for sharing their time and experiences so generously and with so much good cheer. Thanks also to Nitaben Patel, who invested a great deal of her time in explaining not only her area of work, but also the entire purview of SEWA, as I was just beginning to get my bearings. I also thank Monaben Dave, who not only furthered my understanding of SEWA, but also helped maintain positive spirits, even in the sweltering summer of Kutch. It was an inspiration to be witness to the determination and dedication of all of the SEWA staff and members with whom I worked. I know of few places where friendship and work come together so harmoniously.

Finally, I would like to extend my deepest gratitude to Reemaben Nanavaty. Her patience, strength, wealth of experience, and wisdom have been my main source of direction. More importantly, her capable leadership has played a crucial role in all of the events described in the pages that follow.

Chapter 1

THE SEWA MOVEMENT

The sun reflects off the white desert sand like a mirror, bringing with it the sweltering heat of summer in the Rann of Kutch. Few trees are visible on the flat horizon. The only motion is the illusory specter of the melting air rising from the ground, rippling as it goes. It, too, is trying to escape the scorching heat of the sands. Nothing offers any shade.

Jamu is resting from her journey through the desert that started just after the sun began its journey downward in the sky. Her infant son is resting on her hip, sleeping from either the exhaustion of the heat or lack of food or both. His hair is bleached and dry, from malnutrition and overexposure to the sun. Jamu's bare feet are crusted in salt, the mark of her trade. salt-farming. She lives and works in the desert eight months out of the year, extracting the white grains in the white heat of the white desert.

Now, she is traveling the 6 kilometers between her mud hut in the desert and the nearest village. In Patanka, the village, she hopes to find the rice and millet she needs to feed her family. There is a government fair price shop (FPS) in the village, but there is no guarantee that they will have even the basic items she requires. In fact, they rarely do.

If not, then she will have to pay the bus fare of Rs. 4 to go to the next provisions shop. She makes Rs. 15[1] a day working in the saltpans. Today's trip will cost Rs. 8. The food will cost Rs. 15. The loss in labor for the hours she is gone amounts to Rs. 5. She will have to borrow from the shopkeeper again. This means that she will have to pay five times as much later in interest, but her family has to eat.

She has to make this journey every day. Every day the sand doesn't get any cooler. The distance doesn't get any shorter. The debt just keeps getting bigger.

Ten years later, Jamuben Ahir is the Chairwoman of the BDMSA Watershed Committee in her village. When she wants extra income, and the conditions are right, she collects gum from the trees surrounding her

village where, until recently, there was only desert. Otherwise, she makes
over Rs. 700 a month doing embroidery in her home: her home with a concrete floor, a tile roof, and plaster walls. Her house is in her name, the same
as on her savings account. She buys her food from the Shakti Packet shop
near her house. It always has what she needs. Her two young daughters,
in a setting where daughters are not always welcome and nurtured addi-
tions to the family, have just returned from school. The girls are healthy
and smiling.

Jamuben is a SEWA member.

To appreciate the transition that Jamuben's life has undergone, we must
have a standard of measure. SEWA's 'Ten Points' is the standard by which
its members measure their own success. They are the following:

Have the members ...

1. Increased their employment opportunities?
2. Increased their income?
3. Improved their access to nutrition?
4. Improved their access to health services?
5. Increased their access to childcare?
6. Improved their housing, water and sanitation circumstances?
7. Increased their assets?
8. Strengthened the organization?
9. Strengthened the women's leadership?
10. Increased their self-reliance?

For Jamuben, the Ten Points read like a checklist. She has more employment opportunities by having more options. If she wants to work on crafts
rather than suffer in the blazing sun, she can do that. However, if collecting gum will offer her enough money to outweigh the difficulties, then she
can do that instead. Point 1 is accomplished.

These multiple sources of employment offer Jamuben bargaining power.
If salt merchants want her to help them produce salt, they have to pay her
as much as she could make working in the fields. If the landowners want
her help in the fields, they must offer her more than she can make with her
embroidery. They have to pay her much more actually, because embroidery
is a much less arduous task and she is less willing to work in the fields
unless the compensation is that much better. As a result, her income
increases. Point 2 is accomplished.

The health of her daughters is a good indication that her increased
income is being put to good use. If the most vulnerable members of the

family are well fed, then it implies that the whole family is enjoying access to good nutrition. Good health is a significant result of improved nutrition. Jamuben's daughters' ability to concentrate in school is another result of the health that nutrition that affords. But, just in case good nutrition isn't enough, a SEWA mobile health van comes twice a month. Points 3, 4, and 5 are accomplished.

Similarly, Jamuben achieved two goals simultaneously when she renovated her house. The loan for the floor, roof and walls was given on the condition that the house would stand in her name. Anxious for the improvements, her husband agreed. Now her house is not only improved, but it is her asset. Points 6 and 7 are accomplished.

Jamuben's neighbors have inevitably seen the transition in her life and want the same. They have become SEWA members as well, and have added to the collective strength of the organization. Jamuben now leads those women in developing the economy of the whole community through improving their access to water. Points 8 and 9 are accomplished. Point 10 is the cumulative effect of all the previous points.

A Brief History of SEWA[2]

The SEWA movement began in the city of Ahmedabad, the principal city in the state of Gujarat, on the western coast of India. Ahmedabad gained prominence at the turn of the 20th century as the center of India's burgeoning textile industry. Known as the Manchester of the East and compared to England's textile megalopolis, the city had over 60 large textile mills operating at its peak, employing tens to hundreds of thousands of people both directly and indirectly.

It was also in Ahmedabad that Mohandas Karamchand Gandhi settled in 1915, after gaining prominence in South Africa for promoting the cause of the oppressed Indian community in that colony. On the banks of the Sabarmati river, which divides the city in half, Gandhi established an ashram, which he used as a base to struggle against the unjust colonial policies of the British Empire and the self-destructive practices of the Indian people. Perhaps most memorably, Gandhi began his Great Salt March from the Sabarmati ashram, and the event in many ways represented the initiation of the satyagraha (Sanskrit: 'truth force') movement, the driving force behind India's struggle for independence. The Salt Tax law forbade anyone from using salt that had not been processed and therefore taxed by the colonial government, including the severely impoverished people living and working on the salt flats of Gujarat, where salt crusted the ground in consumable form. In protest against the law, Gandhi argued that salt was essential to human life and that the regressive, flat tax disproportionately impacted the poor. It was from Ahmedabad, in what was to become a characteristic Gandhian form, that the Mahatma and a modest contingent from the ashram marched to the village of Dandi on the Gujarat coast, setting out at 6.30 a.m. on 12 March 1930. The 241 miles were covered in 24 days. Once they arrived at the salt flats by the sea, they simply reached down and collected the salt, at once defying the British law and mocking its absurdity with the simple, non-violent, but illegal gesture.

Gandhi also left his mark in Ahmedabad as one of the founding forces behind the Textile Labor Association (TLA), one of the first labor unions in India. The TLA had its beginnings in the plague epidemic of 1920. As the plague spread through the population, productivity in the mills declined as workers either fell ill or feared exposure to the disease from their coworkers and so avoided the mill. Facing financial disaster, the mill-owners promised the workers double salaries if they came to work despite the dangers of the disease. Many workers accepted the offer and worked through the epidemic, keeping the mills open and productive. However, by the time the epidemic was over, the mill-owners reneged on their pledge and refused to pay the promised salaries. A strike, debilitating to both sides, ensued, and Gandhi was invited to arbitrate. In addition to settling the dispute by finding a compromise acceptable to both sides, Gandhi, along with Anasuya Sarabhai, a dedicated advocate for the poor and herself from one of the most prominent mill-owning families, helped organize the workers into the TLA. For decades to come, this institution would strike a balance with the powerful mill-owners to help secure just and equitable conditions for the textile industry's workers.

In 1955, a bright young lawyer named Ela Bhatt, a woman largely inspired by Gandhi and Anasuya Sarabhai, joined the TLA and assumed the role of representing the organization in court and advocating at the policy level for improved labor laws. By 1968, Ela Bhatt had become the head of the Women's Wing of the TLA. As the head of the Women's Wing, Ela Bhatt's responsibilities primarily included organizing sewing, typing, and other classes for the wives and daughters of the textile workers. However, she was also acutely aware that these women were in need of much more than what the TLA was then offering. Though their husbands were earning wages, these were not enough to sustain a family, so these women found additional work of their own, most often in the 'informal sector'. This meant they worked from the home or on the streets as cart-pullers, head-loaders, vegetable vendors, bidi-rollers, construction laborers, and in many other jobs. These women had neither contracts nor regular wages, nor job security nor even recognition. In addition, Bhatt knew that there were many other women whose husbands did not work in the mills, and perhaps did not have any jobs at all. These women worked at the same jobs in the informal sector, and, as such, were vulnerable to manipulation, overwork, disease, and misery.

In total, 93 percent of the Indian labor force was and is believed to be self-employed. Of Indian women, a slightly higher figure of 94 percent are self-employed. This means that more than half of the Indian workforce, both male and female, were comprise self-employed women (Ela Bhatt, personal communication).

By 1968, although these women were large in number, they suffered their fates individually, isolated from their fellow informal sector workers. Cart-pullers, who spent their days loading, lugging, and unloading their carts of textiles from the mills to the warehouses and merchants, were not considered employees of the mills. Instead, they were independent laborers who were hired on a job-to-job basis, denied the security of regular wages. Similarly, for those who could not afford to own, or (as was more frequently the practice) rent one of the primitive carts, smaller loads would be balanced on their heads and carried to the specified place, as head-loaders. All these women, instead of being coworkers, had to compete with each other for work, and accept the low, and sometimes withheld, wages. They were unorganized and, as such, simply outnumbered themselves. If someone demanded better wages, then the next one would be willing to accept the work for a lower amount.

The cart-pullers and head-loaders, acutely aware of their predicament but unsure of how to help themselves out of it, approached Ela Bhatt, specifically concerning their poor housing conditions. When Elaben[3] went with these women to investigate the problem, she observed the housing conditions, as well as many other difficulties. The women were paid the same meager rate, regardless of whether their trip was a few blocks away or all the way across the city. Sometimes, the merchants who kept accounts of the work and paid the cart-pullers and head-loaders, would only pay the women part of the wages that were due to them, taking advantage of the workers' illiteracy and lack of bargaining power. To compound these difficulties, most of the women did not even own their carts, and had to pay the cart-owner a significant portion of the daily wages as rent. All of this translated into continuing drudgery in an unending cycle of poverty.

Elaben responded by writing an article in the local newspapers, highlighting the plight of these women. This statement elicited a response from the merchants that was used as ammunition in the ensuing struggle. The merchants professed their innocence, citing the wages they purported to pay and the other fair practices they supposedly showered upon the women. The merchants' reply was reproduced on cards that were distributed to the women. These cards were then presented to the merchants any time they went back on their word. As a talisman against unfair practices, the cards had a positive effect.

The word of this initiative spread to other women in the informal sector. Within a few days of the newspaper article, a vendor of used clothes named Chandaben approached Elaben to enlist her support for the sisters in her own trade. They traveled around residential areas, trading objects such as cooking vessels for used clothing. Then these women repaired the used clothes and resold them to lower-income buyers. These women were exposed to harassment from the police and, with marginal income, were vulnerable to the same problems that poverty brought to cart-pullers and head-loaders.

Recognizing the common issues, a meeting was held and attended by women of the many occupations that constituted the diverse informal sector. This meeting led to the birth of a union and the unheard-of concept of organizing the informal sector. SEWA became a branch of the TLA, with the leadership of the TLA assuming the leadership of SEWA as well, and the women of the informal sector filling its ranks.

The early years of the union were highlighted by victories for the cart-pullers and vegetable vendors, among others, a greater visibility in general for the issues affecting the self-employed, and the establishment of a bank catering specifically to the needs of the poor women. Like the cart-pullers, vegetable vendors faced many difficulties. The primary difficulty was police harassment. For generations, vegetable vendors had lined the streets of the markets with their baskets or plied the streets with their carts. Many market spaces were, in fact, occupied by granddaughters of women who had sold in the same spot two generations ago. However, in the eyes of the law as represented by policemen, that heritage did not constitute legitimacy. In the absence of a licensing or permit system, some policemen extorted bribes from the vendors, kicking the women's produce or physically harassing them if they did not comply. The bribes thus demanded could sometimes be over half of the daily profits.

To make matters worse, many of the women had to borrow money from moneylenders in order to purchase the day's stock of vegetables. This usually meant interest rates that could be as high as 10 percent per day. For example, a woman might have to borrow Rs. 50 at the beginning of the day in order to purchase her stock at the wholesale market.

Then, by the end of the day, she would have to repay Rs. 55 back to the moneylender (Rose 1992: 47). Considering the effects of the obligatory bribes and the interest payments, the daily gross profits of Rs. 15 are not much for a day's work.

To combat the bribes, police harassment and issues of legitimacy, SEWA did what it does best: organize. At first, there were several little successes: for example, one bold SEWA member grabbed a policeman's badge and sat on it when he leaned over to extort a bribe, only giving it back after the man's superior officer officially apologized for his subordinate's behavior. Another time, a SEWA organizer, who was at the market in response to members' complaints of official abuse, grabbed a policeman in the act of taking the bribe. She began pulling him and his pocket full of rupee notes toward a rickshaw, telling him they were heading for the police station to take the issue up there. These instances were effective on a small scale, but the root of the problem — lack of empowerment and legitimacy for the vendors — remained unsolved.

The issue came to a head when a large number of vegetable vendors were evicted from a market on the pretext of an attack on a cyclist and an ensuing riot, though the incident had had nothing to do with the women. The whole market was closed temporarily but, when it reopened, the police blocked the vendors from resuming their trade. The police argued that the women were a nuisance, blocking the pedestrian traffic and plying their trade without official permission. SEWA and its members argued that the women were an established and vital link in the consumption chain, providing a service that almost every person in India relied upon for food. They did not have official permission because no such apparatus for granting that permission existed.

For days, the women waited to return to their work, led on by promises from officials that they would do something about it 'tomorrow.' Finally, exasperated by unkept promises, and getting deeper in debt as the days went by without income, SEWA members decided to enter the market the next day with or without official permission. The members of the SEWA vegetable vendors' union were accompanied by members from the other SEWA unions and organizers. Police officers arrived on the scene, ostensibly to maintain the peace but, in reality, several of them tried to instigate reactions from the women. Ultimately, the show of collective force succeeded, the police left, and business resumed. This type of collective action continues, and has to continue, in the face of official and unofficial harassment, even after the Supreme Court of India recognized street vending as a fundamental right under the Constitution of India.

To combat the problem of moneylenders, which severely affected not only vegetable vendors but every poor person in India, the SEWA Bank was founded in 1974. Recognizing the need for capital for the poorest classes, the then Prime Minister Indira Gandhi obligated state banks to allocate up to 1 percent of their loaned funds to people living below the poverty line. Many banks deftly avoided the obligation while others obliged but simply wrote off the loans as losses, never expecting to see the money again. Some banks in Ahmedabad approached SEWA to assist in recognizing eligible loan recipients and help recover funds from defaulters. However, regardless of the efforts made by all involved, SEWA realized that the conventional banking system was simply not conducive to addressing the needs of the poor. Illiteracy was the first obstacle. Most SEWA members would not be able to read the signs telling them which queue to stand in, would not know how to fill out the necessary forms, or even sign their names. Furthermore, the small amounts the women were working with, relative to the usual banking patron, and the numerous children that the women brought with them and their bedraggled appearance, all invited the ire of the bank personnel.

After a few years of trying to make the conventional system work, some SEWA members came up with an unconventional idea: why not have a bank of our own, a bank exclusively for poor, self-employed women? The first obstacle was the Rs. 100,000 required for share capital in order to charter a cooperative bank. For women who made Rs. 10 to 15 per day, such a feat would be difficult, but not impossible. They were poor, but they were many. Within a few months, the members had raised the necessary funds among themselves. Within a few more months, they had convinced the Registrar of Cooperative Banks that poor, illiterate women could constitute a viable bank, and they registered the Mahila SEWA Sahakari Bank, better known as the SEWA Bank, in July 1974.

To adjust to the unique needs of its shareholders, this cooperative bank has adopted several innovative practices. First of all, photo identity cards have overcome the necessity of personal signatures for records and verification. The bank staff use these identity cards to access the account files of the members and are also accustomed to deposits and withdrawals of Rs. 5, as well as processing loan applications for Rs. 100 or lower. If a woman misses a loan payment, rather than penalize her or write her off, loan recovery officers (many of them previously impoverished, self-employed women themselves) first talk to the borrower to ascertain why she missed the loan payment. Often, an adjusted repayment schedule can be worked out in response to a temporary and unforeseeable difficulty, such as death in the family, loss of work, or a health problem. Rather than defaulting, the women continue to repay their loans while still being able to feed and clothe themselves and their families.

The SEWA Bank has also found ways to support the shareholders by offering support services with the loans. Linkages to government subsidies and other programs, identifying raw materials merchants with better prices and better marketing, help the women put their loans to the best use.

SEWA, the bank, the unions, cooperatives and other institutions, have grown substantially since the association's founding in 1972. Bidi-rollers, who manually prepare bidis (Indian cigarettes) from dried tobacco leaves, have secured a more equitable access to raw materials and more fair prices for their finished product. Construction laborers, of whom women constitute the vast majority, have been collectively assured fair wages and access to skill training beyond the pack animal-like roles they had previously played. Now, for example, some women have become masons and welders, acquiring skills previously reserved for men. Street sweepers, water concessionaires, acrobats, paper-pickers, fish vendors, industrial cleaning women, block printers, weavers, kerosene vendors, and makers of agarbatti (incense sticks), are among the other member groups that have come together to become part of SEWA.

For the first decade and a half since its founding, SEWA devoted most of its efforts to the urban self-employed. Within Ahmedabad, the membership grew rapidly and also contributed and benefited greatly. However, outside Ahmedabad lay the rest of Gujarat and India, most of which was poor and rural. This was to be the next major challenge for the quickly evolving and progressing SEWA. Thus, the next decade and a half would bring significant progress for SEWA and for the rural poor where it became active, as the two joined to initiate the process that is the focus of this book.

To fully capture the meaning behind SEWA in one word or phrase can be a challenging exercise. Non-Governmental Organization is far too official-sounding a word. It fails to convey the nature of SEWA's primary characteristic, the self-employed women who make up its membership. Membership-Based Organization is much more fitting, but it still doesn't capture the full scope of SEWA's activities.

It is best to turn to the choice words of Ela Bhatt. As she has described it, SEWA is a 'movement'. The word is large enough to encompass all of SEWA's parts. From the activism of the SEWA Labor Union and the innovations of the SEWA Bank to the scholarship of SEWA Academy, the 'movement' embraces them all. Now, the BDMSA, and Kutch Craft

Association, two of SEWA's rural kin, have been added to the family. To describe the process of the birth and maturation of these two organizations is to share the implications of their experiences and achievements for rural development elsewhere. The book will focus on the work SEWA has undertaken in the districts of Banaskantha and Kutch in particular. However, the experiences gained in these two places, and described in the pages that follow, have much to teach us in general.

The Movement

As with people, institutions and concepts can be related. In the SEWA movement's family tree, organization and struggle are the parents of change, development, and progress. The movement has furthermore adopted into a family of ideas such concepts as activism, capacity-building, asset-building and empowerment. Who says women can't procreate on their own?

The SEWA family is made up of 220,000 members and 16 organizations. Despite SEWA's size and diversity, it is these concepts that hold the different parts together as a movement. First of all, there are the members. Although they are geographically spread across the state of Gujarat and beyond, they are not isolated from each other. They come together often, in numerous forums. They travel great distances to witness each other's successes and share each other's experiences. They share the characteristics of poverty as well as the demand to end it. Similarly, they share the means to achieve their goal.

The different organizations the members form also share the family traits. As mentioned before, their goals are organization, capacity-building, asset-building and empowerment. The relationship to their members is found in these organizations' means to achieving their goals. The programs are demand-driven and need-based. The members identify their wants, and formulate and implement their strategies together. Thus, there can be no question about the responsiveness of SEWA to the community: they are one and the same.

The SEWA staff is another key to the movement's propulsion. The members are poor, but they have to work hard even to maintain that status. Though they always find ways to provide time for the movement, the demands of survival allow time for little else. SEWA organizers and administrators, who are also SEWA members, work on behalf of their sisters. They use their education and dedication to further the other members' demands. They work to keep the membership informed and to inform others, at the policy level, of their membership.

Before beginning the narrative of events, it would be useful to outline the general structure of SEWA's efforts in rural development, and to mention the major government agencies involved. A clearer understanding of the logistics will facilitate an easier journey through the pages that follow.

A key to SEWA's efforts is its team of organizers. They are the catalyzing agents that bring about the desired changes. Most of the organizers are from the districts in which they work, such as Banaskantha and Kutch, though some are from Ahmedabad. Many are from poor families themselves, though a few are from the middle class. The vast majority are women though, in Banaskantha, some men have joined the ranks. However, one of the characteristics they all share is that they work hard because they believe in their work.

These organizers are divided among the different activities in which SEWA participates, such as dairy development, artisan production, and using water as a regenerative input. But both within these categories and outside, they discharge many different functions.

The organizers' title derives from their primary responsibility, which is to organize the members. The process begins with the organizers making the first foray into the villages. They are armed with a passion for the movement they represent and the ability to convey this sentiment to others. Theirs is the task of igniting a flame of interest in the women of the villages so that they themselves recognize the need for change and the potential path to it.

The job of fostering an interest in change can be a challenging one. The women in the villages of Banaskantha and Kutch live in an environment steeped in tradition. Some of these traditions are practical adaptations to a challenging environment, and should continue to be preserved. However, other traditions are in need of change. Literacy, nutrition, control of assets, and many other rights are denied to the impoverished women of the villages. Furthermore, because these denials have become such a way of life, the women often fail to recognize their own deprivation. Instead, the men have an almost exclusive access to education, as well as a privileged access to nutrition and control of the assets. Whether they do it intentionally or not, the men's monopoly of such resources serve to perpetuate their dominant role at the expense of the women.

An early step for the organizers is to inform these women of their rights. A great deal of time is spent just talking to the women about this one issue. These initial discussions can last hours, and often take several meetings in the same village before the women are moved enough to act. But the organizers possess the skill to convey their message and the patience to see their goal through.

Once the village women are awakened to the possibilities, the organizers then take them to the next step. The organizers build the women's collective strength by fostering the formation of groups. Then, as a group, the women are in a better position to determine their own destiny. The knowledge of what resources are available to the rural poor and how to access them is the organizers' tool for tapping the collective strength of the women they organize. There are a number of government programs that aspire to help the rural poor. But the providing agencies' abilities to deliver these resources often fail as a result of their top-down structure.

The organizers seek to manage the delivery system of development resources from a different angle. Instead of the traditional top-down system, the organizers seek to empower the poor women so that the system is oriented from the bottom up. To facilitate this, the organizers not only organize the women, but also give them access to information and ideas. The initial meetings, discussing the women's neglected rights, are only the beginning.

Even after the first stages, the organizers meet the women several times a month. Take the "Water as a Regenerative Input" program as an example. As will be discussed in detail later, this program utilizes traditional, as well as new, water-harvesting techniques to supply the vital resource to the villages. In 1999, the organizers for this program covered eight villages in Banaskantha.

At least once a month, an organizer travels to each of the eight villages. Along with the leaders and other members of the respective village water committees, they hold meetings. As a contact point for the expanding government Watershed Development Program, the organizers are always up to date on the latest initiatives in the program and what resources are available to the villages. The organizers present these options to the water committees and together they discuss the possibilities. Would the village be better served by recharging its wells, or should they strive to construct a check dam or a new village pond?

The decision made by the committee is then put into action. Another of the organizers' functions is to communicate with the government agencies supporting the program about the wishes of the different villages. Many organizers spend a great deal of time traveling between their respective districts, Ahmedabad, the primary city in Gujarat, and Gandhinagar, the state capital. They write reports and maintain records consistently. In the process, the "Water as a Regenerative Input" organizers, for example, articulate the decisions and demands of the village water committees to the government and assure the delivery of the appropriate resources.

Simply put, the primary role of the organizers is to convey information. They inform the village communities of the possibilities that are available to improve the present circumstances. Then, because most of these villagers, especially the women, are illiterate and busy working to feed themselves and their families, the organizers inform the government of the villagers' decisions, filing and reviewing the necessary documents. The organizers constitute the mechanism that ensures an informed demand, and sees to it that the supply meets that demand.

SEWA's original work pattern in rural areas, before they became involved in Banaskantha, included commuting organizers. SEWA's rural organizing experience, prior to Banaskantha, was limited, but they did learn that the commuting work pattern would not work. The fact was that, as an urban center and home base to SEWA's activities, Ahmedabad was the prime recruiting ground for potential organizers. However, these women were inevitably viewed as outsiders when they came and went from the areas in which they were working. As they began in Banaskantha, SEWA realized it needed a different approach.

Banaskantha and Ahmedabad are separated by over 200 kilometers of roads that are sometimes bumpy, and always occupied by just about every type of creature imaginable, the more effective traffic-blockers including camels, bullocks, water buffaloes, elephants, donkeys, horses, and wedding parties. Sometimes, the three-way traffic on a one-lane highway can be a bit slow, but always interesting to the uninitiated. In addition to the time needed to navigate all that territory, there are also the different accents, dialects, customs, and apparel that can serve to increase the conceptual distance between Ahmedabad and Banaskantha.

Until a local pool of women could be recruited, and their abilities developed, the new strategy for SEWA required a great deal of commitment from the initial organizers. The early organizers left their homes and families in Ahmedabad and made Radhanpur, a primary town in the district of Banaskantha, their new headquarters. Their sacrifice helped establish a rapport with the rural community and gain the trust of the villagers. In the process, these organizers also gained a much more profound understanding of the area, which greatly enhanced their work. Then, as these experienced organizers came into contact with the local community, they eagerly identified local women who had the potential to lead the organization to independence and self-sustainability. And, so, the process began.

However, organizing is a process that never ends. Once the village women are formed into groups, their organization is not complete. In fact, it is just the beginning. The organizers' role is not just to bring them together, but also to lend a purpose and a direction to their unity. As the available resources continue to grow, and the communities develop, the organizers facilitate the connection between the two sides.

The key role the organizers play must be remembered. This is not only so that credit is given where credit is due. For those interested in truly understanding or, perhaps, even replicating the success of SEWA's efforts for rural development, the organizers must be the starting point.

Next come the spearhead teams. With the weight of responsibilities the organizers carry, they cannot do their jobs alone. Nor do they have to, especially after the women they help organize begin to develop their own leadership abilities. To employ the experience, devotion, and creativity of the empowered village women, SEWA developed the concept of the spearhead team. In each of the rural activities within SEWA's purview, there is a spearhead team. Each team usually consists of 10 people: two organizers and eight leaders from the various village groups from the respective activity. For example, eight leaders from the different savings groups in Kutch comprise 80 percent of the Kutch Savings Spearhead Team. The other 20 percent (two persons), are organizers. These 10 then orchestrate all the savings and micro-finance activities in the district, from organizing to the day-to-day functions of the program.

The spearhead teams' abilities are constantly developing, and these women eventually play a major role in the recruitment and organization of new groups. Furthermore, once the groups are organized, the spearhead teams undertake the training of the members. Every training program includes methods of accounting and record-keeping, conducting meetings and business planning. Each activity then poses specific issues that need to be addressed in the training. Craft groups need to acquire methods of quality control and raw material distribution. Watershed groups should be well versed in various matters of watershed dynamics and the options for improvement. Savings groups, of course, require a more sophisticated familiarization with accounting and record-keeping.

The spearhead team members do receive a wage for the expertise they acquire and provide. However, it would be impractical and costly to pay the trainees as well. Instead, the spearhead teams developed a system of on-the-job training. Whenever possible, the knowledge is passed along as the new groups work, produce and earn. That way, the income of the trainees is maintained through their own productivity. Nothing has to be disrupted in order to conduct the training.

Beyond the training, the spearhead teams continue to play a role with the groups by monitoring their efforts. Most of the women in the villages are both illiterate and innumerate, so building their self-sufficiency in issues of management can take time. As both the trainers and the monitors, the spearhead teams are the perfect answer to the challenge. They train the groups to perform and allow them to be productive at the same time.

Working with the Government

There is much global debate about the role of government in society. This dialogue is particularly intense in India, where the government has always played an especially overt and central role in the development of the nation. Thus, an initiative for a reduced government role in society is combined with the legacy of a multitude of government programs for the alleviation of poverty. The result is a strategy of delivery of services that relies heavily on non-governmental organizations.

As will be elaborated in this book, SEWA provides linkages for government programs based on the needs of the community members. Different government programs have different goals, different structures and differing degrees of flexibility. As such, the dynamics of development work in Banaskantha, Kutch, and other districts are greatly affected. Some programs are impractical and unresponsive bureaucratic mazes that do more harm than good. However, the majority of the programs are valuable and widely utilized. SEWA's approach is to link the existing programs with the underutilized skills latent in the communities, rather than initiate parallel structures. The government programs are then bolstered through local resource mobilization and organization.

Since the 1980s, several programs have been developed and have risen above other rural development initiatives. Among them are the TRYSEM (Training of Rural Youth for Self-Employment), the DWCRA (Development of Women and Children in Rural Areas), and the Watershed Development Program. All three are programs coordinated through the DRDA (District Rural Development Agency) in the respective districts. All three represent a new generation of government development programs that have the flexibility to adapt to local needs. They also focus on opportunities for employment as the foundation of rural development.

The TRYSEM has been a valuable resource in support of building the skill-base of the rural poor. It provides funds for training programs, as the name indicates, as well as tools and raw materials as start-up capital. Similarly, the DWCRA offers start-up capital and training. However, the latter focuses more specifically on poor women and children, the most neglected section of the population.

The Watershed Development Program, as briefly mentioned earlier, supports the creation of traditional as well as new methods of water-harvesting. From check dams to village ponds, well-recharging and contour bunding (land-leveling for the purposes of reducing run-off and erosion), the program assists in cost-sharing schemes with villages that have limited access to water. The importance of this program will be explored in depth in the next chapter.

Also, the Government of India Development Commissioner for Handicrafts has supplied funds as well as expertise for craft development infrastructure.

This book will deal with all these programs. But what deserves special attention here is the cumulative effect they have had on SEWA and vice versa. Working with the government has required SEWA to be flexible and to plan well. Government funds offer invaluable support, but their management may not always be timely. SEWA has had to work around this matter to make sure that government delays, and other complications, do not hinder progress.

SEWA has also had to learn to juggle the varying demands of the government, international development agencies, and the poor rural community members. In many of these circumstances, the demands of the community are the more substantive, and it is a struggle not to compromise their interests. Each group has its individual constituency. But SEWA's constituency — which comprises its members — is the most directly involved. Thus, the need is to build their knowledge base and bargaining power, and make their voices heard.

SEWA's determination not to sacrifice the interests of its members has had its impact at the policy level. The DWCRA itself was the outcome of a special government-sponsored committee that included Ela Bhatt, founder of SEWA, as a member. Furthermore, in 1996, the National Consultation on the DWCRA was held in Ahmedabad, with the SEWA DWCRA programs as the showpiece. Dealt with in greater detail later in this book, the recommendations SEWA made in that consultation have been largely implemented in the program on a national scale.

But the adoption of SEWA strategies and objectives is not unnatural to the government. Local organization-building is being increasingly recognized as the best path to sustainable development. Previously, highly centralized, large-scale government programs were the common method for development of any kind. Now, more recognition is being given to the local communities' own ability to manage their progress. SEWA has been among the strongest proponents of this shift.

The simple fact that most rural development programs focus on employment opportunity as the starting point is also largely a credit to SEWA. The result is well known when you "give a man a fish."[4] Unfortunately, the rest of the adage was not incorporated into most development programs, and most people could only "eat for a day." But SEWA helped these women to develop their "angling" skills, and has also helped them with things such as acquiring a license and developing a market. This document details that process in a much less metaphorical way, but the government has begun to get the hint as well. Removing unemployment has become the government's new mantra, in the place of removing poverty. The government is now attacking the disease rather than the symptoms, and SEWA was among those leading the way in making the original diagnosis.

Similarly, previous programs tended to offer charity-type schemes to the poor, with or without the support or knowledge of the 'target' community. The complaint was that the poor never paid for the services provided. Yet, the poor were never consulted about the provision of those services, nor their content and manner. SEWA's approach has been to bring the poorest of the poor in from the beginning stage. Though it sounds basic, it had rarely been done before. For example, the 1996 National Consultation on the DWCRA, the principal instrument for improving the lives of impoverished rural women in India, included not a single impoverished woman from a rural area on its panel. Among the recommendations SEWA made to that panel was the inclusion of these women in meetings that were meant to determine their future. This was a logical conclusion, but one that had not been reached till then. Now it has been.

Working with the government has brought its challenges and its rewards. SEWA and its members have been able to influence the government's developing development strategy. Their recommendations are often heeded and their example is often followed. Programs like the DWCRA, which have failed elsewhere, have succeeded with SEWA. As a result, the government is often responsive to SEWA's success and, therefore, that success is spreading.

The Practical Philosophy

The last thing needed to appreciate fully the impact of the process most of this book describes, is to understand the ideology behind the actions. This ideology finds expression in the physical implementation of SEWA's activities, but it is also present in the spirit. It is this spirit that deserves elaboration here.

As a membership-based organization, SEWA must be responsive to the parts that make up the whole. The members are the ones who choose the organization's leadership, make the organization's decisions and form the development strategy. Conversely, they are the ones who are in need, so their leadership and decision-making combines to create a more naturally effective strategy.

All of SEWA's programs are demand-driven and need-based. The programs described in the following pages have evolved through a process of natural selection. Those creating, implementing, and managing the programs are the same as those benefiting from them. The rural poor are the ones who can best identify the needs of the rural poor. They are also the people who can most effectively voice their demands. SEWA incorporates this process into an institutional structure.

This book will also mention several examples of training programs, exposure trips and other means of capacity-building. To cover them all in detail would need another, much larger, document in itself. The goal of these exercises is to build the capacity of each member to the point where she is capable of supporting herself and her family in a healthy and productive life. Training programs range in their focus from business planning to craft production to quality control. However, they all seek to build the skills of the members so that they can become not only more effective workers and producers, but owners and managers as well.

The exposure trips seek to give the women, who have until recently lived isolated lives, a greater perspective on their work. For example, members of the dairy cooperatives in Banaskantha made a trip to Banas Dairy, the regional milk-processing facility. There they witnessed the operation of the milk production chain after these women got the milk from their cattle. They saw the chilling and pasteurization process. They saw how the milk was packaged and shipped. Also, on the same campus stood a fodder farm, an innovation they had directly adopted. The impact of the trip was widely felt. Understanding the whole process and its magnitude gave the women a stronger sense of the importance of their work. It also gave them a better understanding of the market in which they were involved.

It must be remembered that the women receiving the training and exposure had been denied any such knowledge and experience up until then. The learning curves were vertical and the opportunities to put the lessons into practice were immediate. The impact of the efforts at capacity-building should not, thus, be underestimated.

This investment in human capital ensures that the benefits will continue to increase well after the various agencies' investments end. The developments described in this document are sustainable. Through capacity-building, the women's bargaining power is increasing to the point where they can maintain their progress independent of outside help. As an organization, they can control their own destinies and defend their own interests.

The DWCRA may cease to be, but the people of these rural areas will continue to develop. Well after the Watershed Development funds have dried up, the watershed development will continue to flow. That is the best tribute that these programs could hope for.

Beginning in Banaskantha

Since 1989, SEWA has been involved in organizing rural development programs in Banaskantha. In this arid, drought-prone district in northwestern Gujarat, water is scarce and so are employment opportunities. But, in a land where people had once argued that "nothing grows," the Banaskantha DWCRA Mahila SEWA Association is now flourishing.

Since its founding as a labor union in 1972, SEWA has been an organization of women who work in the informal sector, vegetable vendors, bidi-rollers, head-loaders, and paper-collectors, among others. These people are the poorest of the poor, who work for meager wages and are, thus, the most vulnerable to fluctuations in the labor market. SEWA, for over two and a half decades, has struggled to empower these members through a twin strategy of labor union struggle and development through income-generating activities.

SEWA has been very successful in its struggle and continues to lead the members and their families in achieving their common goals. Yet, from the beginning, the district of Banaskantha has presented a unique set of challenges to the organization. SEWA first became involved in

Banaskantha in answer to a request from the Government of Gujarat. The district had been the site of a water pipeline project jointly undertaken by the Government of Gujarat and the Dutch Government. Eager to assess the impact of their project on the local population, the state invited SEWA to take a closer look. What SEWA found was that the pipeline largely failed to improve the lives of those it intended to help. The problems were rooted both in the project's conception and in its implementation. The water was not getting to the people, but the bigger problem was that the people had no work. After it identified these problems, SEWA was further invited to help improve the situation, and it accepted the challenge.

Much of SEWA's experience was centered around urban labor union activity, namely, advocating for better working conditions and wages for self-employed women. Banaskantha is not urban, nor is much of its population employed in the first place. Surplus supply in the rural labor market is a widespread phenomenon in India. Even after the Green Revolution, most of the agricultural work remains labor-intensive, but it still cannot absorb the burgeoning rural population. Furthermore, agriculture in Banaskantha, such as it is, relies largely on rain-fed water resources. Thus, frequent droughts aggravate the employment situation even more.

Migration is one of the major results of the unreliable environmental circumstances. Entire families have to leave their homes in search of water, food, and work. This migration makes school attendance for the children impossible. Consistent income is difficult to secure for parents. Access to health services is hindered for the whole family. Every day spent traveling is another day of productivity lost and another day removed from the comforts of home. In general, it eats up the energy, hope and resources of everyone involved.

Though the same drought and migration are present in the urban areas, they are issues of a lesser magnitude in the cities. City water supplies can dry up, and migration certainly disrupts the lives of the urban inhabitants. However, agriculture is not as important in the cities, so the water needs are less essential to the economic well-being of urban society. In terms of migration, the cities are experiencing a large influx of migrants. However, most migrants are those who migrate from rural areas to other rural areas in search of agricultural work. Hence, this is also a rural issue. These and other differences are more significant than they would first appear to be.

SEWA traditionally approached most issues by doing what it did best, by organizing. As a labor union, SEWA utilized the collective strength of its members as leverage against exploitative people and policies. However, in the rural areas, even when organized, the rural poor do not have the collective strength to acquire that leverage. Their needs are even more fundamental. They cannot call for better working conditions or better pay. First, they simply need work; they simply need pay. For SEWA, this required a different strategy.

To fill the gaps that the urban labor union approach could not, a new sister/daughter organization (in India, where the elder sister frequently assumes a maternal role for her siblings, the lines can be blurred) was fostered. That new organization was the BDMSA. In the process of this foster relationship, SEWA itself has changed from an urban labor union to a labor union for the whole spectrum of self-employed women, urban and rural. Today, SEWA's total membership is 220,000 strong, and the rural members constitute two-thirds of the rolls. This broadening of scope has had a significant effect on SEWA, Banaskantha and the many other people and institutions involved.

Banaskantha before:[5] A Brief Look at Some Available Information

In the 1991 census, the population of the state of Gujarat was 41,309,582 people, of whom 2,162,578 lived in the district of Banaskantha. The literacy rate in the state was 61 percent combined, 73 percent for males and 49 percent for females. In Banaskantha, the literacy rates were 39 percent combined, 55 percent for males and 23 percent for females.

Of all those recorded as employed in Banaskantha, 78 percent were working in the agricultural sector. But, under a drought that lasted from 1985 to 1988, crops consistently failed. Thus, the agricultural sector, where thousands found employment, suffered the worst impact of the drought.

The livestock population had actually decreased from 1,298,024 head in 1977 to 1,251,017 head in a little over a decade. After that decade, during which other regions of India significantly increased their herds, Banaskantha's declined from want of food and water, among other things. Meanwhile, the number of electric motors used for pumping water out of wells, to compensate for the lack of rain, went up from 3,983 in 1977 to 24,329 in 1988. By 1999, 46 percent of the state's power used in the agricultural sector was consumed by four northern districts, including Banaskantha, solely for the purpose of pumping groundwater

(*The Economic Times:* 3). The vast majority of those pumps belonged to the wealthier farmers, the only ones with the resources to purchase such machinery. The smaller farmers have had to deal with the compounded effect of drought and over-tapped underground water resources. The drought conditions have cost the state and region dearly, but it has cost the poorest the most.

Santalpur and Radhanpur talukas ('taluka' is the administrative level just above village), the focus of SEWA's work in the district, reflect even more destitution, relative to the rest of Banaskantha. Of the two resource-poor talukas, Santalpur and Radhanpur, the former was the poorer. 23 percent of the women in Banaskantha could supposedly read, as against 17 percent and 16 percent respectively in Santalpur and Radhanpur respectively.

The gender ratio, a useful standard for measuring gender equality, is lower in these two talukas than in almost all other places in the country. In Radhanpur, there were 918 women per 1,000 men. In Santalpur, there are 914 women per 1,000 men. This discrepancy points to severe inequality, as will be discussed in detail below.

In terms of agricultural potential, although only 68 percent of Radhanpur's total land area was cultivable, Santalpur could only cultivate a meager 55 percent of its land. But, with a rise in irrigation and mechanized farming (1977: a total of 754 tractors; 1988: a total of 3,526 tractors), a large proportion of the uncultivable land was being encroached upon. This was good in that it raised production, but it did so only temporarily. As the farmed soil was leached of what little nutrients it had, it would be abandoned by the cultivators and left exposed and vulnerable to the encroaching desert.

Industry was not noticeably present in Banaskantha (employing only 7 percent of the employed population), least of all in the two talukas that are the focus of SEWA's work. If major progress is to be made, it has to be land-based. It is partially the poor condition of the land that is reflected in the population's poverty.

Within that population, there are severe, gender-based divisions. In the census, 74 percent of the women in Banaskantha were recorded as 'non-workers'. This meant that, officially, as defined in the opening pages of the 1991 District Census, each of those women constituted 'a person who had no economic activity during the reference of one year preceding the date of enumeration'. Considering traditional views of women and work, the validity of this statistic is debatable, but, either way, it sheds light on a sad situation. Their contributions to the labor market were either intentionally discounted or unconsciously ignored. In either case, the value of women's work was unrecognized and one could assume this was reflected in other ways as well. Indeed, other statistics bear this observation out.

Perhaps, the most illuminating of all is the male-female ratio, already mentioned but here, for analytical purposes, considered in Banaskantha as a whole. According to the census, for every 1,000 males in Banaskantha, there were 932 females. Considering that women have a physiological survival advantage over men, other things being equal, this statistic is tragic. In societies where the gender divide is less unequal, women have a measurable survival advantage in the first crucial months of infancy, as well as a tendency to outlive their male counterparts. This is universally attributed to women's biological superiority in terms of survival capability. That there are fewer women in Banaskantha indicates that the harsh realities of poverty in that district are disproportionately borne by the women.

To put this last statistic in more vivid terms, we can compare the gender ratio of Banaskantha to that of Kerala, a state in India where the gender ratio is considered to be more on a par with the natural rate, 1,036 women per 1,000 men (UNFPA 1999: 23). Assuming that Banaskantha could have achieved the same ratio, if women there were equally valued in society, there would be 104 more women per 1,000 men in Banaskantha today. That is a total of 116,414 more women who would be living in Banaskantha today. But, the fact is that these women are not alive. They are missing. Because they were the victims of infanticide due to their gender, or died young of malnutrition and neglect in favor of older or younger brothers, they are missing. Because they survived a precarious infancy so that they could struggle through a double workload, responsible for both making an income and maintaining a household, getting less food and less sleep than they would if they were male, they died young and they are missing. Because they died several years earlier than they would have if they were male, despite their natural survival advantage, they are missing.

True, 87,311 would have been labeled 'non-workers' despite fighting to find employment every day since they were 14 years old (74 percent of the missing women). True, 89,639 of those missing women, at least, are missing out on a lifetime of illiteracy (77 percent of the missing women). And they are missing out on many more of life's difficulties that are less quantifiable. However, they are also missing out on the caprice of adolescence, the joys of motherhood, and the satisfaction and the respect old age brings, among an infinite number of other things.

However, 40,000 of their surviving sisters, now members of BDMSA, are realizing those dreams and struggling to claim their rights to many more. Since 1989, they have been reviving a devastated economy, reclaiming a declining ecosystem, reshaping local politics and society, and rebuilding their communities. Let us see how they are doing it.

Notes

1. At the time of writing, Rs. 42 was roughly equivalent to US$ 1.
2. Much of this section is directly and indirectly indebted to *Where Women are Leaders*, an exceptional history of the first two decades of the SEWA Movement, authored by Kalima Rose and published by Vistaar Publications in 1992.
3. In the Gujarati language, the word 'ben' translates to 'sister.' It is also attached to a woman's first name as a suffix, as in 'Elaben.' As such, it is meant to indicate a combination of respect and affectionate familiarity.
4. The reference is to the popular Chinese proverb 'Give a man a fish and he will eat for a day. Teach him to fish and he will eat for a lifetime.'
5. Unless otherwise noted, all figures in this section are from the Banaskantha District Census 1991.

Chapter 2
WATERSHED DEVELOPMENT

Roughly two-thirds of India is subject to drought conditions, that can have a devastating effect on the economy and society. The state of Gujarat experienced a prolonged drought from 1985 to 1987 as three successive monsoons failed to materialize. In 1983–84, two years before the drought, 5.7 million tons of food grains were produced in the state. In 1984–85, the year before the drought, 5.3 million tons of food grains were produced in Gujarat. In 1985–86, the year the drought began, the total had dropped to 2.7 million tons, followed by 3.1 million tons the next year. By the third year of the drought, the total was down to 1.4 million tons (Chen 1991: 167). In short, the final year of the drought produced only 26 percent of the food grains that had been produced in the year before the drought.

Going further back in history, in a drought that had lasted from 1899 to 1901, an estimated 15 percent of the population of Gujarat had died over the two-year period (ibid: 168). Fortunately, droughts in India are less devastating to life today, but they still have a tremendous impact on lifestyle. Thanks to lessons learned from previous centuries, human consumption patterns in drought rarely decline to a fatal level. However, production as well as income, along with other benefits that come with it, are still susceptible to a precipitous decline in times of drought.

Furthermore, the belt-tightening that does take place affects women from poor households most of all. In one study based on a village in Gujarat, it was estimated that women had to spend as many as three hours collecting fodder for their husbands' cattle and fuel for their cooking fires during the drought. This figure should be compared with the hour or less they would have normally spent doing the same tasks (ibid: 179). Added to the amount of time they had to spend fetching water, this is a substantial amount of time that could have been used performing any other of the multitude of tasks these women must otherwise perform every day.

As a reward for their increased workload, when there is less food for the family, it is the women who have to cut down on their food intake most substantially. When a loan needs to be procured from the moneylender in order to buy food, it is the woman's only property — her jewelry, which is the equivalent of a bank account in an impoverished household — that is mortgaged first. Water is an essential part of the people's lives and its absence infects every aspect of their existence, especially the women's.

It is clear that water is a necessity for survival. But less apparent are the repercussions if it is not easily available. In Banaskantha, there was a time, before human and natural elements combined to desertify the environment, when water was more readily available. The roots of the trees and other vegetation retained the rain that fell from the sky, naturally maintaining the quality and quantity in the water table. Likewise, with the retention of moisture in the ground, more roots were nourished and more greenery thrived. Such was the foundation of the thriving life cycle on the border of the desert.

Yet, this balance was fragile and, in the 20th century, the loggers and farmers were insensitive to the vulnerability of their environment. The clearing away of the trees for lumber and the tilling of the soil for crops tipped the scales out of balance. The moisture evaporated from the exposed soil and, when the rains came, the water would erode the soil rather than get absorbed by it. So, as time went by, droughts became more frequent and the water table began to drop, and the people found themselves adapting to the changes. Women responsible for getting the household's water had only to go as far as the village well originally. But, as time passed and these wells either dried up, or their upkeep was neglected, successive generations of women would find themselves traveling further and further to secure their supply. Granddaughters would walk 4 kilometers when their grandmothers only had to walk a few hundred meters to perform the same task. But, because this was a gradual change, the succeeding generations of women probably found the increased time spent on the chore less objectionable. What you don't know can't hurt you?

To the objective observer, who has to travel only as far as the nearest faucet, the idea of spending up to five hours toting several liters of water for the day's supply would seem intolerable. Yet, this is the reality for some of the women in Gujarat. When one considers this in the light of the time that could be spent in other productive activities, this situation seems doubly ludicrous. If a third of a woman's waking hours are spent collecting water, that means that she has that much of time less to harvest the crops, collect gum or salt, or tend to the multitude of family needs. For these reasons and more, better water supply was clearly a viable option for initiating a development program with the greatest effect.

The Santalpur Regional Water Supply Scheme

Those who first undertook the development effort in Banaskantha in the late 1970s focused on the water supply. A water supply pipeline was initiated in a joint effort between the Gujarat State Government and the Royal Netherlands Government in 1978. Over a course of 10 years this pipeline was constructed and, in theory, it supplied 102 villages in Banaskantha with potable water. In practice, the water was not extended to all the villages and, more importantly, the water alone did not unlock much of the region's potential.

The nationwide Indo-Dutch Rural Water Supply Scheme took the form of an ambitious pipeline water supply program in Banaskantha. The local effort was named the Santalpur Regional Water Supply Scheme. The program was initiated with the Gujarat State Sewerage and Water Supply Board as the implementing body. Over a course of 10 years, six large tubewells were dug within the drainage area of the Banas river. This water was pumped into one pipeline first, and then two pipelines, and ultimately three, across the Santalpur and Radhanpur talukas of the Banaskantha district.

Getting water, let alone economic progress, to the villages proved a more elusive goal than originally expected. Leaks that developed, punctures made by vandals, flaws in design, and even hotels that illegally tapped the water—all these reduced the water pressure in the pipeline so that many of the villages at the tailend of the scheme got little or no water at all. Despite a significant investment, the pipeline was not running as desired.

Furthermore, the combined effect of the six tubewells, in addition to the other wells that were constructed by wealthier farmers near the Banas river, was a measurable drop in the water table of the region. Village wells that had been working dried up and needed to be dug deeper. Many village water users were simply excluded from getting water from their own wells. Depending upon the location or the season, only wells of a significant depth could provide water, and this depth could only be achieved through the expensive process of getting the proper machinery to dig a borewell. However, the resources required to make borewells, or other expensive water-harvesting structures, were not generally available to small farmers.

Lastly, concurrent with this drop in the water table was a decline in the quality of the water available. Fluoride began to rise to levels that made the water undrinkable. Besides, the salt content began to increase to a degree that made the water not only undrinkable, but also detrimental to the crops in the fields in long run. Thus, not only the lack of water but also the poor quality of the available supply had a wide and detrimental impact.

The goal of the Santalpur Regional Water Supply Scheme was not simply the supply of water for its own sake. The water availability was expected to unlock the human potential that had dried up with the decrease in water supply. However, what the Santalpur Regional Water Supply Scheme seemed to have assumed was that, with the availability of water, the rest would automatically take care of itself. Thus, the entire focus of the program had been on the supply of water alone. Little or no attention was paid to the other ingredients necessary to implement a complete program that would lead to an improvement in the quality of life of the local population.

By the late 1980s, the Dutch Bilateral Aid Program, which funded the water supply scheme in Gujarat and other areas of India, was heavily criticized both in India and the Netherlands as inefficient, poorly prepared and monitored, as also for its nexus with Dutch business interests and its generally low impact on poverty alleviation (Schulpen 1997). To the critics' credit, such honest self-criticism was rare by that time. In 1981, the Annual Consultation on the water programs, carried out by a Dutch delegation, called for a more 'integrated approach,' including community participation and an emphasis on income-generating activities. In 1984, however, the minutes of the Annual Consultation was talking of the 'passive attitude of the Indian authorities on this point' (ibid: 124).

The problems of water salinity and fluoride content, poor community participation, and poor impact on poverty alleviation, were pandemic across the other regions where the water supply schemes were undertaken. In Uttar Pradesh, Andhra Pradesh, Kerala, Himachal Pradesh, and Karnataka, there were similar difficulties (ibid: 124). Yet, it still took over a decade to begin addressing these issues substantively.

It was eventually apparent that a more grass-roots approach was required to complement the new physical infrastructure of the Santalpur Regional Water Supply Scheme. Hence, the BDMSA program itself had its foundation in the Water as a Regenerative Input program. Originally, SEWA and the FPI were invited to do a study on the impact of the pipeline on the local people. What they found was that many of the villages were not only not getting the expected water from the pipeline, but had also become dependent on the supposedly forthcoming supply. Relying on the promises of the scheme, many villages had neglected to prepare for the probability that the promised water would not come. This resulted in the exacerbation of the water problem rather than its alleviation.

Also, it was found that the physical planning of the program was not only faulty as mentioned before. The location of the water stand-posts, where the people could access the water, was often found to be in an inconvenient area. Either it was too far from the houses, or it was on land claimed by those who sought to control access to the water for personal gain. In many villages, the location of the stand-post was as far as 2 kilometers from some of the houses, not centrally located, but at one extreme end of the village.

On the basis of the findings of the impact study, and the difficulties it brought to light, the GWSSB began to explore the possibility of adopting a more grass-roots approach. For this reason, an invitation was extended to SEWA to initiate a program that targeted the needs of the rural community more directly.

Because SEWA was invited to join the Rural Water Supply Scheme well after the construction of the water pipeline had begun, building from the existing resources was the most practical strategy. Hence, in the spirit of grass-roots development, SEWA and the FPI undertook a program of 'action research.' They tried to understand the specific needs of the community by interacting with the people, with the goal of formulating the most effective intervention strategy together.

The Pani Panchayat

SEWA first focused on the status of the pani panchayats, or village water committees: 'pani' means water in Hindi and Gujarati, and 'panchayat' is the title for the village-level, elected government body. What they discovered in their action research was that the pani panchayats were, without exception, non-functional, existing only in name. Initiators of the Indo-Dutch scheme had first developed the concept of the pani panchayat in 1979. However, beyond issuing the government directive and informing the village leadership that they were responsible for organizing the board, little had been done to actually foster its development. There was no effort to encourage establishment of the pani panchayats by outlining its goals. There was no interest in training the members or reflecting with them upon what would be the best way to be effective.

In response to the government inquiries regarding the members, the village sarpanch, or head of the panchayat, would simply list the names of appropriate villagers, without ever informing those named. Thus, when SEWA went through the list of pani panchayat members in a particular village, they often found that those on the list were not even aware that they were part of the board, let alone what their responsibilities were. Needless to say, they did not meet on a regular basis, if they met at all. Because so many of the development activities were water-based, it was clear that this situation had to be rectified.

The root of the problem was the traditionally top-down organization of the water supply system. Since India's independence in 1947, the government has tried to actively encourage development through central planning. 'The Five-Year Plans,' a regular governmental fixture, have dictated a centralized role in the economic development of the nation. This strategy has put the resources of the whole country behind the effort, but it has also given rise to several problems. One such problem derived from the government's penchant for focusing on one particular area of development at the expense of another. In the case of water, the first Five-Year Plan's focus on industrial development secured the majority of the national water resources for commercial use. In Gujarat, this meant that the textile mills and chemical plants, for example, got over 70 percent of the available water. In the 1970s, with the advent of the Green Revolution, the major allocation of water shifted to agricultural use. However, those who benefited the most were the larger farmers who could afford access to irrigation materials and technology. Whether the money resources went to industry or large-scale agriculture, it was the small-scale water user who lost out.

SEWA sought to address the issue by empowering the local communities so that they could advocate their own needs and ultimately increase and manage their own resources. But this is a process that would take time, and time was at a premium when monsoons were unpredictable and water was running out. Furthermore, the GWSSB looked to SEWA as the body responsible for encouraging pani panchayats to collect payment from the villagers for recovery of the pipeline program's cost. For the GWSSB, this became the first priority.

SEWA and the FPI began to invest a lot of time and resources in reviving the pani panchayats. Training was arranged and so were meetings, but the problem was more the system than the personnel. A common complaint about development programs is that the 'poor don't pay'. But, after 10 years of unreliable water supply, it was impressed upon the pani panchayats that their first task was to collect the fees for 10 years of water. This did not make the pani panchayats a popular group. Nor did they themselves believe in collecting money for 10 years of water that rarely arrived. Also, in the course of those 10 years, the villagers were never informed that they would have to pay for the water. The demands put upon the pani panchayats by the GWSSB were simply unreasonable.

However, in defense of the GWSSB, the demands were being put upon them from a higher source. A Finance Committee comprising persons from the World Bank, Government of India, and the United Nations performed an analysis of the entire water supply scheme and was very critical of the program's neglect of cost-recovery considerations. Considering the stature of these three bodies, the GWSSB had to take these criticisms very seriously. Immediate and resolute steps had to be taken to collect payments from the villages, apparently regardless of how amenable the circumstances were.

In search of an expeditious solution, the GWSSB sought to implement a cost-recovery program without sufficient preparation. The issue of payment then became an obstacle to progress on any other issue. The pani panchayats were reluctant or unable to collect the money, and the GWSSB refused to go any further until the cost-recovery issue was resolved.

Realizing the predicament, SEWA undertook a mediating role between the pani panchayats and the GWSSB. The difficulties were many and extended beyond the collection of money from the villagers. Another responsibility of the pani panchayats was the repair and maintenance of the pipeline in their respective domains. This included patching up holes in the pipes, replacing broken or defective taps and clearing up blockages. All this necessitated tools and parts, which the pani panchayats were responsible for requisitioning. The process, to be strictly followed, was that, if any part was needed, the pani panchayat had to fill out an application and submit it to the GWSSB office. If the GWSSB did not have the needed item in stock, the pani panchayat would have to wait until it was available. The panchayat was not allowed to seek out the item through a local merchant, although it might have been procured there more quickly, closer to the village, and at a lower cost. All the while, the villagers would still be responsible for paying for the water they were not receiving.

A more practical approach, which the pani panchayats and SEWA proposed, was that, of the funds collected from the villages for water, the pani panchayat keep a small portion in order to cover the maintenance costs and responsibilities independently. For the pani panchayats to consider such an undertaking was a tribute to the progress they had made in fulfilling their function. However, the GWSSB was not keen on relinquishing their complete control over the program, even though it meant the cost-recovery would not be fully implemented.

Meanwhile, SEWA and the pani panchayat members remained dedicated to improving the status of water availability in the villages. To achieve these ends, the panchayat members, as well as other representatives of the originally neglected communities (primarily of the lower castes) were invited to join new village water committees. In coordination with establishment of income-generating programs, to be discussed later, SEWA advocated augmentation of the pipeline water, using traditional water-harvesting techniques. By improving or establishing village ponds, digging or recharging village wells, in addition to introducing innovative techniques such as roof water tanks, smaller-scale projects would increase the capacity of the villages to harvest water and earn an income, with which they could pay the GWSSB, among other things. The expanded water committees sought to develop these ideas. They wanted to mobilize the funds independently and orchestrate the operation and maintenance of the water resources. This, however, was to prove a bureaucratically arduous task.

SEWA was immediately criticized by the Dutch officials for taking up work beyond its technical ability. SEWA responded by underlining that traditional technology was to be the base of the program. But the Dutch Embassy felt that this was not a legitimate approach. They, therefore, cut SEWA's budget for all water-based activities. SEWA and the Water Committee members then turned to the GWSSB for support. But, because the proposed ponds and wells were meant to serve several village functions beyond drinking water, such as irrigation for small-scale agriculture, the GWSSB was not interested. The additional functions were beyond their mandated role.

Without the support of their original partners, the Dutch and the GWSSB, the group turned to the Minor Irrigation Department, only to learn that the department exclusively supported the construction of check dams. Next, the State Groundwater and Sewerage Department would not get involved with the construction of surface sources, which eliminated the inclusion of village ponds as a possibility. At that point, on three occasions, SEWA and the village water committees pooled their resources and hired private engineering firms to carry out the work. However, on all these occasions, the senior engineer on the project disappeared with the funds, and the project remained unimplemented.

Finally, the group met with success through the help of the Indian Petro-Chemicals Limited (IPCL). The IPCL wanted to test a new pond lining material and technique of application. Their product was 'agrifilm'. A plastic based material, it acted as a barrier between the sweet rainwater and the saline soil if placed on the walls and bottom of the pond. By keeping the rainwater and soil from mixing, the agrifilm would keep the pond from being tainted by salt.

The IPCL was confident in its product, but needed a showcase. Gokhantar village needed a feasible solution to its water problem. Its only village pond was extremely saline and retained water only for a few months out of the year, in good years. Thus, the village was chosen as that showcase. With SEWA and Gokhantar providing the funding, and the IPCL providing the technical expertise and agrifilm at cost, work got under way.

Construction began in 1993, but ran into a snag when it was discovered that the site selected, the old village pond, still retained moist, saline soil which would corrode the lining material. Since this discovery was made late in the dredging process, by the time the site was shifted to a more appropriate spot, the monsoon rains were threatening to arrive before work was done. Indeed, the first wave of the monsoon passed before the pond was finished and the water escaped harvesting. However, the lining was in place in time for the second wave of rains and the water saved from those rains lasted until the next year's monsoon.

In a similar fashion, a lined pond was constructed in Datrana the following year, with even greater success. Two more ponds in two other villages were planned for 2000, and seven in the next three years. The success has convinced others as well. The National Watershed Development Program, to be discussed presently, and the United Nations Development Program's Community-based Pro-Poor Initiatives have now joined the village water committees in ensuring construction of the lined ponds.

Other technical experience was gained through a trip to Israel, in which three water committee members from the program were included. The knowledge these women gained in this water-starved, expertise-rich country included techniques for planting nurseries on the rims of the ponds, and reducing the exposed surface area of the ponds all in the interests of minimizing evaporation. A delegation of Israeli experts was then invited to Banaskantha to evaluate the progress here and make further suggestions. In five short years, SEWA and the water committees overcame the criticism of the Dutch and others that they lacked the ability to undertake the proposed utilization of traditional resources. With these experiences and their newfound technical knowledge, the water programs were well poised to progress with any opportunities that arose.

The Watershed Development Program

In 1995, the water program entered a new phase. The Watershed Development Program is a national government program that integrates several water-based development strategies in arid, semi-arid, and drought-prone areas. The BDMSA began participating in the program in 1995. Since then, a consistent source of funding has been available for water-based activities, and this has greatly enhanced the productivity of the program. All the traditional activities the BDMSA had previously undertaken are still utilized, but now on a larger scale. In addition, activities that restructure the land surface to reduce rain run-off and erosion have been added. These include construction of check dams, tree-planting, land-leveling and contour bunding.

With the freedom to implement the program from the beginning, the BDMSA was able to bypass the failed pani panchayats and organize the village women directly to take the leadership role in watershed development. They have now formed new water committees independent of the previous constraints put upon the pani panchayats. Since then, the program has been implemented in eight villages with notable success.

The program makes a portion of the required money available to the villagers according to a budget prepared by the village water committee. The funds are used for the construction of water-harvesting structures, on the condition that the village contributes a similar amount of money. The program is implemented over a course of four years with a fixed budget, to be spent in a well-planned manner and at the discretion of the village. Each of the eight villages has its own committee—consisting primarily of women—which conducts the business and planning for the watershed program. Together, they manage mobilization of funds as well as the operation and maintenance of the water resources.

In every village, the program follows a similar structure. The work begins with one or more village-level meetings with all the villagers and a team of SEWA organizers. The SEWA organizers explain the whole program, and then open up the discussion, ultimately mapping a collective course of action. Members of the water committee are chosen, with representatives of all the different sub-communities in the village included. All castes, 'outcastes' and religions, as well as small farmers and agricultural laborers are provided representation, with at least a half of the members of the new committee being women.

After the committee is chosen, they select an entry-point activity; a small project, such as building a village crèche, that will give the community experience in working together. Upon the success of this activity, the larger water project is undertaken. For the village's portion of the project funds, engineers ascertain the catchment area for the proposed water structure. Those who would benefit directly are made responsible for raising the funds. A typical check dam, for example, would directly supply water to all the landholders within a half-kilometer radius. They would either then contribute the funds in the form of labor, cash or a portion of their subsequent harvest.

In Banaskantha, the communal structure of the program is particularly important. In part because the value of the land is so low, Banaskantha has a large number of small landholders, relative to districts with richer agricultural land, where high land values exclude those with fewer resources. Thus, one check dam may supply water to a dozen or more landholders within a half-kilometer radius in Banaskantha. Cooperation between all those interested parties is then essential to the overall success of the activity.

Because of the structure of the program, the support of the villagers is required and represented through their contributions to the funding and labor for the projects. That way, with each person having a vested interest, each is encouraged to have his or her voice heard, and each has a reason to listen. The chances of success are reinforced by the collective involvement as, over the course of the program, the different activities undertaken in a village spread the benefits.

In the first year Rs. 62,500 is made available to each village, Rs. 100,000 in the second, Rs. 62,500 in the third, and Rs. 25,000 in the fourth. This typically allows for several different activities, with one check dam typically requiring Rs. 90,000 from the government program. Thus, through the four years of the program, several portions of the village and the surrounding area are covered, with the sites being chosen primarily by the outside engineers, who determine the most technically suitable locations for water-harvesting structures. These sites are then reviewed by the water committees.

Difficulties have inevitably arisen within the villages. Everyone obviously wants the direct benefit of the program, and some are reluctant to pay. However, because the whole village ultimately benefits, most of these difficulties are worked out. In cases where landowners avoid contributing to the effort, the water committees have, without exception, been able to work out an arrangement agreeable to all parties. In some cases, the water committees have even been creative, extending loans, for example, to the reluctant landowners and allowing them to pay their portion on an installment basis.

On two occasions, the program was forced to stop completely. In both cases, the difficulty was not individual but communal. In the village of Vauva, for example, different communal factions divided by caste and political party affiliations tried to win control of the water committee. When the Ahir caste won out, all others pulled out, and work never began for lack of communal support. Similarly, in the village of Bamroli, Thakurs and Muslims refused to work together halfway through the project, and progress had to be abandoned. However, these two exceptions are outshone by numerous other success stories.

Extensions to the four-year program are currently being considered. The suggestion for extensions has come from government officials, satisfied with the success so far. However, the original goals have been fulfilled and the villages involved have made many gains. The potential for the extension does not reflect the need to finish what remains undone, but rather to expand the achievements already made.

The benefits of the BDMSA members' activity in improving the rainwater-harvesting techniques are many. First and foremost, it has provided the members and their communities with a year-round source of drinking water. Second, it has decreased the amount of time the women must spend in getting the daily water. This, in turn, has freed them to invest more time in income-generating activities.

Third, it has enhanced the village-wide capacity to earn income throughout the year. Since the economy of the area is primarily agricultural, the impact of a year-round source of irrigation is significant. Because of the check dams, land-leveling, and well improvement that has taken place through the program, many villages now have a year-round supply of drinking water, and enough surplus to produce two to three crops a year on some fields, instead of only one meager crop.

Fourth, village health risks have been reduced. Water is the essential factor in matters of hygiene and sanitation. At a meeting in Mar del Plata,

Argentina, where the nations of the world declared the 1980s to be the "International Drinking Water Supply and Sanitation Decade," it was estimated that 80 percent of the worldwide child mortality is due to poor drinking water and lack of proper sanitary conditions. Without water, regardless of how health-conscious a person may be, there are few options

Plate 2.1: Women collect drinking water from a well constructed under the Santalpur Regional Water Supply Scheme

for maintaining a clean living environment. Similarly, an excess of water not managed correctly, collecting in stagnant pools for example, can become a breeding ground for diseases such as malaria. The watershed activity has managed to make water available and to manage it in a manner that is safe for the community.

The total benefits of the watershed program are difficult to enumerate. Since water is such a central factor in everyday life, the program's impact is felt in countless ways. For that reason and others, the watershed program is the first discussed in this book. In relation to all the programs, whose descriptions follow, it must be remembered that the availability of water has in some way made them possible.

Biography: Too Busy to Migrate

It is late in the evening, the sun has set, and Rajiben, from the village of Garamdi, is done with most of her daily duties. Her day began before the sun rose. She prepared breakfast, swept the floor and milked her buffaloes, depositing the milk with the village cooperative. After breakfast and cleaning up, she headed for the fields, collecting fodder and firewood. After she returned with the wood and fodder, she quickly left the house again to get the water. The village tap was actually flowing today, a rare event. Garamdi is one of the villages at the tail-end of the Santalpur pipeline.

The women of the village crowded the tap, filling their jugs in turn. To take advantage of the auspicious arrival of the water, Rajiben and the other women made several trips to the stand, with pots stacked and balanced, three-high on their heads. They need to get enough water to last for at least four days. The water comes twice a week under the best of circumstances. But sometimes it does not come at all for several weeks.

Rajiben is a leader of the Garamdi Water Committee. Once a week she has to go to the GWSSB office in Radhanpur to ensure that her village gets water. She first stops at the SEWA office and together, with an organizer, presents a request for water at the GWSSB. The request, in writing, is usually answered and her village gets its water twice a week. However, without this constant agitation, the village would likely get nothing.

Tonight, a few people have gathered at Rajiben's house, sitting around, talking about the past—the women around the cooking fire and the men hovering near the door, smoking bidis. There is no electricity in the village, but the light from the hissing kerosene lamp illuminates the group of men and women reminiscing. The year before SEWA became involved in Banaskantha, Rajiben and her family had to migrate out of Garamdi, as was the case for most people in the village, as was the case in most years. It was the final year of a prolonged drought, and the family left the village with five buffaloes, coming back a few months later with only three. Two had died of starvation and thirst on the way to Saurashtra district. This constituted a major loss in income and assets for the family.

In those days, Rajiben recalls, the water pipeline came to the village, but almost never worked. She jokingly looks at the men in the room and chides them about their inaction on the issue. There was a pani panchayat, all men, but they never met. They never did anything about the lack of water. To them, there seemed to be no lack of household water. If they wanted a drink, then there was always a jug of water in the house. They were not the ones who had to walk 3 kilometers to the hotel near the highway in order to get the water and carry it all the way back, Rajiben exclaims. The men sitting nearby mumble, smirk and look at the ground for lack of a good response.

Regardless of the scarcity of drinking water, everyone felt the impact of the lack of water in the fields and for the animals. This required improvement beyond the scale of what the pipeline intended, let alone actually accomplished. Therefore, when Garamdi began implementing the "Water as a Regenerative Input" program, their choice of activities reflected a high priority for improving their income and checking the push factors for migration. They have since focused on irrigation resources and contour bunding. A well has been dug and the land has been leveled, so that, when the rains do come, it will be absorbed into the soil rather than eroding the soil away.

The village water committee is also making plans for a new watershed development project. Their neighbors in the village of Datrana have an agrifilm pond. Garamdi is in agreement that they want one, too. They are already preparing to procure the funds among themselves and gather the technical inputs. They expect to have their pond by the year 2002.

Will she have to migrate again? Rajiben has taken a loan from her SEWA savings group and purchased a new buffalo. This is a drought year again and she worries about her investment. But she also realizes that things are a lot better than they were. She gets fodder at a reasonable price as part of the SEWA dairy cooperative, so her cattle will survive. She also gets better access to drinking water to free her and her neighbors from the burden of spending a few hours a day just to get it. This is time that can be used earning income, or taking care of household work. Besides, she feels she owes it to her village to stay and keep the pipeline flowing.

Despite the drought, she will not migrate. Even the progress that has been made thus far, after only a few years, has made a significant and positive impact on her life. She will stay and she will continue to work towards a better future where, perhaps, even the question of whether or not to migrate will become obsolete.

Chapter 3

FORESTRY AND MINOR
FOREST PRODUCTS

Approximately 75 million hectares of India's total landmass of 318 million hectares is recorded as forested land. Of this, it has been estimated, through satellite imagery, that 64 million hectares actually have forest cover. However, only 35 million hectares have adequate forest cover. The National Forestry Policy calls for a 33 percent forest cover for India, and the call is seconded by international standards. However, by these estimates, only 11 per cent of India has adequate forest cover (Chen 1993: 23). Banaskantha has perhaps even less than the national average.

The environmental conditions in Banaskantha are not entirely of geo-climatically natural origins. Time was when much of this now arid region was more widely covered with trees. It has taken a few generations for the circumstances to degenerate to their present condition, but there are those still living in the villages who remember a greener time. Since then, primarily through commercial wood harvesting and transient agriculture, humans have invited the Rann of Kutch desert to spread its sands more extensively over the district.

The consequences of deforestation in Banaskantha have been thoroughly destructive. The indiscriminate felling of trees has brought about the decline of other vegetation. Without a protective canopy, the soil has been laid bare. Erosion and exposure to the elements, without the nutritive regeneration of the natural cycles of growth and decay, leaches the soil of most of its organic content. Once this decline sets in, droughts naturally become more severe, and floods more devastating. There is no vegetation to store the moisture that invites the rain. Nor is there any vegetation to absorb the run-off when the rain does come.

People whose ancestors had managed to reap their harvests for centuries have now been reduced to a struggle for survival, trying to eke out a living in an increasingly harsh environment. The dominant traditional Indian method of forest utilization is intermediary consumption. Rather than felling trees, people collect fallen twigs and leaves for fuel, or products such as gum from living trees, leaving the trees standing. These trees, left standing, then offer a protective cover under which grasses and other plants grow and thrive, providing food for the people and fodder for their animals. Tree species such as prosopis and neem grow quickly and extensively, offering a large, lush biomass and many by-products. Prosopis provides gum that can be harvested and sold as a source of income. Neem provides leaves and seeds that have medicinal value and are used to combat everything from malaria to tooth decay. However, these trees have often been cut down to clear space for agricultural fields or plantations of teak and eucalyptus for commercial timber production.

In many cases, the hearty and well-adapted prosopis and neem have disguised what in reality was poor soil. Often, a farmer would dispose of the trees and plant his crops in their place only to discover that the soil was poor and saline. Sometimes, this realization can take more than one season. The trees improve the condition of the topsoil by naturally providing biodegradable fertilizer in the form of fallen branches and leaves. However, when the trees are removed, the bare, pre-planting season fields are exposed to the monsoon rains and the equally bare, post-harvest season fields are exposed to the winter winds. Thus, that layer of topsoil soon erodes away.

Similarly, commercial timber tree species are sought for their tall, straight trunks, rather than their lush canopies and beneficial by-products. From such tree species there is little coincidental wood-fuel production, nor much protective cover for ground-level vegetable growth. The tendency toward monoculture plantations also makes the trees vulnerable to being universally wiped out by pests or diseases. This vulnerability, and the more certain possibility of tree-cutting, means that the soil will inevitably be laid completely bare and depleted.

The impact of cutting down forests for agricultural use, and in order to make space for commercial timber, is compounded by the increasing population pressure, which makes even more demands on the dwindling resources. It is estimated that India, as a nation, derives 33 percent of its energy from wood-fuel resources. In the context of the rural areas alone, the amount increases to 80 percent of all energy consumed (Chen 1993: 25). In addition, the rising cattle population creates an increasing demand for fodder. These two trends (decreasing supply of, and increasing demand for, wood resources), juxtaposed against each other, indicate a problem of tremendous proportions.

Government Forestry
Policies and Initiatives

Soon after Independence, the Indian government nationalized the country's forests in the interests of revenue and conservation. However, in terms of conservation, even by the 1950s, the tide was not in their favor. In the first half of the 20th century, the agricultural land in the country increased rapidly by as much 45 percent in some areas, particularly in the north, while land with forest cover rapidly declined, by as much as 40 percent in those same areas (Chen 1993: 22). This was less a sign of the failure of conservation activity and more a sign of successful revenue activity. Devastating famines loomed large in the history of the subcontinent and India was determined to avoid these disasters by expanding food production to the point where it could even afford to export an agricultural surplus. Although agricultural growth came a distant second to industrial expansion in the early years of the nation, it was, nevertheless, a national priority. Unfortunately, this was sometimes at the expense of India's trees.

The national and state forestry departments all date back to British Indian institutions, and many retain some of their original attitudes. Forestry in the colonial era was often a militant affair. As a precious and essential resource to the British, who relied heavily on sea power and thus wooden ships to sustain their empire, Indian forests were a closely guarded resource. In a largely misguided anxiety over local populations felling the trees, forestry officials in the British era often armed themselves and literally guarded the forests.

Furthermore, like many colonial government institutions, the forestry departments became highly profitable agencies, levying lucrative fees on timber exports and leasing forested lands to timber merchants. Both the traditions, of protection and profit, linger on. State and national forestry departments represent some of the most impenetrable bureaucracies, and one of the very few government agencies (if not the only one) that now run on a consistently profitable basis. These traditions have had their impact on policy today.

As the decline in forest cover caught the attention of the central government, pressure was stepped up on the forestry departments to reverse the trend. The departments responded by supporting people to plant more trees and, more specifically, by encouraging private landowners to plant timber-producing trees on their property. The policies outlined schemes by which the forestry departments would supply saplings to people and buy back the grown trees when they were ready for harvesting. These schemes implied that the people involved would have land to grow the trees on, and that the trees would be of commercially viable timber varieties.

These schemes were successful in that many landowners adopted the schemes and benefited from it. However, the scheme inadvertently hurt the rural poor. To make room for the plantations, agricultural land was supplanted with trees. This was, of course, the positive aim of the scheme, but it had its adverse effects. It displaced agricultural labor. The trees were much less labor-intensive in comparison to annual crops and so left many of the rural poor jobless. It seemed a no-win situation, with deforestation balanced against unemployment.

Furthermore, the timber plantations contributed relatively little to the local economy, other than putting money in the pocket of one local landowner. For agriculture, money was distributed from the local labor pool, to the local farmers, to the local merchants. However, in the timber business, the local labor was largely excluded, and the network of local merchants was not as widespread as in the agricultural sector. Instead, timber was often handled by merchants at the regional level and elsewhere by urban exporters and industries. Thus, timber plantations contributed to a widening income gap between the landless and the landowners, and the rural classes and the urban.

Lastly, timber plantations contributed as minimally to the local ecology as to the local economy. The commercial timber species, such as eucalyptus and teak, did little to regenerate the soil or provide a canopy under which ground vegetation could thrive. Thus, there was room for improvement in the forestry policy.

In the early 1980s, the Government of Gujarat took these shortcomings into consideration and several changes were written into law. Most importantly, government land was made available to the landless as individuals, cooperatives and parts of institutions, such as schools or voluntary agencies. The reforms in Gujarat culminated in the January 1987 Government Resolution, stipulating that government fallow land, wasteland, sandy land and saline land would be offered on a lease basis. These leases would be extended to applicants, with priority accorded to the Scheduled Castes and Scheduled Tribes, landless persons and marginal farmers (Dhagamwar 1993: 215).

Later, under the 1988 National Forestry Policy, the Indian government called for an end to the commercial exploitation of forests for industrial purposes. Instead, forests were to be utilized for the conservation of the soil and environment, and to serve the subsistence needs of the local population. The policy stated that: "The life of tribals and other people living within and near forests revolves around forests. The rights and concessions enjoyed by them should be fully protected. Their domestic requirements for fuel wood, fodder, minor forest produce and construction timber should be the first charge on forest produce" (as quoted, Kalipada 1997: 173).

The impetus for this explicit change in policy came after the Planning Commission for the Eighth Plan concluded that previous attempts at social forestry showed signs of success, but were too small and scattered to be significant. Thus, efforts were to be expanded, influencing statements such as the one just quoted, and helping to create the National Watershed Development Program (Kalipada 1997: 174). All this left the door open for SEWA and its members to engage in forestry activity.

Women and Reforestation

With the introduction of forestry reforms, the SEWA members were in a sound position to make the most of the opportunities available to them. Since they were organized, they were in a better position to negotiate the application process, gain access to useful training and information, and accumulate leverage in marketing. But, most of all, they were simply at an advantage as women.

The rural poor women are the primary collectors and users of minor forestry products. The average woman in an impoverished rural household will often spend more than an hour collecting wood for the cooking fire and fodder for the animals. In areas where drought and deforestation have had an impact, the time so spent can increase significantly. In addition, some women collect fodder, gum or wood for sale as income. As these women spend a greater portion of their time collecting minor forest products, they can be even more severely affected by drought and deforestation. In either case, adverse conditions will mean that the women have to spend even more time collecting, while at the same time not necessarily being able to collect as much. Both consumption and income can decline, as well as the amount of time available for other activities.

While the women are more vulnerable to the negative impacts of these adverse conditions, they are also more aware of how to overcome them. Because women have long traditionally been assigned the task of collecting and utilizing forest products, they are the ones most aware of which of the products are useful and how to use them. Thus, women are in a better position to determine what kinds of trees would be most useful to a local economy, since they are more intimately aware of the consumption patterns of the economy. While a patriarchal society will base its decisions for nursery and plantation varieties, for example, on the profit of a three-year-old teak tree, women are more likely to see the more subtle but significant short- and long-term advantages of day-to-day fuel and fodder.

In addition, in the early stages, tree nurseries demand a lot of attention. Any new life is fragile and demands the constant attention of caring hands. Trees are no exception and the women are no strangers to this concept either. As mothers and older sisters, they are already well prepared for the type of work required. With training and the opportunity to work, they are naturals. Forestry activity, through nurseries and plantations, is a challenge taken up by the members of SEWA. Aware of the conditions, the women have sought a way to combat the deforestation trend. Tree nurseries and plantations represent a dynamic solution, offering an environmentally conscious activity that can also potentially be a source of income generation and direct consumption.

SEWA Tree Nurseries and Plantations

SEWA began to look into the possibility of establishing a tree production program run by the women members almost as soon as it became involved in Banaskantha. The Gujarat Agricultural University in Disa, Banaskantha, offered its expertise in the field and participated in a comprehensive training program. Trips were arranged for the members to go to the university grounds, and students and professors at the institution also ventured into SEWA's Radhanpur office and the different villages. The women were taught about the various types of trees available and their specific needs, such as techniques for proper watering and protection from the sun.

However, water shortage proved a major obstacle to the program. Because SEWA had focused mainly on 'tail-end' villages that did not receive much water from the pipeline, the nursery members could not get the required amount of water to keep their saplings healthy and alive.

The consequences of water shortage became apparent in the first season, when the women tried to sell their trees to the Gujarat State Women's Development Corporation (GSWDC). The nurseries were not allowed to sell their trees in the open market, but were rather obligated by law to sell their produce to the GSWDC. The GSWDC had a height requirement for the trees they would purchase from the nurseries. Any trees under that height were rejected. The Banaskantha groups, due to the scarcity of water, had a large percentage of their trees below the specified height. As a result, in the first year, 20,000 of the 100,000 saplings were rejected.

The rejection of 20 percent of their produce was devastating to the cooperatives, basically eliminating their profit margin. Most of the rejected saplings were very healthy, the height being a somewhat arbitrary measure of a tree's health. After much follow-up by SEWA, and after an expert from the Gujarat Agricultural University who testified to the health of the saplings, the GSWDC did agree to purchase some of these plants, but it was obvious that difficulties lay ahead.

Unfortunately, many of the original groups that had undertaken nursery activity were forced to close down. Lack of water was the major factor, but other issues contributed. In most cases, the land used for the nurseries had to be leased from the Gujarat State Forestry Development Corporation (GSFDC). However, the lease offered was only for a period of three years. Incorporated into the nursery activity was the plantation phase of the program. The groups could not rely upon selling all of their saplings, nor would they want to. They were a source of continuing income and by-products, providing fruit, wood fuel and shade for fodder. Some of the unsold trees would still be cultivated to the point where they would yield these benefits. However, this process required more than three years to mature. It would take at least four years for the trees to grow to the extent that they could even begin to be substantial sources of such harvests. Without a guarantee that the land would be available for at least 10 years, particularly in the light of other GSFDC policies and inconsistencies, the investment seemed risky.

Some groups did succeed in those first three years, and other groups in villages that could more easily support such a program replaced the ones forced to shut down. Today, in addition to outside sales, trees from BDMSA nurseries and plantations border many village ponds, themselves created through the Watershed Development Program. In addition, fodder farms for the BDMSA dairy cooperatives find the shade they need under the canopy of these trees, in the aisles of the plantations.

Early efforts at tree nursery and plantation activities were also the foundation for a "Feminize Our Forests" campaign that SEWA began in the mid-1990s in several districts. Campaigns have been an essential tool for SEWA since its inception. Knowledge is power, and part of SEWA's approach has always been to empower through knowledge. For this campaign, such empowerment took place on several levels.

Campaigns are a way to create visibility for unrecognized, under-appreciated, or misunderstood causes. Since SEWA's inception as a union of self-employed women, two of its primary functions have been to gain visibility for its members and to create a common vision. Grossly under-represented in census figures, unrecorded in payrolls, absent in government policy decisions and ignored by society before coming together under SEWA, self-employed women were a large but invisible population in India. Once organized, they began to announce their presence, sometimes as individuals or small groups that stood up to abusive contractors, for example, or as groups marching in the streets or occupying a market-place.

With the announcement of their presence, the women have sought to tell others not only that they are here, but also who they are. They did this by sharing knowledge about themselves, the crucial role they play in the econ-omy, how many they are, the lifestyle they live, the conditions they live under, the changes they want to effect and the power they have to effect them. In the process, the self-employed women have recognized those very same things more profoundly for themselves.

In the three decades of SEWA's existence, they have gained a great deal of visibility, and campaigns have been an effective tool in achieving it. As the movement has grown, their campaigns have been able to press beyond issues now considered more fundamental, and embrace a multitude of other issues related to the larger general struggle. The "Feminize Our Forests" campaign was a major example of how SEWA embraced a broader range of issues into its campaign strategy. Focusing on the environmental benefits of reforesta-tion, this program also sought to highlight the capabilities of women have in leading such a program, and the impracticability of government policy in forestry.

With government policy, particularly Gujarat state policy, as a direct target, an issue was made of the paradox of the government on one side encouraging cooperative plantations and nurseries, but at the same time inefficiently engaging in the same activities themselves. The government, in the form of Forestry Department nurseries and plantations, competed with the same people whom they were supposedly helping. If the trees were for research purposes or reforestation of government lands, that would be a different issue. However, most of these trees were being produced for sale. Even while deliberately encouraging the impoverished people in the rural population to engage in nursery and plantation activity for income-generation purposes, the government was directly competing with them.

The government has obvious advantages in land and capital. Their production capabilities are high, which serves to reduce the price of the saplings in the open market. However, the cooperatives cannot sell directly in the open market. Rather, they have to sell to the GSWDC, which sells to the Forestry Department, which then sells in the open market. However, the Forestry Department's first priority is to sell its own saplings before procuring more from the cooperatives. Thus, when the sales are down, the losses are passed on to the cooperatives, with little to no impact on the Forestry Department's revenue.

There is a portion of the trees procured by the GSWDC that are not sold, but instead are given away free of charge. Some of these trees go to places where there would otherwise be no trees, achieving a laudable goal. However, the issue is more complex than that and merits further thought. Although the natural market price of the trees could be at a rate that could sustain the cooperatives at a much more feasible level, the government demands that the cooperatives sell their trees to the GSWDC at a low price, as the corporation gets no returns in giving them away. If the cooperatives were simply allowed to sell in the open market, and did not have to compete with the government giving away the trees at a loss, their prospects would be much brighter.

Furthermore, although most nursery and plantation cooperatives are forced to rely upon the government land for leasing, they are only leased out, as a matter of policy, for a maximum of three years. The absurdity of this policy is evident when one considers how long it takes to transform barren land into a productive nursery, let alone a plantation. Hopefully, once released from the fetters of forestry policy, the nurseries and plantations will be more able to unlock their full potential.

The campaign continues to call attention to the benefits of reforestation and the difficulties in pursuing it. Meanwhile, SEWA members find other ways to utilize what forests there are.

Plate 3.1: Women at work in a nursery and plantation cooperative

Biography: Cause for Optimism

Menaben's early history is a chronology of dismal struggle, and she looks back with anguish. As the eighth of nine children, one of her earliest memories was migrating across the desert to Pakistan as a 10-year-old to find work. For four years in Pakistan, she contributed to the scant family income by working as a laborer in different farmers' fields, making very little money since she was only a child. But, by the time her family left to come back to India, she was 15, old enough to be married.

Much of her early married life coincided with successive droughts. She and her new family, including one small child, had to migrate out of Banaskantha to eastern Gujarat to find work. However, it was still hard for her to find income because of the stigma of her child. The child was seen as an inhibitor to productivity, and she was paid half as much as her fellow-workers. Yet, in reality, she feels, she was just as productive as the rest.

Through years of this kind of unrewarding toil, Menaben developed a hardened, skeptical outlook on life. When a SEWA organizer first came to her village to set up a nursery program, Menaben doubted the benefit of such a program. But her pessimism was a double-edged sword. On the one hand, the program would probably fail like the government programs. But, on the other hand, what did she have to lose? Her work at the time still consisted of field labor, as well as making mud utensils in the off-season months to sell in surrounding villages. She took a chance and joined the group.

In so doing, she also became a SEWA member. It took her five attempts with the help of the organizer before she could pronounce the name of the organization, but this future member of the SEWA Executive Committee did finally manage. The nursery also took multiple efforts. The first nursery failed due to lack of water and the small plant size. But the group then switched to plantation work and found success.

In both activities, Menaben underwent training. For the first training, she was doubtful that her husband would let her go. The training was at the Gujarat Agricultural University in Disa, a day's journey away. Her husband originally rejected the idea, as did other people in her family and village. But the SEWA organizer came, talked to them and convinced them of the value of the experience. After her visit to Disa, she went to Dantiwada Dam. She visited the university nurseries and learned how to graft and prune the trees, as well as water them properly and provide them with sufficient shade.

When Menaben got back to her village, the men and women asked her endless questions about what she saw. She explained it all slowly and in detail, gradually winning their confidence. This left her free to attend other SEWA trips and meetings, eventually taking a leadership position in the organization.

Now she works in the village DWCRA nursery from 8 A.M. to noon. She prunes the trees, applies fertilizer, water, and organic insecticides. She also plants and grows fodder in the aisles between the trees. This she learned about on an exposure trip to Banas Dairy's fodder farm. The trees will not bear fruit until next year, but in the meantime the fodder provides income for the program.

For this work, she gets paid Rs. 125 per month. The rest of the time she works in the fields like she always has. But, with her assured income, and the benefits of the savings group and insurance scheme she takes part in, she has more bargaining power with the farmers. Before becoming a SEWA member, she used to make Rs. 5 to 10 per day. Now she works for no less than Rs. 40 per day. These days, she can be more optimistic that she will find that work.

In fact, Menaben's outlook on many things has become more optimistic. In 1997, she won the World Women's Summit's 'World Laureate' award for her work in SEWA's 'Feminize Our Forests' campaign. Menaben led 10 villages in growing 30,000 seedlings, the equivalent of 100 villages' worth of production. It was particularly her motivational skills that were recognized by the award, which brought her US$ 500. This has in turn motivated her, and enabled her, to achieve even more ... and finally enjoy life.

Gum Collection

Some of the most arduous work done in Radhanpur and Santalpur, yet done by 80 to 90 percent of the women, is gum collection (SEWA Half Yearly Report). In this arid region, one of the few trees that grow on the saline soil is the prosopis juliflora, a type of gum tree from the mesquite family. The tree, with gum oozing out of the stem joints on the interior section, is a valuable source of off-season income for the region. When the crops are harvested, the fields are bare, and no other work is available, the gum tree is a main option for employment and income.

Despite its benefits, gum collection does have its disadvantages. Many of the women, even girls as young as 10 years old, have to walk several kilometers in desert conditions to get to the gum trees. Some have to do it barefoot, on hot sand, even while carrying an infant and enough water to survive the day. Heat stroke, dehydration and plain exhaustion are only a few of the dangers the women have to face.

The income for this work can range from Rs. 4 to 25 per day, depending upon several factors. The peak season for gum is right after the monsoon, from October to December. At that time, the gum is white in color, considered to be of a higher quality, and more plentiful in quantity. The white gum, used for human consumption, draws the highest price per kilogram. As the dry season progresses, the gum becomes darker, from red (January to March) to black (April to May). In the process, the amount of gum that the tree produces decreases, as does the price. The red gum, used in glues and screen printing, draws the median price. Black gum is used in firecrackers and in the color chemical industry, and draws the lowest price. The whole season can last six to eight months in a year.

The difficulties of gum collection extend beyond fluctuating prices and the impediments of the location. The gum tree itself has long, sharp thorns. Because the women often have to probe deep within the tree, these thorns can puncture their skin or tear their clothing. Infected wounds, particularly on the hands and feet, are common and can be dangerously debilitating. They are dangerous partly because they can prohibit a primary income-provider from working in a family living at a survival level.

The working conditions are hazardous and difficult and the compensation is minimal. There is much room for improvement. For those reasons, one of the first activities in which SEWA got involved in Banaskantha was organization of the gum collectors. But, this was not easy. The initial obstacle was the gum collectors' fear that the SEWA women were government officials.

Policies, again dating back to the British colonial period, had claimed many directly uninhabited areas, sometimes whether forested or not, as official forest area, and off limits to the general populace. Therefore, anyone who made any effort to cut down a tree on this land, gather dead branches, or even collect gum, was essentially breaking the law. Considering the militant legacy of the forestry departments, this was a considerable concern.

When SEWA came to the villages, the gum collectors feared that the organizers had come in order to enforce the forestry laws. Because of this, the women that the organizers encountered would not admit that they collected gum. In some cases, when the SEWA jeeps were spotted heading for the villages, the women would abandon the village until the organizers left. It took several visits to the villages, sometimes even resorting to stealth tactics, such as coming at night, before the organizers began to make progress. The discussions that did ensue brought to light the full magnitude of the disturbing policies that the GSFDC followed.

In addition to their difficult working conditions, the women were exploited by virtue of the government-engineered legal structure of the gum trade. Because the gum collection took place in the 'forest area,' the GSFDC had domain not only over the area where the gum was collected, but also over the sale of the gum. All gum harvested in Banaskantha had to be sold directly to the GSFDC. Furthermore, the gum had to be sold at the price the GSFDC dictated. This price often had little resemblance to the actual market value of the gum.

To have the privilege to sell gum to the GSFDC and, therefore, to sell the gum at all, one needed the necessary license. This license could only be obtained through that same institution with the necessary help of money, time, and influence. None of these entities were readily available to the women, who had to struggle every hour of the day in order to ensure that they had enough money to feed their families.

The system growing out of this policy centered around a middleman. An enterprising village merchant, often the local government ration shop-keeper, as a side business, would acquire a license and purchase the gum from the women who collected it. Because the women had no other outlet for their 'illegal' harvest, they were compelled to sell to the middleman at a very low price.

Realizing this predicament, SEWA struggled to create another option for the collectors. Together, SEWA and their newly organized members obtained a license so that the women could sell gum directly to the GSFDC. In eliminating the middlemen, the gum collectors overcame a major obstacle. Previously, they sold their daily harvest, which was

2 kilograms on a good day, for Rs. 4 to 6 per kilogram, depending on the gum quality. Instead, selling directly to the GSFDC, they could sell their gum for Rs. 10 to 14 per kilogram. Their income was double to triple what it had previously been.

However, this change did not come without its difficulties. As mentioned before, those who had previously purchased the gum from the collectors were often the same people who ran the village ration shop. This was a position of significant power. In response to the women organizing themselves, some shopkeepers refused to sell food to the women on credit, a heretofore common and necessary practice with these government-supported ration shops in places where the economy was seasonally based. In fact, issuing credit was a method by which the shopkeepers obligated the collectors to sell gum only to them. The merchants would capture the women in a cycle of debt by delaying payment for the gum, but offering credit on the government-subsidized food instead. By manipulating the benevolent intent of a government program, these ex-middlemen sought to reassert their parasitic position in the gum trade.

Also, after the cooperatives were formed, these traders would buy gum from villages that did not have any organized women. The traders would buy the gum at a very low price, and then sell it to some of the SEWA members at a slightly higher price. These SEWA members would then sell the gum to their licensed group. Though these SEWA women were making a profit from this chain of transactions, it soon became apparent to them that it was at the expense of other women who did not have the opportunity to organize. This was not acceptable and they sought to rectify the situation.

Fortunately, the organizing strength of SEWA in this new sector was substantial enough to stand up to these tactics. The SEWA members contacted the GSFDC and informed them of the illegal, unlicensed purchases that were taking place. A surprise inspection was the result and the practice of illegally buying and selling gum was curbed. As for the practice of shopkeepers denying credit to the women, the spot payment the women now received for their gum alleviated the problem. The women had no need for credit when they had access to money.

The Fall in the Price of Gum

In February 1992, shortly after the women obtained their license, the GSFDC price offered for gum fell from Rs. 14 to Rs. 12, then Rs. 10, Rs. 6, and ultimately to Rs. 4 per kilogram. This precipitous drop in price was due to the formation of a cartel among the wholesalers who purchased the gum from the GSFDC.

The gum is sold at a closed auction to the highest bidder. The GSFDC undertakes no advertisement for the sale. There are no attempts to gain access to a larger market. Without an aggressive marketing methodology on the part of the government, the bidders are inevitably a small group that is easily organized and hardly monitored. Under such conditions, the cartel manages to consistently acquire the gum at an unnaturally low price. This means that the GSFDC then procure gum from the collectors at an even lower price. Meanwhile, the open-market price for gum of similar quality remains unchanged at Rs. 22 per kilogram, a difference of Rs. 18 from the Rs. 4 at which the gum collectors are obliged to sell.

Despite ardent calls from the organized gum collectors of SEWA to end the government monopoly on gum sale in the face of such blatant inefficiency, little has been achieved. When SEWA first approached the GSFDC over the issue of the price decrease, they were told that the price drop was due to a glut in the market. Indeed, the drought of 1991–92 did push many of the villagers to gum collection, who did not normally engage in the activity. In addition, with the decline in sales to private traders who sold much of their gum illegally in the black market, sales to the GSFDC increased. The result was a harvest exceeding any previously recorded total. The GSFDC complained that the gum collected had begun to accumulate without enough buyers. However, SEWA later discovered that, despite the glut from domestic production, the GSFDC was actually importing gum!

This issue remains unresolved till date. Through a persistent follow-up, SEWA negotiated an increase to Rs. 8 per kilogram. Meanwhile, the price of gum in the open market has increased, climbing as high as Rs. 40. Furthermore, in 1995, to compensate for the low price paid to the women, relative to the open market price, the GSFDC promised to procure gloves, shoes and collection bags to protect the women collecting the gum. This four-year-old promise is also yet to materialize.

Present negotiations are an attempt to strike at the heart of the issue. The law, which prohibits the gum collectors from selling at the much higher prices in the open market, is a law passed by Parliament, not the GSFDC. The current SEWA proposal is to sell the gum to the GSFDC at the prescribed price, and then purchase it back at the same price, essentially working within the constrictions of the law. The cooperatives, through their own registered marketing organization, would then be free to legally sell the gum on the open market.

Although this is a practical solution, the GSFDC so far insists on raising the price at which they sell the gum back to the collectors. Thus, negotiations are stuck on that point. Meanwhile, SEWA has already had offers for several contracts for large quantities of gum at the open market price. But, as the government stalls, the contracts are lost.

Though they have had little success in obtaining a fair price from the GSFDC, SEWA has made progress in other ways on behalf of the gum-collectors. An aggressive program for planting gum trees along roads and near villages has cut down on both erosion and the distance that women have to travel to get to the gum. Also, still at the experimental stage, but soon to be fully utilized, is a chemical injection developed by the Development Technology and Science Institute in Bangalore. At the end of a two-year pilot phase with 100 BDMSA trees, this injection has tripled the gum output without sacrificing the health of the trees.

Biography: Working Together

In the village of Anternesh, like every other village in the region, the people work at many different jobs throughout the year in order to make ends meet. Field labor, salt farming, craftwork, charcoal production, and dairying are just a few of the activities the people of this village undertake. But, it is gum collection that is the most common source of income among the women.

Most of the women in Anternesh began collecting gum when they were little girls, accompanying their mothers. There was not enough fieldwork available to employ all the people of the village and the men were paid more for the labor anyway. Instead, the women turned to gum collection.

It is arduous work. The heat can be overwhelming, the distance punishing and the long thorns unforgiving to a weary and wavering hand. They have to carry water and sometimes even their children, who are either too young or too fatigued to walk themselves.

Other dangers are also ever present. The death of a child a few years back still weighs heavily on the villagers' minds. A young boy, five years old, accompanied his mother as she was collecting gum. The boy soon wandered out of his mother's sight and, when she called to him, he made no reply. Not knowing which way he went, the mother spent hours searching in all directions. As her own life came into danger from lack of water and over-exertion in the hot sun, the woman staggered back to the village, hoping her son had returned there or to get help. Despite the efforts of her neighbors, he was not found until the next day, too late.

On this March afternoon, the women are just beginning to return to the village from a day of gum-collecting. The women had left home at 6 A.M., before the sun rose. In eight hours, they have managed to collect roughly one kilogram of medium-quality gum each. That will sell for around Rs. 12 to their SEWA cooperative. If they were selling to traders, they would be getting Rs. 20 for every kilogram. But they can't do that.

Anternesh has had a gum cooperative for several years. The village has been with SEWA through all the struggles with the Forestry Department. When the villagers finally got a license to sell gum directly to the department, they thought they had won a victory. They did not foresee the problems ahead.

When they got their license, they stopped selling gum to the traders. Instead, they collected it as a group and sold it to their own association. They were initially getting better prices for their gum and more informed of the larger issues that surrounded their work. This empowering awareness gave them a greater sense of control over their own destinies.

Soon, however, other realities imposed themselves. When the prices offered by the Forestry Department began to fall, the women clearly understood why, but felt they had little control over it. Poor management by the Forestry Department was costing the women a lot of rupees. They began collectively discussing what to do, and this led to lobbying efforts at the association level. But, this lobbying proved to be a long and unpredictable process. Meanwhile, the gum collectors and their families had to survive.

The women were forced to consider selling to the traders, but the traders would not buy from them. The traders knew the women's predicament and were still spiteful over the women's acquisition of a license. Furthermore, the Forestry Department had the names of all the gum collectors in the village from their DWCRA registration. With this, the forestry officials closely monitored the women's gum-collecting activities. If they did not sell their gum to the association, the officials announced, the decrease in the BDMSA's production would be interpreted to mean that they were selling the gum illegally and the BDMSA would be penalized.

Fear of the department, however, was not the primary factor in the women's continuation of work with the cooperative. Asked why they continued to collect gum through their BDMSA group, despite the lower prices, the women pointed to several locations near where they were sitting. They pointed to the underground water tank, the Shakti Packet shop, and their cattle, tile roofs and concrete floors that they acquired through loans. They talked about what it meant to be organized, to be leaders and to have control over their own destiny. 'Because of these things, we are SEWA members. It is more than just the gum license. We are willing to wait until the gum situation improves because, meanwhile, our lives are still improving.'

Salt Farming

With the difficulties in other areas of forestry activity, many SEWA members are forced into even less desirable means of income generation. Included under the aegis of forestry land is much of the land used for salt farming. Despite the problems it causes in agriculture and in water potability, salt is a necessary part life. We, of course, need it in our diet to keep us healthy, but it is also a key ingredient of many industrial products, including metals, a wide range of chemicals, and many food preservatives. India produces 10 million metric tons of salt every year, over 60 percent of which is produced in Gujarat. Most of Gujarat's salt production takes place in the Little Rann of Kutch, which borders Banaskantha and lies primarily in the district of Kutch (Singh and Bhattacharya 1996: 122).

It is estimated that around 15,000 people from Radhanpur and Santalpur participate in the salt production process. From September to March, people either commute or migrate entirely to the Little Rann of Kutch from the surrounding villages. The process begins with the digging of a well. For the salt farmers who can afford it, a borewell is drilled, sometimes 130 to 140 feet into the ground. For farmers with less capital, the well is dug, by hand, 15 to 20 feet into the ground. Although the Little Rann of Kutch is India's largest source of underground brine, the raw material that salt is extracted from, there is no guarantee that the brine will be where the hole is dug. Thus, the smaller farmers are effectively excluded from taking the risk of spending the money for a borewell.

The difference in terms of production between a borewell and a regular well is significant. One borewell lasts as long as two seasons and employs 20 to 25 laborers at a time. The more rudimentary wells need to be replaced two to four times before the season is through. The quantity of salt each produces also follows the same trends. Unfortunately, the costs and subsequent risks of drilling a borewell prevent smaller producers from taking advantage of the more efficient methods. This is a major obstacle for those trying to expand their production and increase their income.

Regardless of the difference in the well type and its impact on the scale of operation, salt farming throughout the region uses similar means of production vis-à-vis its laborers. The brine is extracted from the ground and pumped into storage pools. At that point, the salt content in the Little Rann of Kutch brine is between 15 and 22 degrees brine concentration (bc).[1] The brine is then stored in the pools as the blazing heat of the desert sun evaporates the water, leaving the salt behind. For this purpose, several individual pools, surrounding the well, are prepared.

Once the brine in an individual pool reaches roughly 24 degrees bc, it is transferred by the men through a series of ditches with precisely calculated gradations and flow patterns to the nearby earthen salt pans. There, it is usually the women who are responsible for trampling on the brine barefoot to render the floor and walls of the pan impermeable, preserving the harvest. As more water evaporates from the pan, the men add more brine. This is done until there is no brine left and the bc rises to 28 degrees, at which point, the salt crystallizes. Then, the salt is raked by the men to extract the sand and stones, and piled for transport.

The conditions under which this labor is performed are the most challenging in the area. In the heat of the desert sun, the laborers have no natural source of potable water nearby. For the laborers living at the work-site, the problem is particularly acute. Water has to be brought to the site at great cost, and so must be used sparingly. For example, the workers can bathe only once or twice in a week, leaving themselves crusted with salt the rest of the time.

The days in the desert are excruciatingly hot and the nights are frigid. The laborers live in huts made of mud and sticks that have to be rebuilt after any wind or sand storm. The ultra-luminous sun, reflecting off the sands, also causes night blindness among a large number of the salt producers. The prolonged and intense exposure to salt invites lesions and fungus on the feet and legs, particularly for the women, who are most frequently in contact with the brine. In the salt camps, it is common knowledge that the feet never burn completely in a salt worker's funeral pyre, due to the high salt content.

According to a survey done by the Sabarmati Salt Farmers' Society, a group devoted to the improvement of salt farmers' conditions, the infant mortality in the salt farmers' community was 150 per 1,000 for boys and 200 per 1,000 for girls. This points not only to the extraordinarily poor condition of the community (the average IMR in India is roughly 100 per 1,000 births for both girls and boys), but also to the harsh gender inequalities. That 50 more girls than boys die per 1,000 births is a particularly startling fact, considering that, as noted before, female infants have a measurable advantage over male infants in terms of natural ability to survive the first crucial months of infancy. This statistic indicates the perhaps subtle, but certainly direct, denial of care and nutrition to female infants.

All the effort and suffering of salt farming is, for most, compensated with very little gain. The large salt traders have a lot of leverage in the industry and use it to exploit the others involved in the salt production process. The system largely in use is that the traders lease land from the government, since salt lands were nationalized shortly after Independence, and then turn around and rent that land to the salt farmers, commonly called 'agarias.' Depending upon the agaria's available capital, he (very rarely a 'she') may then have to borrow money from the trader in order to buy tools, materials, and wages for the laborers. The agarias will then use their family members as laborers and perhaps hire one or more other people at a rate of Rs. 15 to 20 per day. The debt from these loans has to be paid back in salt, at a price the trader dictates, usually Rs. 10 to 15 per ton. This amounts to about 2 percent of the price the consumer pays at the other end of the production cycle. a price that barely sustains the salt farmer. In fact, it can often fail to lift the farmer out of the debt that obligates him to sell to the trader. In that case, the farmer has to sell his salt to the same trader for years to come until his debt is cleared. Thus, the salt farmer is captured in a sharecropper-like relationship. Agarias and laborers alike find themselves working under the poorest of conditions with little to negative returns.

SEWA Intervention

In 1989, in response to the appalling conditions faced by the salt workers, SEWA decided to get involved. The field staff held meetings with the salt workers, and together they decided to approach the Rural Labor Department in Ahmedabad and the Salt Commissioner's Office in Gandhinagar. Part of the latter's job was to collect a tax of Rs. 3.50 for every ton of salt sold by producers having over 100 acres of productive land. Out of the funds from this tax, which in 1990 totaled Rs. 12,240,000 in revenues, an amount of Rs. 2,264,540 was supposedly allotted for improving the welfare of the industry's labor force. SEWA hoped to put these under-utilized resources to good use.

Both offices instructed the group to submit details concerning the number of people involved, their backgrounds and productivity. SEWA promptly conducted a survey and responded with the required information and waited. In response to their immediate compliance, SEWA and the salt workers were delayed. After much follow-up, the response was a nominal allocation of Rs. 20,000 to run a two-month-long health program. With the equivalent of US$ 450, they were expected to fund a physician, medicines, medical supplies and support staff, among other requirements, for two months. This would have been impossible. But, alas, even these funds were lost in the shuffle of bureaucratic paper work.

Despite the disappointment, the women salt workers from the villages of Madhutra and Datrana took matters into their own hands. They traveled to the SEWA office in Radhanpur, and proposed establishment of a cooperative. An application was prepared and submitted to the District Registrar and a fund was collected with all 55 members contributing Rs. 10 each. Upon approval of their application, the group leased 10 acres of land from the District Collector, and this was partly covered by the group funds. With the collateral of group support and SEWA backing, they were also able to receive a bank loan of Rs. 40,000 that was used to dig a bore-well and purchase a diesel pump.

Success appeared at hand, but the future had more challenges in store. With the harvest completed, the cooperative members prepared to sell the salt. Upset over the formation of the cooperative, and the easy money it cost them, the traders blocked all means of transporting the salt. The traders, accustomed to a hardball industry, had formed an influential cartel that contracted all the private trucks to the exclusion of the new cooperative and other small traders. Furthermore, SEWA discovered, too late unfortunately, that the cooperative could not, without ownership of the land they worked, reserve the necessary train wagons to transport their salt to market.

By law, in order for a salt producer to be able to reserve a train wagon, they must have the title to an amount of land sufficient to indicate they can produce enough salt to merit the commitment of the transportation resources. The large salt traders get around this by owning the token amount of property and then leasing it out to small salt farmers. As for the small farmers, who lease land from the traders or the government, the law excludes them from much of the process on the ground of their lack of land. This gives the traders the ultimate leverage, since small farmers are not able to sell their own produce at full market prices and bypass the middlemen.

For SEWA, the disaster was complete when early rains that year washed away the cooperatives' stockpiles as they waited for transport to the market. In the open, not able to move it anywhere, the salt dissolved with every raindrop. The loss was nearly the entire harvest. Serious improvement needed to be made in order for the program to be successful. By that time, the DWCRA program had proved itself valuable for the artisans and gum collectors, so the salt workers decided to register. Since all the women salt farmers qualified as below the poverty line, they were quickly registered into several groups with 12 members each.

However, despite the useful DWCRA support, the BDMSA was aware, from past experience with the government program, of their reluctance to release funds on time. Since salt farming was a time-bound activity, the dilatory payment schedule had to be overcome. Otherwise, the groups could not lease their land, purchase their pumps or compensate their members.

The BDMSA and the cooperatives set up a structure by which the association loaned out the allotted funds to the individual cooperatives on time and did not require repayment until the DWCRA program released the promised amount. The cooperatives submitted their total budget to the BDMSA and, upon review, promptly received 50 percent of the requested funds. The balance was then released mid-season, after the quality and quantity of the production was assessed. When the DWCRA released its funds, the BDMSA deducted the amount they had loaned to each cooperative and distributed the remainder. No interest was charged on the BDMSA loans, the DWCRA program was put to good use, and the salt production calendar of the cooperatives was not disrupted. As a result of this adaptation, almost all of the cooperatives were able to begin the subsequent year of salt farming with their own capital.

However, much remains to be done. A legal controversy between the Forestry Department and the District Collector over the establishment of a Wild Ass Sanctuary, covering almost all of the Little Rann Of Kutch, has put a hold on all new land leases while the courts sort out the issue—at the speed of bureaucracy. Meanwhile, the salt traders' cartel remains strong and unchecked, and the red tape that precludes the procurement of a railway car remains to be cut. Without a free, fair and competitive market or transportation, the salt trade remains a difficult one to enter.

Considering these constraints, SEWA has made efforts in other ways to compensate for the salt workers' difficulties. To address the startling health conditions among salt workers, a mobile van cum doctor, medicine and support staff visit the villages where salt farmers live. Since December 1994, the van has been making three trips a week to Santalpur, visiting two villages on each trip (six villages a week). Though the van serves other villagers who are not salt workers, the route selection intentionally favors the villages that border the little Rann of Kutch, where there is a higher percentage of those who participate in the salt industry.

Funded jointly with the Salt Workers' Welfare Board, balwaadis, or day care centers, have been established in the villages where salt workers live. In addition to educational instruction, breakfast and snacks are given and immunization services coordinated. Among other benefits, the infant mortality rate has dropped perceptibly. The villages are guaranteed access to food and health care. They are less susceptible to overexposure to the sun. And their parents are freed to get more work done.

SEWA also made efforts to close the gender gap in salt production. Salt production is a process that requires a surprisingly high degree of technical expertise. Understanding and creating the proper flow pattern from one pan to another, as well as managing the brine once it is in the pans, are complex matters. Traditionally, the men have been the ones to learn and execute this process. The women have traditionally been limited to the more menial tasks of higher risk to health. By coordinating training with the Center for Salt and Marine Research in India, SEWA has helped to build the capacity of some women to undertake the whole process of salt production themselves.

The SEWA women have attended training sessions that explain the steps necessary to improve the salt production process, and the science behind them. In some cases, the women have been able to share this knowledge with the men who have been in the business for years but based their work on raw experience and instinct, with little awareness of the science behind the process. With this knowledge, both the men and the women can be not only more productive, but more independent as well.

As living and working conditions slowly improve for the salt workers, they will hopefully be able to gain the leverage needed to improve the situation where the salt traders' unfair practices and the government policies reinforce an inefficient system. When one is struggling for their next meal, it is difficult to struggle against an exploitative system. But, with more assured health, a promise of education and nourishment for children, and a glimpse of a way to an improved life, there is greater hope for the future.

Forestry Epilogue

In March 1999, SEWA held a 'sammelan' (large meeting), attended by over 3,000 SEWA members and the Chief Minister of the Gujarat. The Chief Minister first listened to the SEWA members who presented their reasoned perspective on some unproductive government policies. Those who spoke out included gum collectors, salt farmers, and tree nursery producers. Many issues were touched upon, but it became clear that one major issue consisted in the counterproductive policies of the Forestry Department. Gum collectors were obligated to sell their harvest to the Forestry Department at prices well below the market value. Salt workers, landless in an otherwise barren land, were barred access to a desert devoid of vegetation but rich in salt, because the treeless landscape was territory claimed by the department. Tree nursery producers had to compete with the heavily subsidized department nurseries to sell the fruits of their labor. All these policies limited the opportunities for the women. The policies monopolized trade, stifled production, and quelled open competition. All this was done by the department in the name of protecting forests where there were no trees and protecting profits for a non-profit government entity.

The Chief Minister listened to the women's testimony. When it was his turn to speak, he promised change. As the only person outside the Forestry Department with the power to intervene, he promised to do just that. SEWA took note of the promises and followed up. They soon found that the Chief Minister was sincere in his promises. With the stroke of a pen and the determination to see that the memorandums' words were heeded, the Chief Minister reduced the Forestry Department Raj.

The gum collectors have since been given a one-year period in which they can sell gum directly on the open market. With the success of this pilot program, the SEWA gum collectors would be able to continue to sell their produce continuously. Since then, SEWA has procured a contract through a Mumbai trader for up to 5,000 kilograms per month. Other contracts on the horizon include one for as much as 14,000 tons a month with the Postal Department (glue for the stamps). While SEWA gum collectors would in no way be able to fill such a large order, it is an indication of the vast potential available.

Tree nursery cooperatives have prepared to sell their stock for a fair price in the open market as well. They also have prepared to extend their leases on the nursery land beyond the three-year limit arbitrarily set by the Forestry Department. Thus, their fruit-bearing saplings will have the opportunity to mature and provide income in addition to the sale of seedlings. Similarly, the opportunities for the salt farmers to lease land have also opened up, giving them access to salt. These official leases also give the salt farmers access to rail transportation. Space in a freight car is offered only to those who own land or lease from the government, opportunities the poorer salt farmers did not previously have.

The progress that developed as a result of the sammelan is significant for the changes it achieved. However, it is also significant for the way in which these were achieved. The first issue SEWA had to deal with as it became active in Banaskantha was: how does an urban labor union effect change in a rural area? Banaskantha was a region where it would be hard to improve the working conditions when the workers had no work to begin with. The surplus in the rural labor market meant that workers had little bargaining power and their problems were more fundamental than better pay or better working conditions. They simply needed work.

SEWA began by simply initiating employment opportunities, but still set its sights on the day when the Banaskantha members would have the collective strength to pick up the union-type struggle. In March 1999, after the sammelan, the long-awaited day dawned. No doubt, the responsiveness of the Chief Minister to the SEWA members' demands was a major factor. It was the well-thought-out, articulate demands, and the strength with which they were presented, however, that elicited the Chief Minister's response. In a decade of involvement with SEWA, the rural members have learned to recognize their own rights and have the courage to demand them. The sammelan and the subsequent policy changes are reflections of that courage.

Biography: From Laborer to Owner

Somiben lives in the village of Piprali. On the fringes of the desert, Piprali has many salt producers, and Somiben is one of them. Before she was a SEWA member, she used to work for salt merchants under a type of agreement that is still common. She and her family would borrow food and money from the salt merchant in return for the obligation that they sell the salt they produce only to that same merchant.

The arrangement with the merchant was often binding for more than one season because the accumulated debt was not always cleared by the salt harvest. The reason was twofold. First, the costs of setting up salt production were high. Somiben and her family were responsible for investing in the set-up costs, but had to borrow from the salt merchant to cover it. Second, the price at which the salt merchant purchased the salt from Somiben and her family was never the full market value. As part of the agreement, the salt merchant dictated the price at which he bought the salt. The last year Somiben worked for a salt merchant, she recalls, the market price was Rs. 15 per 100 kilograms, but the merchant only paid Rs. 7 for the same amount of salt.

Two years ago, Somiben and several other SEWA members formed a DWCRA group for salt farming. The Rs. 25,000 provided by the program as start-up capital was not enough, but the BDMSA gave them an interest-free loan of Rs. 40,000 to compensate. With this money, they dug a well, purchased a well-pump and rented a tractor to dig the salt pans. Once production was underway, the women made enough salt for each of them to make Rs. 150 per day. This work lasted for over three months.

In addition, the women were in the middle of the desert, but near several other salt farms. Able to serve several people in the area, a doctor came once a week, and a school was set up nearby for the children of the salt farmers. Somiben took advantage of both these facilities. Her children went to the school and the whole family visited the doctor. In her case, she had several sores on her legs, the scars of which still remain. However, the ointment she was given was unavoidably washed off as she worked in the brine.

Most important of all, Somiben was not only a worker, but also an owner. This made a great difference, especially in the salt industry. The work is hard and the risks are great, but so too are the potential benefits. Wages for the laborers are predetermined and assured, but low. As an owner, with a little luck, but especially with good management, the profits can exceed many other sources of income open to these women. Somiben was willing to take the risk, as long as she had some control.

However, difficulties lay ahead. When the big salt merchants monopolized all the trucks, and the train wagons were denied to the BDMSA, there was no transportation available for the group to take their salt to market. Consequently, the group's harvest was partly dissolved in the early monsoon. Most of their profits were never realized and they could barely clear their debts.

Next year, the group decided not to work together. Instead, Somiben worked for a merchant. This time, she worked as a simple wage-earner on a large salt farm. It was a relatively good job. The wage used to be Rs. 8 per day a few years ago, but now it is Rs. 30 per day. But she still hopes to work with her group in the coming season.

Somiben and the BDMSA have learnt from the difficulties of two years ago. Now they know the need to secure transportation before beginning production. They have no capital saved from the last time. But, they have managed to maintain their good credit, and the BDMSA has agreed to provide another Rs. 40,000 loan; interest-free.

Furthermore, she and several of the members attended a training program about salt production organized by SEWA. Among other things, the group learned to separate the brine into three separate pools, dividing it into different stages of completion, rather than continuously adding new brine and delaying the crystallization stage. The three pools speed up the process and allow for a more efficient mode of production.

The salt farmers have learnt many lessons the hard way, but learnt them nonetheless. With more efficient methods of production and timely arrangements for transportation, they are ready. This time, Somiben feels, she and her group know more clearly how to ensure their success. She looks forward to the coming season.

Note

1. Brine concentration (bc) is a standard of measure for the salt content in a given amount of water. For the reader's reference, drinking water, optimally, has 0 degrees bc. Seawater is between 3 and 4 degrees bc.

Chapter 4

DAIRY AND CRAFT COOPERATIVISM: DEMAND-DRIVEN, NEED-BASED

In an impoverished, agriculturally based, drought-prone area, one of the greatest assets a family can have is a year-round source of income. Crops such as cumin, cottonseed, and castor, the main crops of Banaskantha, only require attention three months out of the year. Therefore, they offer employment and income only for that same relatively short period of time. Because the agriculture is mainly rain-fed, it is specifically the three months after the monsoon that are very busy. However, the rest of the year is often a hard struggle to find work. That struggle often results in migration.

In India, migration is, in many ways, a misunderstood phenomenon. The urban sprawl—its slums and squatters—is well known to urban Indians who live next to these migrants, more than much of the rest of the world that catches only glimpses of the subcontinental reality of the overburdened metropolises. In contrast to the ever-changing cities, village life is often thought of as static and sedentary. These impressions may in part be attributable to basic urban unfamiliarity with rural reality, or a subconscious refusal to surrender some idealistic notion of the village life, as portrayed in Bollywood films. However, the truth is that village life in India is far from static or sedentary.

Migration in the rural areas is widespread and at least half of the migrants move not to the cities, but to other rural areas, in search of employment and food for themselves and their animals. Furthermore, the majority does so not on a one-time basis, but consistently, year after year, following the same routes and sometimes stopping in several places for temporary work or grazing grounds.

The scarcity of year-round employment and poor grazing prospects are the root causes of the exceptionally high migration rates in Banaskantha. In the 1980s, the migration rate for 700 families in Banaskantha surveyed by the FPI was over 30 percent (210 of the families) in the dry season (SEWA 1993). Migration becomes a necessity for survival when there is no source of employment or fodder nine months out of the year. More specifically, it is a necessary evil. Without migration, there is starvation, but, with migration, the economy is disrupted, children's education is discontinued, and communities are torn apart. A great deal of energy is spent moving to find work rather than actually working, and much of the cattle's calories are spent looking for fodder, thus making them even more hungry. Some livelihoods are more affected than others, but the whole community is affected.

Migration has only been taking place on this large, cyclical scale in India for the past three decades. Better roads and a greater awareness of opportunities beyond the local boundaries have made migration an inviting option (Chen 1991: 152). The winter months, after the November harvest, are the peak migration season for agricultural laborers, because of the decrease in employment opportunities in the fields. This will usually last until March, when the planting season presents opportunities for employment closer home. The migration season then picks up again in the pre-monsoon summer months of June and July, the peak migration period for those with livestock, since fodder is most scarce at that time. However, in times of drought, migration is a year-round affair.

There are many detrimental effects of migration on village life. The social support network in rural communities, where there are fewer public resources and a greater degree of communal intimacy, can foster a degree of interdependency that overcomes the challenges of rural life in many ways. On a microcosmic scale, the common familial and cultural heritage can engender a degree of trust and compassion not usually shared among neighbors in an urban setting. While nostalgia can sometimes lead urbanites to over-idealize this phenomenon, it does exist. But, migration negates these benefits for half the year while the communities are separated, and it erodes the ties by the time the communities are reunited.

It is in times of economic distress that this communal support is most important. However, it is also in such times that people are forced to migrate and abandon those communities. Neighbors lose the opportunity to borrow food or funds from other generous neighbors. Mothers lose access to childcare from extended families. Pregnant women have to forgo the future services of dais, the local women who traditionally assume the role of assisting in child delivery. Children have to leave their classmates and playmates. Small farmers have to leave their fields. Everyone has to leave his or her home.

Furthermore, access to public resources is limited when migrants are on unfamiliar territory. There is less familiarity with the location or quality of things such as water, provisions shops, health facilities, or schools. Either the families have to take their chances with the first place they come across, or somehow temporarily make do without such necessities. Similarly, they are forced into compromises for shelter and employment, taking what they can get in sheer desperation. With surprising speed, word spreads as to where there is work and food. Any place that presents an opportunity may soon be flooded with migrants who invest a significant amount of time and energy in getting there. As such, they are anxious for work and short on leverage, willing to accept a bare minimum of compensation for fear that another person will arrive the next day and seize the opportunity for less.

These circumstances are in many ways even harsher for women. Jaded notions of women's capacity to work, as compared to men's, translate into wage discrimination on the migrant labor trail, with women making a fraction of what men make for the same work. This income disparity, in turn, both lowers the status of the women and heightens the pressures upon them to work harder and longer than their male counterparts. In whatever ways such discriminatory practices may be justified, such as the smaller physical size of women or the childcare responsibilities that slow them down, the amount of work that women do is still undiminished. Yet, their burden is still heavier and their status is still lower.

When organizers and researchers from SEWA and the FPI initially went to the villages of Banaskantha, they did so on the premise of assessing the watershed development activities. But the scale of the migration and the devastation it was wreaking upon the communities could not escape their notice. Nor, obviously, did it escape the notice of the villagers who were the victims. The need, expressed in the form of a demand in village after village, was employment. In particular, the community needed and demanded a local economy that could provide them with a year-round source of income, eliminating the need for migration and allowing the communities to rebuild themselves.

In the course of discussions between community members, SEWA, and the FPI, two particular sources of income-generating activity arose as the most viable options for sustainable employment: dairy production and craftwork. Dairy production showed promise because a very large percentage of the residents of Banaskantha had milch cattle, or at least did before the drought. Some had to sell their cattle at throwaway prices during the drought, some lost them to starvation, and others migrated to other areas to keep them alive. Nevertheless, all had the experience and ability to make dairy production a productive undertaking.

Furthermore, by improving the locally based resources behind dairy production, the community would be addressing one of the leading push factors for migration, cattle survival. Despite the hardships that cattle ownership brought upon people, cattle had value as milk producers and beasts of burden, as well as producers of fuel, fertilizer and building material with their dung. The blessings that the animals provided meant that the hardships were to be endured in order to gain the benefits. With the abandonment of cattle ownership an unwise and unlikely prospect, the logical approach was to make the best of the situation. Establishment of productive dairy cooperatives was therefore adopted as one of the first income-generating activities.

The second such activity that looked promising was craft production. As the watershed meetings progressed, the unique style of the women's apparel stood out to the visitors from SEWA and the FPI. Their clothing was the result of hours of work undertaken by the women themselves, in line with a tradition passed down by their mothers, grandmothers and beyond. Such handiwork clearly constituted a skill, and perhaps one that could serve not merely to clothe but also to feed the women and their families. Like dairy production, craftwork was a skill shared by a large proportion of the women in Banaskantha. However, unlike dairy production and other land-based activities, craftwork was free of the limitations of seasonal rains, poor soil and physical exhaustion. In some instances, once the hint of a suggestion was made to the women that their craftwork could be the source of income, the organizers were literally mobbed by craftswomen and anxiously implored to help.

In both cases, with the dairy and craft cooperatives, the programs were demand-driven and need-based. A central part of SEWA's ideology—the responsiveness to demand and need—ensured that the communities, that would immediately begin to assume ownership of the activities, would embrace the initiatives. This sense of ownership then meant that the women were willing to invest time in building their capacity to deliver, and that the work would be sustainable and their self-sufficiency ultimately established.

Dairy Cooperativism

Banaskantha has a tradition of cattle-breeders who lead a nomadic or semi-nomadic lifestyle. Some groups lead their herds from place to place throughout the year, while others only leave their native village when there are not enough resources there to ensure their productivity. The former migrate out of choice. The latter, and by far the more numerous, reluctantly migrate only when there is no other choice. It is these reluctant migrants that this section focuses on.

Having little or no private land, poor cattle-breeders are largely dependent on communal land for grazing. Because of the unique way in which land has been devolved to the mass population in India, causing the decline of a society with rural areas characterized by a few large landholders and a large number of landless people, some land has been set aside for communal use in every village. Usually, this land is relatively poor in quality and so less productive than most private lands. In a study conducted in seven states across India, it was observed that poor households graze their animals on common lands 70 to 90 percent of the time, while more affluent cattle-raising households only utilize the common lands 10 to 20 percent of the time (Chen 1993: 31). Thus, the poor are more vulnerable to the shortcomings of common land.

In an arid place, the grasses and fodder on the communal lands do not last long. In fact, since the common lands in a place like Banaskantha are usually the most saline, eroded and waterless lands, the fodder on these lands runs out much quicker than on most private lands. The dependence of a larger number of families on that land also adds to a rapid deterioration. When the area is grazed out, the poorer villagers with cattle are forced to shift to places where vegetation is more readily available. When the rains come, they stay in their native villages and participate in the local community and economy. However, milk yields are directly tied to the nutrition the cow or buffalo receives. Without ample food for their animals, milk production declines and the cattle-breeders get less and less income. In more extreme cases, though not uncommon in a drought, because of the scarcity of food for the animals, the breeders risk not only a temporary decline, but also a permanent loss of income and assets.

Dairy activity for the poorer families is a definite push factor for migration, making it an almost annual necessity, whether they are nomadic or not. However, dairy production does not have to be such a negative influence. It can also provide a year-round source of secondary employment and income, but this is not common in Banaskantha. SEWA, in 1989, recognized this and looked into the status of the dairy cooperatives in the district. If sedentary dairy production could be made viable, the benefits could be wide-ranging and substantial, reducing migration and raising income levels.

Banas Dairy is the name of Banaskantha district's dairy cooperative system. Based on the highly successful Amul Dairy model, the Banas Dairy consists of several regional chilling centers and one central processing plant. Village-level dairy cooperatives subscribe to this system by supplying

Plate 4.1: Women in Banaskantha gathering fodder for their milch cattle

milk, collected daily and transported to the local chilling center. Every day, these chilling centers temporarily store the milk and send it on to the Banas Dairy central plant where it is homogenized, packaged and distributed for sale. The cooperative members are essentially the owners of the system and hire professional personnel to orchestrate its functioning. The governing body is a board elected from and by the village cooperatives.

Before the Amul Dairy model had been developed and widely applied, milk production was largely at a subsistence level or at best only consumed locally. Operation Flood, begun in 1970, began to spread the Amul Dairy model throughout the country and was especially successful in Gujarat, where the prototype had been created in the town of Anand, in Kheda district. However, Operation Flood took time to implement thoroughly. As late as the early 1980s, milk in the urban areas was strictly rationed. In Ahmedabad, the milk lines extended for hundreds of feet, beginning at 4:30 P.M. There were few local resources for milk and, without proper facilities, bringing in milk from surrounding areas was difficult. Most of the producers were and are small-scale, and most were too far away from the cities for the milk to travel the distance without going bad from the hot and tortuous journey.

Once the Amul Dairy model spread, the dairy market was literally revolutionized and the production potential increased immeasurably. The Amul system allowed for a broader distribution of milk, opening up the links between the rural producers' market and the urban consumers' market. The impact of the program is a good example of how urban expansion is in many ways dependent upon rural productivity.

In Banaskantha, the Banas Dairy system revolves around the central plant, located in Palanpur, principal city of Banaskantha. For most of the SEWA members, the nearest regional chilling center is in Radhanpur. So, the milk goes from the village to Radhanpur, and from Radhanpur to Palanpur, and the whole system is now a cornerstone of the local economy. However, there was a time, even after the Banas Dairy was set up, when it was not so successful. The exceptionally adverse conditions of Banaskantha put the Amul Dairy model to test.

Due to the successive droughts, all the 75 Banas Dairy system cooperatives in the Radhanpur and Santalpur talukas of Banaskantha had become defunct. The monsoons spanning 1985 to 1988 had all failed, destroying much of the district's production capacity. In the final year of the drought, roughly 200 out of the 1,000 milch cows in the surveyed action research area died. Furthermore, most of the surviving animals nonetheless lacked proper nutrition. This malnourishment substantially decreased the productivity of the surviving cattle. Because of the subsequent decline in milk production, the Radhanpur Chilling Center was forced to close down.

The reason for the closing was twofold. On one side, with the shortage of milk being produced, its price in the open market increased. However, when the Banas Dairy collected the milk, they did not alter the rate paid to the producers. The result was that either the individual members of the cooperatives would sell to the private traders, who were offering a higher price, thus weakening the village cooperative, or the entire cooperative would sell to the traders, weakening the entire cooperative system. This loss of business to the private traders, in addition to the simple decrease in milk production, made the maintenance of Banas Dairy's procurement routes an increasingly burdensome endeavor. Village by village, the procurement routes were retracted until, finally, no village cooperative was supplying milk to the Banas Dairy.

When the milk cooperative system collapsed and all the milk producers had no other option but the trader, two new problems arose. First, the traders lacked the production and distribution facilities of the Banas Dairy.

So, the scale of operation was significantly reduced, almost back to the level of earlier days when rural producers were also the major consumers, while milk in the cities was rationed. Many of the previous cooperative members were thus reduced to subsistence production once again. Second, because so many dairy producers suddenly lost their market, the traders had the leverage to lower their procurement prices once competition from the cooperative system was eliminated. There was greater supply milk than the traders' demand for it, so the power was in their hands.

By the time SEWA learned of the situation in 1989, milk procurement had been suspended for three to four years. The fact that the cooperatives did not last long into the drought indicates the fragility of the milk cooperative system. In fact, it only took the first drought year for the Banas Dairy structure to collapse. The continued drought years that followed simply made any recovery more difficult to achieve. The loss in dead cattle would extend the drought effects well beyond the dry spell. To rebuild the herds to the previous level would take at least four years of cattle-breeding, assuming that food resources would match the increase in animals. Recovery looked like a long process.

To rehabilitate the system, the FPI, and SEWA made a concerted effort to convince both sides—the Banas Dairy and the village cattle-breeders—that the cooperative method could be made mutually advantageous with some improvements to the system. The FPI first organized a meeting for all the members of the defunct dairy cooperatives in the two talukas. Here, the FPI presented the dilemma and distributed a questionnaire, which sought to determine the production potential lying dormant in the villages. It asked questions such as how many animals the people had and how many they had lost in the drought. This questionnaire was ultimately completed by 24 responding cooperatives.

The results of the questionnaire, indicating a still strong potential for production, were presented in a second meeting. This meeting was attended by the Banas Dairy Development Officer, and provided a sufficient argument for the reopening of the procurement routes. It was agreed in this meeting that the chilling center procurement in Radhanpur would be reopened and collection reestablished.

Meanwhile, SEWA began the process of restarting the cooperatives from the producers' side. To achieve this goal, exposure trips were arranged to the Banas Dairy, so that the cooperative members could gain a better understanding of the entire milk production process, from the cow to the consumer. They saw how the milk was pasteurized, chilled, stored, and packaged on a large scale. Thus, with a clearer conception of the enterprise in which they were engaged, many of the members felt more comfortable and confident proceeding with the re-establishment of the dairy cooperatives.

Other issues, too, preempted the resumption of cooperative work. Of the 24 cooperatives that responded to the FPI's questionnaire, it was discovered, 1,555 members were male, and 39 were female. Considering that the care and use of the cattle is primarily the domain of the women, it seemed unjust and impractical that there should be so few of them in the representative body.

In most cases, while the men mind the grazing cattle, women are responsible for collecting the fodder, cleaning the animals and collecting the milk. Women are the more significant partners in the dairy production cycle, yet they were excluded from membership within the cooperative that made decisions concerning the work. SEWA sought to remedy this discrimination by advocating establishment of seven all-women dairy cooperatives in the villages that previously had no cooperatives, as well as encouraging the increased inclusion of women in the existing cooperatives.

However, the revival of the procurement routes was not the only obstacle. While the routes were opened, the opening of the local chilling centers was delayed. Still not fully confident in the production capacity of the new groups, the Banas Dairy did not want to make the significant investment in reopening the chilling centers. Instead, the milk was collected in the tankers and traveled all the way to the Banas Dairy in Palanpur. The whole journey, including collection from the village cooperatives to delivery at the Banas Dairy, took as long as eight hours. Meanwhile, the milk would be stewing in the tanker. By the time it arrived in Palanpur it had often turned bad.

The milk was not considered to have been purchased by the Banas Dairy until it was delivered, in good condition, to their Palanpur facilities. Because of this, the bad milk in the tankers was still considered the unpurchased property of the village cooperatives. Although they turned over the milk in good condition, the cooperatives took the blame and bore the cost. Though it took some time, the Banas Dairy solved the problem by reopening the chilling center in Radhanpur. Thus, the milk ultimately arrived at Banas Dairy in good condition, but not without a struggle that almost ruined the whole enterprise before it began.

With cooperation on the part of both the Banas Dairy and a handful of cooperatives, the entire system was finally revived in the latter half of 1989. The commencement of cooperative activity coincided with the first full monsoon rains in four years. Production grew at a steady rate and, in fact, outpaced the dairy's capacity to process the milk. As a result, the dairy was forced to declare two 'milk holidays' a week in order to ease the pressure on its facilities. On those days, the cooperative members were obliged to cease production and forfeit any opportunity to work.

Furthermore, the over-supply of milk brought the market price down. Although the Banas Dairy had neglected to raise the procurement price in the drought years when the market price had risen, it nevertheless did not hesitate to lower the procurement price in the time of glut. In both cases, in time of surplus and in shortage, the producers were left to bear the brunt of the market fluctuations.

To address the situation, SEWA pushed for several changes. First, SEWA advocated establishment of a powdered milk plant at the Banas Dairy. With such a facility, any excess milk not sold before going bad could instead be converted into powdered form, which had a longer shelf life. The advantages in this case would be many. There would be a safety valve in times of surplus and a reserve supply in times of shortage.

Second, SEWA sought to cushion the blow of environmental and market-based fluctuations by supplying access to capital to the dairy producers. Rural micro-finance is discussed separately in this book; however, it does deserve special mention here. Milk-producing livestock is a highly valued asset in Banaskantha. As mentioned before, it is a source of year-round income in an area where such opportunities are rare. In the face of drought, when cattle die, the loss can be doubly devastating. The owners of the cattle lose not only a productive asset, but also one that would be their main collateral when attempting to recover. Formal loan sources would balk at loaning money to a woman without income or collateral. The only alternatives available to most at this point are the moneylender and day labor. One is exploitative and the other inconsistent, and they both retard the full recovery of an individual and the economy to their pre-drought condition.

By extending rural banking resources to women, SEWA facilitated a more complete recovery from the prolonged drought and prepared them better for future difficulties. The members were able to restock their herds through micro-credit and, in some cases, become more productive than they had been before the drought.

However, all challenges had not yet been overcome. Of the seven women's dairy cooperatives organized by SEWA, not a single one was able to register. The government office responsible for registering the dairy cooperatives, the District Registrar in Palanpur, refused to register the women's cooperatives. According to them, women were not capable of running a cooperative on their own, as evidenced by the fact that there was no precedent.

Never mind the fact that dairy production is almost exclusively performed by women. This situation was similar to that of the pani panchayats that consisted almost exclusively of men, when it was the women who were primarily involved in every water-related activity. Yet, the District Registrar refused to recognize the women's abilities. From 1989 to 1991, SEWA and the cooperative members vehemently lobbied with the Registrar, until finally, after a year and a half, the office relented. Not until then could production commence. Since then, however, the women's cooperatives have become models in the region.

The women's effectiveness has still not prevented further obstacles from arising. Since 1991, five villages with old cooperatives, that failed to revive themselves after the drought, refused to let the women take over. SEWA organized women who were ready and willing to re-establish productivity but, once again, the Registrar refused to register them. This time, the 'reason' was politically motivated and stemmed from the Banas Dairy itself. According to the Gujarat Cooperative Act, in order for a dairy cooperative to be registered, it has to have a positive recommendation from the district dairy union sent to the Registrar. The Banas Dairy is headed by a board of directors that is elected by all the members of the cooperatives. In short, the current board members were fearful that, if the five new BDMSA cooperatives were brought within the fold of the Banas Dairy, they would alter the political structure of the institution and ultimately influence in the elections. So, fearful of losing their seats, some members of the board refused to give the recommendation needed to start the new cooperatives. The issue remains unresolved.

For the cooperatives that were functioning, good monsoon rains in 1993 again resulted in above-average milk yields. Already behind schedule in expanding the facilities in order to keep pace with the production of the revived dairy cooperatives, the Banas Dairy was again unable to cope. During that season, Banaskantha milk cooperatives produced 450,000 liters of milk, while the Banas Dairy's holding capacity was only 20,000 liters. To compensate, the dairy declared milk holidays four days out of the week. On these days, the producers were again forced to cease their production and forfeit any opportunity for profits. In addition, due to the failure of effective resource management, the price of milk plummeted from Rs. 105 to Rs. 75 per unit. Thus, benefits from the good monsoon were reduced to nought for the dairy producers.

In response to the same crisis in 1990, SEWA advocated construction of a powdered milk production plant. With the same issues resurfacing three years later, the Banas Dairy finally commissioned the plant in 1993.

Completed in 1996, this facility can now convert surplus milk into powder. The future need for a milk holiday has since been minimized by offering an alternative for surplus milk production. The advantage of an increased shelf life offered by powdered milk, gives the government an effective tool for controlling the amount of milk supplied to the market. The price fluctuations can now be moderated and with effective management, perhaps even controlled. And, when the cooperatives' production exceeds capacity, there will hopefully be no need for milk holidays. Thus, the dairy cooperatives have a better chance to continue to produce at full capacity.

The Fodder Security System

One last significant development for the dairy cooperatives has been the establishment of a Fodder Security System. As noted before, nutrition for the cattle is a foundation to milk production. Even when there is no drought, the natural cycle of monsoon and dry season causes fluctuations in the amounts produced. To lessen the effects of the dry season, the BDMSA cooperatives devised the concept of the fodder farm. A yearly deposit is collected from the members and used to procure the resources needed to grow fodder. Between the rows of trees of the BDMSA tree plantations, the growing fodder is provided the shade and water it needs. Once harvested, the fodder is stored until the dry season progresses, and is then sold to the members at a substantially reduced price. Similar to the savings and loan program, the Fodder Security System offers the women a tool for sharing and, therefore increasing, their resources and protecting themselves from potential obstacles in the future.

The system itself was a direct result of a community-based innovation. At meetings in the early stages of the program, SEWA, FPI, and the individual dairy cooperatives discussed the decreasing productivity of the groups. The members cited the lack of fodder as the reason. They then elaborated the system they already had in order to address the problem.

Before the introduction of the Fodder Security System, large families or several different families would pool their resources and purchase fodder in bulk from other districts. Because of environmental circumstances in these other districts, they often had a comparative advantage in producing fodder. That way, the price for fodder in these regions was lower and the availability was extended well into the period in which fodder was no longer available locally in Banaskantha. However, the system had its limitations, mainly because the overall organizational capacity of the family groups was limited. The members suggested that this no longer needed to be the case. With their newly organized numbers, they could utilize the same system on a larger scale and with greater benefits.

The plans for a fodder bank were immediately devised on the previous model the members had used. In addition, a small amount of land was procured so that the cooperatives could produce their own fodder. Soon, this was expanded to include 25 acres of land leased from the district authorities and used for the fodder farms mentioned before. The Gujarat Agricultural University offered advice in technical matters, such as the choice of crops, depending on the soil conditions and available shade and water. They also provided, free of charge, seed stock being developed by the university to fit local needs and resources. Both the fodder groups and the university benefited, as the former acquired free expertise and seed stock, while the latter got to test its work under real conditions.

The initial fodder bank proved a particularly effective program and was soon expanded further. The Gujarat State Rural Development Corporation (GSRDC), that had previously managed cattle camps where animals could find water and fodder during the drought, had several defunct fodder farms. The infrastructure still existed, but was not used. In 1995, the BDMSA and the GSRDC entered into a Memorandum of Understanding that handed over four of these farms, a total of 600 acres, to the women's cooperatives. This opened up the possibility for greater expansion of the program and a more stable milk production system.

However, the political winds of change, often unpredictable, blew away any hope of the realization of the promises of the memorandum. In 1997, with a new regime in control of the GSRDC, the four farms were reclaimed. Having invested considerable resources and energy in reviving the fodder production, the members were now denied the fruits of their efforts. With this great disappointment, the BDMSA discovered that it was wiser to avoid such politicized institutions rather than risk similar problems in the future. Unfortunately, in India, where the government plays such a large role in so many things, politics is difficult to avoid.

The fodder fund does continue to grow, as does smaller-scale fodder farming within the organization. Since the inception of the system, the BDMSA has subsidized the program, though at a decreasing rate. Always with the understanding that the subsidy was meant to strengthen the program so that it could ultimately become independent, the subsidy has gone down from 100 percent in the beginning to 25 percent in 1998. The subsidy is expected to end completely by the end of 2001.

To further put the impact of the concept of fodder farming in context, the effects of overgrazing on ecological degradation must be more fully understood. When rangeland is overgrazed, it is particularly the edible vegetation that is depleted. Induced by drought conditions, cattle are obligated to literally root out a greater degree of this vegetation, eating not only the leaves, but stem and root. As the cattle consume these plants to the point of destruction, other inedible plants fill the void. This gradually turns grazing land into wasteland. The process then increases migration as well as the pressure on the more marginal rangeland, already in a fragile state of ecological balance.

In pre-Independence times, under the zamindari system, each villager paid a fee to the local landowner, with the amount based on how many of his cattle used the communal grazing land. These fees were then partially used for maintaining the grazing land, growing fodder, and dividing and rotating the land for different uses. With Independence, the management of this system was put in the hands of the village panchayat.

With the factionalism and ineffectiveness that at times accompanied the advent of Panchayati Raj, the land management system broke down. Communities went from the feudal to the fend-for-yourself stage. For many villages, independence meant individualism. Social disintegration meant that land conservation lost out to private gain. The private cost of the overuse of grazing land was minimal, but the community costs were high. In Banaskantha, the community cost was desertification.

By developing the concept of fodder farming, the BDMSA and its members are not only improving their own productivity. They are also improving the quality of their community's environment by minimizing the pressure on the surrounding natural resources. In a region where the balance between sustainability and destruction is so fine, the impact of this activity is highly valuable.

In sum, the benefits of SEWA's efforts to organize dairy cooperatives are many. It must be understood that the progress made by the BDMSA cooperatives does not exclude the other cooperatives. The reopening of the procurement routes in 1989, thanks to the work of SEWA and the FPI, included 75 cooperatives. Only eight of those were SEWA groups. Perhaps, most importantly, women's participation in dairy cooperatives has increased in non-SEWA groups as well. This implies progress in rectifying the gender perceptions that initially impeded establishment of the women's dairy cooperatives.

More evidence of the women's effectiveness is provided by the recognized distinction of the women's dairy cooperatives. Every year, the Banas

Dairy awards three prizes among the approximately 400 cooperatives in its system. These awards are given on the basis of performance, isolated from political consideration. The prizes are for production quantity, quality and accounting, and administration. In 1996, one of those awards was given to a SEWA cooperative. In 1997, two of the awards went to SEWA cooperatives. Then, in 1998, SEWA groups won all three awards.

The Fodder Security System adds to the list of gains for many reasons. First, the assured supply of fodder prevents the deteriorating health of cattle, and in some instances even the death of the livestock. Second, the consistent supply of fodder supports stabilization of the milk supply throughout the year. A constant supply helps to secure a year-round source of income for the cooperative members and also minimizes the dairy's need to cope with seasonal fluctuations in milk supply. Third, and perhaps most importantly, the guaranteed supply of fodder eliminates a major push factor behind migration in Banaskantha, cattle productivity and survival. This, in turn, allows the cooperative members, who are also BDMSA members, to participate in other income-generating programs, described in the pages that follow.

Biography: Migrations No More

Rudiben is a dairy producer in Moti Pipli. Before she became a SEWA member, Rudiben often had to migrate in the hope of ensuring the survival of her cattle. In 1989, the final year of the last severe drought, she had to migrate all the way to Kheda, over 200 kilometers away from her village, before she could find sufficient fodder and water. Along the way, she lost six of her 10 cows and buffaloes. They died slowly from lack of fodder and water and the susceptibility to diseases that their want had brought.

Afraid of losing the rest of her cattle, Rudiben anxiously joined the SEWA dairy cooperative in Moti Pipli when the opportunity arose. So did 300 other people in her village. Rudiben's story was sad, but not unique. Many had lost cattle and were in danger of losing more.

Soon after joining the cooperative, Rudiben and others went on an exposure trip to the Banas Dairy. There, she saw the whole process of milk production that took place after she procured the milk with her own hands. She saw the milk tanker delivering the milk from the chilling center. She saw how the milk was stored, sterilized and packaged. She was particularly inspired by the fodder farm. She and the other members had to migrate almost every year. This disrupted their lives and their production in so many ways, beyond the loss of their cattle. The fodder farm seemed to be a way out of this cycle.

Since the trip, Rudiben's group has been regularly buying fodder from the BDMSA's Fodder Security System. The fodder is available year-round, so her cattle are more productive and Rudiben can stay in Moti Pipli year-round. She has a daughter and son, who both attend school, which would have been impossible if they had to migrate. She also has time to work in other income-generating activities since she is not constantly on the move anymore.

She has become a leader in her group and a member of SEWA's Executive Committee. With her leadership, the Moti Pipli dairy cooperative has made much progress. One important development is that the village cooperative has purchased an electronic milk-fat tester.

Milk-fat content is the primary determinant in ascertaining the quality and subsequent price of the milk. The cooperative's previous manual device did not properly measure the quality of the milk, and this was a cause of concern. Some women were not fully compensated for their milk when the milk-fat was under-estimated. Meanwhile, others got away with adding water to their milk, adding to its volume and detracting from its quality. The new tester, complete with the first computer to come to this village, has put an end to such circumstances. This investment has made her group's a much more fair and efficient operation.

Rudiben's life has changed in important ways over the past few years. Most importantly, Rudiben does not have to leave her village to save her cattle. Asked what she is going to do with her spare time, since she doesn't have to migrate anymore, she pauses to think and then says, with a sense of irony, that she enjoys travel. As a SEWA Executive Committee member, she has already traveled to all the nine districts in Gujarat in which SEWA is active. Every month, she meets with her fellow committee members in a new place.

The purpose of the travel is 'lateral learning.' Every time she travels to a new district, Rudiben and the others learn about the SEWA activities in that area. She has taken lessons from these trips, as well as shared her own experiences with members outside her own village. Each one is like a new exposure trip, like her first one to the Banas Dairy, and she enjoys the opportunity.

The Artisan Support Program

When SEWA first became involved in Banaskantha, the organizers were immediately struck by the quality of the embroidery and patchwork done by the women in the villages, evidenced by the clothes they were wearing and the decorations in their houses. The design and manufacture of the rich traditional wear were executed with a skill that blurred the line between artisan and artist. The women were conscious of their abilities and proud of them. They knew the work had value. They just did not know how much.

The clothing was normally meant for members of the family of the woman who produced it. Over the centuries, the women of the region developed their unique style to meet the needs of their families. The pieces they produced were often made for the occasion of a daughter's wedding and were among the commodities that their daughters would bring into their marriages. The different designs were a means of communicating identity, family, caste, and village. They were also simply a means of showing off a woman's talent, a source of pride for the family.

When SEWA organizers indicated that the craft products might have commercial value, the women explained that occasionally a trader would come to the village and purchase the work from the women. After more discussion and investigation, it was clear that the prices these traders offered were only a tiny fraction of what the products fetched later in the open market. In fact, the traders often bartered for the women's work, offering steel and plastic vessels in an exchange that was heavily in the traders' favor. The women had suspected that they were not getting the full value of their products, but did not have access to the craft markets. Nor did they have a strong perception of the tastes of the potential buyers. When custom dictates that you cannot travel outside your village without an accompanying male family member, such perceptions are difficult to acquire. Thus began what is potentially the most monetarily fruitful program in the Banaskantha project.

Some women were eager to try and sell their products once SEWA organizers suggested the income it could produce. However, many other women were initially skeptical of the organizers' insistence that there was a way to get more out of their artisan work. Traders had come, but offered very little. It was hard to visualize the benefits that, the organizers said, were possible. After all, these women were outsiders. How could they be trusted?

To overcome this skepticism, the organizers set out to make a point. A handful of the village women were interested in giving the program a try and so were willing to take a chance. The organizers collected their work and gave the women payment on the spot. The organizers then attempted to find a market for the goods. When these organizers met with success through a Dastkar exhibition in Delhi, they immediately informed the artisans about it. The efficiency of this trial effort impressed a few more women, and they joined in. Over a short period of time, several groups were recruited.

Dastkar, an organization that by that time was already a very effective promoter of indigenous crafts, recognized the SEWA products as a promising new development. SEWA had attended several Dastkar exhibitions, offering products such as weaving and block printing made by its urban members. SEWA had come to highly value Dastkar's expertise, not only in marketing, but also product development. This relationship was to serve the Banaskantha craftswomen well.

But, first, to adapt to the smaller atmosphere of the village, SEWA made a direct effort to include the local government. With the government's support, the program would be much easier to undertake. With the interests of not just the artisans, but their families and neighbors at stake, it was logical that the support of the village government should be solicited and tendered.

A meeting was arranged in each of the participating villages, and it was attended by the craftswomen, the SEWA organizers, and the village panchayat. At this meeting, a list of all the skilled women artisans in the village was prepared and then forwarded to the taluka panchayat office. This office identified which women on that list were registered as below the poverty line (BPL). These women would then be eligible to participate in the Development of Women and Children in Rural Areas (DWCRA) program, reserved for poor women as determined by the BPL criterion.

With those eligible for membership identified, the group selected women of energy, experience, and ability who could lead the others. The responsibilities of this job included management of the group bank account, record-keeping, negotiation and purchase of raw materials, division of the workload, and delivery of the finished product. Therefore, it was decided that not only one leader, but also a committee of leaders should be chosen. That way, more women could share the burden of responsibility, as well as gain from the experience.

A finalized list, naming the regular members, women of the committee, and the group leader, was then submitted and registered with the DWCRA program. This program, a sub-scheme of the Indian Government's Integrated Rural Development Program, is meant to facilitate access for women to employment, skill development, credit and other support services for supplementing their incomes. By registering with the DWCRA in groups of 10 to 15, these women became eligible for a fund of Rs. 15,000 for the purchase of raw materials, training and wages in the initial stage. The money was to be used before the group became self-sustaining enough to support the women and their families while they undertook this new activity. After that, skills could be more fully developed and sales secured, and a new livelihood established.

From its experience in organizing groups of artisans, SEWA also anticipated the degree to which financial transactions would take place and decisions would have to be made. The money from sales as well as from the purchase of raw materials, payment for outside labor and the distribution of wages to group members, would all have to be handled. The artisans were still wary of anyone from outside their village handling their precious money. Besides, SEWA's ability to undertake such an endeavor was limited and limiting. Using SEWA organizers to manage this activity would preclude their ability to work on the expansion of SEWA activities elsewhere. Also, the other commitments of the organizers would hinder the artisan groups' capacity to expand. With little time to take on new duties, they would be unable to keep up with the potential for growth among the groups.

On the other hand, if these groups could acquire the skills to manage their group independently, the benefits would be far-reaching. As the income generation increased, the artisans could decide, on their own, when and how to expand. Thus, SEWA and their new members developed a program to match the complex business of craft production and marketing with local initiative and leadership. With the involvement of every group member in multiple aspects of the program, coinciding with intense training, business got underway.

With the groups roughly established, SEWA organizers and an expert from Dastkar would go to each individual village to conduct production meetings. When they went to the village, they would ask the women to bring one traditional piece they owned, such as a blouse, skirt or ornament, and contribute it to the group pile. They would then write down a list of the names of the craftswomen present. With the names listed, there would also be a head count, and the total had to equal the number of traditional pieces provided to the pile. If the number of people exceeded the number of traditional pieces brought to the meeting, then either some women would have to leave until the numbers matched, or go back and bring a piece.

Though this process may seem tedious, it was an appropriate response to the chaos of the early part of the meetings. The women were anxious for work and would push and shove at each other, while grabbing and pulling the women from SEWA and Dastkar. The women were desperate for what by then appeared a promising opportunity. Shouting matches erupted, with the organizers being caught in the wrangle between the women. Few of the women had ever attended school, or meetings of any kind, and had little regard for the type of decorous atmosphere that helped best to get things accomplished as a group. The early ground rules, strictly enforced, tried to set the tone for the type of cooperation demanded of everybody.

Once things settled down, the women would choose a design pattern from the compiled pieces, the appropriate colors, and the type of garment it was to be stitched onto. After a morning or afternoon of work, the best pieces would be selected as samples. The design would then be recorded, as were the colors, and eventually a catalogue of designs, colors and finished products would be compiled as a resource for the craftswomen. After a few such gatherings, the women would be able easily refer to 'design style 17, using colors 3, 21, and 43 for a shawl,' for example. With these basics established, the focus could shift to improving the quality of the work and their group independence.

For the first craft groups, organizers and experts from Dastkar invested a great deal of time in traveling to the villages and working with the women. They would spend months visiting the villages repeatedly, assessing the work and suggesting improvements. The quality of work was the main concern, and required time.

Traders, who had previously purchased the craft products, had long since discovered the value of the women's work. They learned to acquire the products from the women at very low prices, relative to the amount the articles fetched in the market. The low prices offered and the low market aspirations of the traders translated into a relatively poor quality of work. The craftswomen easily discovered that the traders were not interested in distinguishing between fine and rough work. It was quantity the traders were interested in and, if the women tried to produce quality, they would be wasting their time without reward. The system that arose was that the women would produce as much poor-quality craftwork for which they had the time and inclination, and the traders would compensate them marginally for it.

For the first few years of the program, as the SEWA staff in Banaskantha grew, more and more were assigned the task of working with the craftswomen. The craft program provided the most returns of any program for the members, but it also ate up a lot of resources. Organizers would spend a very significant portion of their time sifting through finished work, sorting out the good from the bad and working with the women to improve the work. This devotion to the functioning groups then limited the ability of the program to expand to other villages. Also, other programs such as nursery activity and micro-finance were beginning to develop and demanded attention. Furthermore, the intense involvement of the organizers limited the progress towards the independent sustainability of the craft groups themselves. Lastly, while the improvement of the quality took time, the women and their families needed to eat.

In order to succeed, the women needed to develop a system that allowed them to enhance their skills, quality of work, and independence while still getting an income. After a few adjustments, a re-modeled system was implemented, which achieved these goals. Through initial skill-testing with new groups that were forming, an exceptionally skilled craftswoman was identified in each village. This woman would then be trained in how to help the other women develop their skills. During the initial period, the women were closely monitored by the trained craftswomen. These 'trained trainers' would particularly stress the quality of the women's work and suggest ways to improve, assuming many of the responsibilities of the organizers.

The trainer would compare the other women's work with samples of superior quality. The work would then be classified into three categories: red indicated poor quality, yellow a need for improvement and green a satisfactory quality. As an incentive, the craftswomen were paid for their work, during the training period, in accordance with the quality rating it received. Thus, every woman was motivated to improve her quality within a training structure that allowed her to visualize her goal. Meanwhile, she had an income, the group was more independent, and organizers were free to take on other responsibilities.

Similarly, once the production improved, it was discovered that the original pricing used by all the groups needed adjustment. As some of the women attended exhibitions in Ahmedabad and elsewhere, they compared not only the quality of their work with other producers, but the prices as well. What they noticed was that their products were generally more expensive. A few of the leaders were concerned enough by this to gather all their original samples and re-create them, closely monitoring the costs of the raw materials that went into the pieces. What they discovered was that, early on in the program, they had overestimated the cost of their raw materials. Once this was realized, all the groups quickly checked and adjusted their costing and made their prices more competitive.

Both the training system and the costing adjustments were praised at a conference at the Indian Institute of Management (IIM) in Ahmedabad, India's premier management institution. The IIM faculty lauded the training structure as an advanced system that allowed for production improvement, sustainability and profitability at the same time. The craftswomen's initiative in checking their costing was also identified as a fine example of innovation in conscientious management. Both were identified as models that could be applied in many industries.

Another problem efficiently tackled was that of failing eyesight. A large majority of the craftswomen struggled with poor vision. Poor nutrition and the natural effects of aging or inherently flawed vision, combined with the strenuously detailed work of embroidery in poor lighting (electricity was, until recently, not available to many villages and, if it was, one exposed light-bulb was often the sole fixture), contributed to severe eye problems among many of the craftswomen. To address the situation, several eye clinics were arranged. A local ophthalmologist generously volunteered his services for several weekends, and examined the women's eyes. In the first year of the clinics, over 1,000 women were examined and 876 were provided with prescription glasses, subsidized by SEWA's capital fund.

With these developments, the time soon came when production from the members became abundant enough to require a more effective system of marketing. The occasional exhibitions, as well as the sales to the government program, could no longer match the production capacity of the groups. To address this issue, the idea of a 'craft center' began to be developed.

The goal was the creation of two facilities to fit several specific needs. Sales, of course, had become a top priority. A retail space devoted to the women's crafts would mean no more dependence on exhibition schedules or government programs. Exhibitions required a lot of preparation, consuming a lot of time and resources. But, the exhibition calendar did not offer a stable source of sales. The government programs were potentially unreliable and susceptible to discontinuation. Furthermore, the stable outlet, in the form of a retail shop, would give the women a better platform from which they could more accurately gauge the market in terms of what tastes prevailed and what prices were appropriate.

A second need was for a location from which the women could prepare for exhibitions. While exhibitions were not a sound base for all sales, they did have certain advantages. They offered a place to meet retailers interested in buying large orders, and also an opportunity to see other groups' work of a similar genre. The specific requirements were for an area where the exhibition materials could be collected, arranged and stored, as well as a space devoted to researching and scheduling the events.

Lastly, the diversity of traditional designs, varying from village to village, was being augmented by the new designs. These new designs were variations on a traditional theme being adapted to reflect market tastes.

By producing a catalogue of all the designs, traditional designs could be preserved, progress in new designs tracked, and all the designs organized and made more readily accessible to the artisans and those who prepared the orders.

Each of these three general needs would require not only four walls and a roof, but telecommunications, computer technology, and a prime location, to be truly useful. These resources were costly. However, if they could be housed in two aptly placed facilities, the total cost could be significantly reduced. In addition, computerized inventories and accounts could be more easily cross-analyzed if they were punched in on the same keyboards.

The resulting two facilities are the Banas Craft in Ahmedabad and the Radhanpur Craft Development Center. The Banas Craft serves as a center for marketing research and exhibition scheduling, but it is also occupies a prime location for retail in Ahmedabad, on C.G. Road. This thoroughfare is the premier upscale shopping area in Ahmedabad. Clothing, jewelry, appliances and other items are sold in the shops that line its two miles. There, the Banas Craft is able to appeal to an increasing population of middle-class consumers as well as those just traveling through Ahmedabad and likely see one of the many pamphlets that the Banas Craft has strategically placed in hotels in the city.

The Radhanpur Craft Development Center serves to catalogue designs, collect and store the crafts, as well as the raw materials, and organize a production schedule. Furthermore, the center has become the headquarters of all SEWA and BDMSA activity in Banaskantha. Craftswomen, as well as pani panchayat members, gum collectors, and others, all use the center as a place to come together. Organizers and the BDMSA leadership base themselves there, where they can always be available to the other members, and each other, and share advice, experiences and resources.

The Banas Craft and the Radhanpur Craft Development Center were innovative adaptations of several different government programs. The Banas Craft was built with funds from the Ministry of Rural Development, Government of Gujarat, as well as an IRDP Infrastructure Support Program Grant. In Radhanpur, it was the Development Commissioner for Handicrafts, Government of India, that provided support. There were government resources available to support individual aspects of what the craft program needed, but not in their entirety. However, all the needs and available funding were adeptly and efficiently consolidated into two unique spaces. By creatively utilizing what the government offered, national programs were made to fit local need. Furthermore, the synergistic effect made the two facilities far more valuable than anything that all these programs would have offered individually.

The Craftswomen

The success stories among the craftswomen are numerous. Hiraben, from the village of Vauva, won the Kamaladevi Chattopadhyay National Award for Mastercraftsmen in October of 1998. Her prestigious award not only gained recognition for her, but has also drawn attention to the under-appreciated craft tradition of Banaskantha.

Other group achievements in Vauva further capture the spirit of the program as a whole. Here, most of the craftswomen are from the Aahir community. The women of the Aahir caste are traditionally not allowed to work outside their homes and rarely travel beyond the boundaries of their village. In 1992, the Aahir community held a regional caste panchayat in Vauva. The only way in which the women were to participate was to cook and clean for the several hundred men who attended the meeting. However, at the time of the meeting, the Vauva craftswomen were working hard to fill an order for their craft cooperative.

The women resented their exclusion from the meeting and gave priority to their craftwork. As a result, the men of the community voted to ban the women from further participating in SEWA activities. Any exceptions the women were previously allowed were revoked, such as traveling to and from the Craft Center in Radhanpur to exchange raw materials and finished products or attend SEWA meetings. The women of Vauva refused to accept the decision. A leader among them arose and presented their case to the community leaders. Bhachiben, that leader, pointed out to the men that the women's work was making a tremendous difference in their lives. There was no more need for migration during the droughts, since the work was unaffected by bad weather. The income for the families had risen significantly and, with it, health and nutrition had improved. The men ultimately recognized the logic of her demands and the ban was lifted.

Today, the women members of the craft program have developed an independence that reflects the strength of their órganization. Their confidence has increased as they have all ventured beyond the confines of their village, many beyond the borders of their state, and some to other countries. They have the confidence that knowledge affords: knowledge in their abilities and their value. They also have increased bargaining power, as membership in the BDMSA cooperative does not exclude them from selling to private traders or other government programs if the terms of trade are better.

They are the owners and managers of their individual enterprises and have all the trappings of decision-making power that come with that position. On a consistent basis, the leaders from each individual village get together as a spearhead team to do the business planning. What markets should they target? Where can they get the best balance of quality raw materials for a good price? Should they expand and, if so, how will it be done? These are all decisions they have learnt to make on their own, with valuable experience behind them.

With a program of this magnitude, the benefits are not limited only to the members. Local dyers and block printers have increased their business. Tailors have more work. Even some local boys have found employment selling the members' products locally from village to village.

Perhaps most significant of all, the agricultural wage rate, the foundation of the Banaskantha labor market, has risen in a manner that at least suggests that the rise in artisan-based employment, the most productive of SEWA's income-generation activities, is involved. In 1989, agricultural wages hovered as low as Rs. 10 per day. By 1994, as the craft program gained momentum, offering wages as high as Rs. 40 per day, agricultural jobs fetched up to Rs. 45. By 1999, the artisan activity offered at least Rs. 50 per day, and often more, with agricultural wages as high as Rs. 60 per day. Whether the parallel rise in wages is correlated or not is only speculation at this point. But evidence does strongly suggest the possibility. Meanwhile, agricultural wages in other districts, Kheda for example, an agriculturally rich area with little craft activity, hover around Rs. 20 per day.

The artisans agree. When work in the fields is available for Rs. 60 they will take it. Otherwise, they will sacrifice a few rupees to save themselves the exhaustion of the physically taxing labor. Thus, farmers have discovered they will not find these women in their fields at harvest time for anything less than Rs. 60 per day. The members are not only more capable of bargaining for better prices for their crafts, but have extended the lesson to other parts of their lives as well.

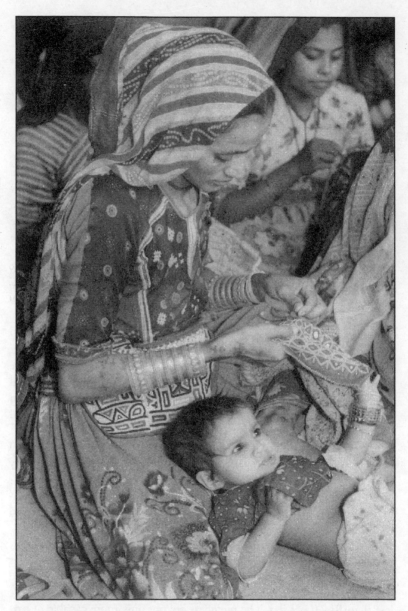

Plate 4.2: A craftswoman concentrates on a traditional mirror work design, while her daughter looks on

Biography: Seeing a Whole New World

Gomiben of Datrana village has been employed by her craftwork for many years. Before she was a SEWA member, she produced patchwork for the Gujarat State Handicraft Development Corporation. In that program, if her work was considered of poor quality, the price paid to her was reduced. There was no training and no suggestion for improvement. Just the lower price.

In those days her brother served as the middleman. He exchanged the raw materials and finished products on behalf of the village group for a small commission. He had to go all the way to Palanpur to do the group's business. The craftswomen could not do it. The women in the village were only allowed to go as far as Santalpur, the nearest town, as a group, to buy supplies. Even then, they could only go once a month.

But that seems like a long time ago. Since then, after becoming a SEWA member, Gomiben has been as far as Ahmedabad and even Hyderabad. The women of Datrana formed a patchwork DWCRA group in 1991. Gomiben became the leader of her group, then a member of the craft spearhead team, and then a member of the subcommittee on marketing.

Her work has improved, as have her income and her other skills. After she became a member of the spearhead team, one of her first activities was to accompany the SEWA organizer to buy raw materials, the role her brother used to fill years earlier. The material needed on that occasion was only available in Kutch. After the journey, Gomiben and the organizer had a hard time locating the right kind of material. Once there, they stopped at several places until they found what they were looking for. Gomiben was then shocked at the high price of the satin-like material, only later to realize the much higher marketability a finished product made of this material had. This lesson was the first of many she took to heart.

Now her focus is on marketing. Her trip to Hyderabad, for a craft exposition, was a part of her work in this capacity. While there, Gomiben saw work from several different groups from various parts of India. She not only worked to sell the Banas Craft's products to people who came to the exposition, but studied the other groups there as well. She saw the different styles and prices, observing what was popular and what was not.

At the Banas Craft's table, she also took special note of what was most sellable. In comparison with other exhibitions she had been to, she noticed that different products were popular in different places. In Hyderabad, for example, light colors were particularly well received. Now, when the Banas Craft goes there for an exhibition next year, Gomiben will make sure they know what to take with them.

Despite all the traveling she has done, Gomiben still remembers her fears about going to Ahmedabad for the first time. She barely slept the night before, wondering if she was going to get robbed or killed. Fears of the big city ran through her mind all that night and for the whole ride there. Now she makes that trip several times a year without losing any sleep. When asked if she wants to go to more exhibitions, there is no question in her mind. Gomiben flashes her characteristically confident smile: "Wherever SEWA sends me, I will go."

Chapter 5

RURAL MICRO-FINANCE

Paramount among the needs of the poor is an escape from the downwardly spiraling cycles that poverty engenders. The world over, poverty all too often brings with it certain conditions that contribute to the continuation of the oppressive situation. It is a tragic irony that the cost of living is often higher for the poor than for those with the resources to avoid the otherwise superfluous expenses of life on the margins. Living on a day-to-day basis, at the mercy of what each successive day brings, the line between survival and suffering can be costly and tenuous. Especially in a drought-prone area, where disaster can strike in so many ways, without resources to fall back on, one's position can be very vulnerable. Without ready access to liquid assets, buying food or medical care often means going into debt. This scenario often includes the moneylender, mentioned earlier but deserving special note here.

A family of means, faced with a medical emergency, does not hesitate to seek professional medical help. When the bill is proffered, they either pay it from funds in their bank account or, in the best of circumstances, it is covered by their insurance. The amount paid is the amount due. If you are poor, however, the amount ultimately paid is likely to be much more than the amount initially due. If you have no access to the required funds, you must borrow. But you have no collateral to speak of, nor anyone you can turn to as a cosignatory on a loan. Besides, which bank would loan funds for such a non-productive purpose? Without savings or insurance to fall back on, you must borrow from the moneylender, and most likely at an exorbitant rate of interest.

A survey conducted by the SEWA Bank in 1988 revealed that more than 80 percent of the rural families, in districts where SEWA was active, had mortgaged their land to a moneylender. Illness, marriage, death or drought can serve to push the family into taking loans on their land, or other assets as collateral, under undesirable conditions. One such condition is that the loan cannot be paid in installments. If it is not paid in a lump sum within the specified period, usually about five years, the collateral becomes the property of the mortgager. In the case of land, the result is that many farmers suddenly find themselves landless laborers. When land mortgages and other collateral are considered, along with what the poorest of the poor owe to the shopkeepers of the provision shops, the debt disease appears to be of epidemic proportions. With interest rates that sometimes exceed 100 percent annually, a small loan can mean a lifetime of paying off debts.

However, it must also be understood that the institution of moneylending, though it is often exploitative, is a vital part of the financial infrastructure for the poor in India, particularly in rural areas. Though it is only the lesser of two evils, debt is better than starvation. Under these circumstances, the moneylender is in some ways a lifesaver.

The moneylender represents an age-old tradition in many parts of the world. In India, the tradition even dates to pre-Vedic times. Like sharks, moneylenders are perfectly suited to their function and environment, and so have needed to evolve little though the ages. They are only a few doors away at most, intimately familiar with their clientele since they live in the same small communities. Their hours are flexible, making them available at any time to those who urgently need funds. Flexible, too, are their terms of lending. The size of the loan can be as small or large as would generally be required by a small farmer or landless laborer. The range of assets used as collateral reflects the scope of objects that are of value to the impoverished borrower, from land, to jewelry, to farming implements. If no collateral is available, the interest rate can be raised to accommodate the circumstances.

The loans from moneylenders are not limited to productive purposes, but can be extended for a health emergency, wedding or funeral, reasons conventionally deemed non-productive and grounds for rejection by most loaning institutions. For a loan from a moneylender, there are few papers to fill out. No waiting in lines. There is no need to formally review one's credit history. The repayment schedule can be accommodating towards the seasonal fluctuations in an agricultural economy, and can even substitute labor or produce for cash payment. And, perhaps most importantly, a flexible agreement can usually be reached on the spot, and the access to the funds is immediate.

The people who provide this efficient service can range from relatively prosperous farmers, school-teachers and shopkeepers to people who make a living on their moneylending activities alone. For the purposes of this discussion, the term 'moneylender' refers to all these people, the flexible use of the term mirroring the flexibility of the system.

Unfortunately, under most circumstances, the borrower is in the weaker position. Particularly when the need for funds is urgent, the flexibility of the system can work decidedly in the favor of the moneylender. A comprehensive study of rural micro-credit practices was conducted in both the Banaskantha and Kheda districts of Gujarat by Sharmila Murthy, a visiting Fulbright scholar. She found that most loans from moneylenders had an interest rate of about 5 percent per month. However, this interest rate, which comes to almost 80 percent annually, barely reflects the egregious extremes to which the system can go. Some moneylenders will gauge how desperate a potential borrower is, and exploit their desperation accordingly. With 5 percent per month as the mean, the extent of the upper extreme can be reasonably inferred. Therefore, in an emergency situation, when the borrower has no time or alternative source, an interest rate of well over 100 percent annually is a conservative estimate at best. Of course, with limited resources to fall back on, and living an emergency-prone lifestyle, the poor are the most vulnerable of all to such exploitative practices.

Furthermore, the illiteracy and innumeracy of the average clientele of a rural moneylender are often exploited. With the passage of time, accounts can too easily be manipulated and debts increased to well beyond the legitimate amounts. For this reason, many moneylenders seek to perpetuate the ignorance of those in their community, and have a vested interest in a social system that continues achieve these ends.

The importance of the moneylender, and the parasitic impact of those that are abusive, is further emphasized if one more fully appreciates the importance of banking infrastructure to a rural, agrarian economy. Agricultural activity, which dominates the rural economy, often engenders economic instability. Drought, flood and various other sources of crop failure can devastate entire regions in the worst of times. In the best of times, seasonal peaks and valleys in cash flow, as well as fluctuating levels of employment and consumption, are all a natural part of the yearly rural economic cycle. Then, if the region itself is not directly hit by adversity, adverse conditions elsewhere can cause fluctuations in crop supply and prices. Finally, the difficulties of getting perishable goods to the market add an element of urgency that diminishes the number of marketing options available to a rural farmer, and therefore a great deal of his leverage.

Under such circumstances, the role of banking infrastructure is crucial. When there is a surplus, as after a harvest, savings services would provide the farmer with a safe and productive place to manage his profits, or a laborer her wages. These then could be drawn upon throughout the year when there are no crops in the fields or work to be done. Conversely, when a drought leaves the seeds withered and dead, with no prospects for wage labor in sight, a reasonable and reliable source for loans would be a lifeline, supporting the rural economy in its time of need. Without it, the funds for new seed stock would be dried up, just like the fields. More importantly, the individuals that make up the marginalized labor pool could use such a loan source for human survival.

The practical reality is that it is difficult for banks to provide services in rural areas as comprehensively as in urban areas. The size of the geographic area, compounded by the lower population density, means that the population a bank branch can serve in a rural area is significantly smaller and more spread out than in an urban area. Therefore, the distance that bank customers would have to travel in order to conduct business is much greater in a rural area. Since the poor have no means of private transportation, that distance is stretched even further.

A multitude of other banking difficulties also affect the rural poor far more severely than any other sector of the population. They have little, if any, assets considered of value as collateral to a conventional bank. The poor, living on a subsistence basis, can only make small deposits into a savings account, at best. Any debts they could reasonably incur would also have to be similarly small. The administrative costs of processing such deposits or loans would tax the resources of most banks, and they would likely be hesitant or unwilling to assume such tasks. Considered along with the complications that the illiteracy and innumeracy of the rural poor would present to the conventional banking process, the attitudes of even the most sympathetic bank staff might well be expected to wear thin.

To take the analysis a step further, the difficulties of banking affect women most severely of all among the rural poor. If very few assets are available as limited collateral for loans, even fewer are entrusted to women. In the budgeting of a subsistence household, it is particularly the women's income that is used to purchase the necessities of survival. Therefore, it is rare that any of their income remains to be saved. If illiteracy and innumeracy present obstacles to navigating the banking process, it is women who are most widely lacking in these areas. Lastly, the attitudes of bank staff are influenced by the fact that it is traditionally the men who are regarded as responsible for conducting the household banking.

Between the services offered by moneylenders and those of conventional banks, the rural poor (especially the women) are caught in a void. With poor nutrition, one is more prone to health problems. Without a consistent source of employment, with work that is dependent on substandard land, loss of income is not just a likelihood, but a certainty. It is the poor who are most in need of equitable financial services. But, it is also the poor who are most often denied such services. It is this void, and the vulnerability to disaster and financial distress, that perpetuate the downwardly spiraling cycle of poverty.

SEWA's Rural Approach

When the SEWA Bank was founded in 1974 in the city of Ahmedabad, it began to implement what has since been recognized as one of the best adapted banking structures for impoverished women. It was founded as a cooperative bank, by and for poor, self-employed women. Deposits and loans were expected to be small, relative to conventional banks. Accommodations were made to circumvent the challenges that an illiterate clientele would present. Photo-identification and thumbprints substituted for signatures. Also, a more supportive approach was adopted toward those members who had difficulty repaying loans on time. When banks in India were nationalized in the 1970s, they were obligated to set aside 1 percent of their loanable funds for the poor. Those banks that complied often disregarded that money as lost, and either dealt harshly or not at all with the defaulters. Rather than foreclosing or forgetting, the SEWA Bank sought to nurture a sense of financial discipline. Loan officers, often previously self-employed women themselves, went to the homes of the defaulters and discussed the loans with them. Usually, it was a case of hardship, such as an illness in the family, which precluded payment. In that case, a new schedule of repayment, or some such adaptation, was worked out.

Furthermore, the definition of 'productive purpose' for a loan was expanded in the case of the SEWA Bank to include house repairs, paying off old, high-interest debts to moneylenders and rescuing mortgaged assets. These innovations took into account the realities of poverty and the unique challenges the poor had to face. By the usual standards, such use of loaned funds would be deemed unproductive because they seemed unlikely to generate income with which to repay loans, among other things. But, founders of the SEWA Bank realized that an ill-constructed house failed to protect the assets housed within, let alone the occupants. Not just furniture, clothing and stores of food, but also productive assets, such as tools of trade, raw materials and finished products were kept within the house. Whether a man's house is his castle is sometimes debatable, but that a woman's house is her factory is often a fact! The bank saw loans for housing improvements as productive because they served to protect productive assets.

Similarly, loans used to pay off loans were seen by the bank as productive because the members of the cooperative bank were keenly aware of the difference between a SEWA Bank loan, at a reasonable interest rate, and a loan from a moneylender. This was a difference not often experienced by the conventional bank patron, who had little use for a moneylender, and so the conventional bank failed to see the practical side of the issue, or at least saw the risk of defaulting as too great. For the SEWA Bank, it was the risk to the way of life of the member that took precedence, and there was a greater degree of confidence in the borrower that, once freed of the burden of exploitative interest rates, she could regain financial control.

These and other innovations helped the SEWA Bank and its members grow and prosper. The synergy between the bank and the labor union helped to consolidate the benefits of both their activities. However, just as SEWA's new involvement in rural areas necessitated something beyond the labor union struggle, the SEWA Bank quickly realized that rural banking required adaptations to their original, urban model. After a decade and a half of urban success, the SEWA Bank faced a unique and formidable challenge in trying to extend its services to a rural area.

Just as with conventional banks, the SEWA Bank in Ahmedabad was oriented to an area of high population density, where every shareholder could venture to the bank premises with relatively little inconvenience. One location was all that was needed to facilitate the shareholders, and this also meant that all the necessary accountants, tellers, loan officers and actual deposits could be housed in one place. In terms of banking convenience, these were luxuries that Banaskantha and other rural areas did not have.

By the time the critical momentum had built up in Banaskantha for savings and credit activity, many of the income-generating activities, like craftwork and watershed development, had already begun to get under way. In conversations with SEWA organizers, and even with urban members whom the new members met on exposure trips, the activities and benefits of SEWA Bank were discussed. Though many of the new, rural members were indifferent to the idea, as too focused on earnings and too little on savings, some picked it up. They began to pressure the organizers to help make progress on the issue. In response, SEWA organizers went to several of the villages to introduce the women to the idea of the savings and credit groups. However, instead of enthusiasm, these organizers were greeted with general apprehension and outright suspicion. When you have no money to spare, any group of strangers that proposes that you 'deposit' your money into their hands for 'safekeeping' will have a hard time convincing you. So, it was no surprise that the initial efforts met with resistance. What was a surprise, however, was that the organizers encountered a handful of women who were inspired by the concept and took upon themselves the task of convincing their neighbors. In some cases, these women even promised to compensate the other savings group participants out of their own pockets if the 'city women' disappeared with their money.

With this spark of interest, the first savings schemes were begun. But, the structure was different from anything SEWA had devised before. While it was an innovative approach to banking for the poorest of the poor, the SEWA Bank in Ahmedabad still had some parallels with the traditional banking structure, parallels that served its urban members well, but would not fit into a rural district as effectively. Furthermore, the bank was limited by licensing laws in the nature of direct rural activities in which it could participate. Banaskantha required an even greater departure from known banking practices. But, if planned well, the results would be far-reaching.

The primary obstacle for a rural banking structure was the dispersion of the members over a wide area, with poor roads and scarce public transportation stretching those distances. A bank housed in a single structure would be an impractical facility. The members would find it difficult to make such a journey, sacrificing a day's work while incurring the expenses of the travel. Because the schedules of the buses from the villages to the towns range from infrequent (often only twice a day at best, once there and once back) to non-existent (during the monsoon season, some roads are impassable), villagers with no other option often find themselves at the mercy of those with private cars or other, lesser vehicles. The costs of such services can be exorbitant, relative to the income of most members. To undertake the journey on a regular basis, to make a monthly deposit, for example, would be highly impractical, if not impossible.

The other challenges, such as illiteracy and innumeracy, lack of experience in banking practices, and the advance of loans without collateral, were not new to SEWA. Combining past experience with a progressing understanding of rural needs, SEWA developed a model that could make banking accessible to the isolated. They literally brought the bank to the members' doorsteps.

As mentioned before, the organizers who went to the villagers to initiate the program met with resistance and distrust. It was still an early stage in the program and confidence in the organizers was still in the process of development. To overcome the villagers' fears, SEWA invited the women to Ahmedabad to visit its bank. Despite rumors that the SEWA organizers would sell the women once they got them to the city, some did make the trip—husbands in tow. What they found was a bank that had been in existence for over a decade and a half, swarming with activity, members making deposits, getting loans, socializing, and sharing experiences. Something so big could not disappear with their money.

Those who went on the trip returned to their villages and talked with their friends. Though still reluctant, the number of those interested in giving it a try began to grow. With the awakening of community interest, the organizers began to arrange meetings. The groups would discuss their needs and establish the structure under which the savings and credit schemes would function. Training would take place throughout that period, preparing the women to become independently capable of managing their accounts.

It became apparent from the initial group meetings that the most practical way to manage the program was as a group. Though some sacrifices would have to be made, they were outweighed by the advantages. First of all, the group apparatus would eliminate the necessity of every member traveling back and forth to make deposits at the district level office. If the deposits could be consolidated at the group level, only one such trip would have to be made in a month. Also, as a group, those able to keep accurate records could take a leadership role, while others learned to develop those skills. In addition, the encouragement, support and discipline that was required to make sure everyone was getting the most from the program, could best be established through a communal effort.

With the organizers' assistance, each of the groups, consisting of 15 and 20 members, discussed the rules under which the group would function, trying to anticipate possible challenges. Because the organizers worked with several groups, and because the groups from different villages increasingly began to interact with each other, not only as savings groups, but in other activities as well, many of the rules were shared in common. One such rule was that no loans would be given out in the first year after the group was formed. Instead, the time would be used to familiarize the members with the discipline needed in order to save.

The primary and initial function of the savings and credit groups was perceived to be saving. The idea was that the members needed to acquire the saving habit and the familiarity with the system and self-discipline that comes with such a habit, before exploring other options. In many cases, the women had little or no economic power in their own households, even with the money they had earned themselves. For these women, in addition to the usual benefits of accumulating interest and self-discipline, the savings account had the added function of a safety deposit box, protecting their earnings. Among other things, a savings account would protect the funds from the caprice of husbands and sons who could all too often drink or gamble away the hard-earned money of the family. Plus, the savings account in her own name also meant a greater sense of economic independence.

These savings would be collected on a monthly basis, with each member contributing an equal amount. The amount for each deposit, decided as a group, usually beginning with Rs. 10 to Rs. 20, was the same for each member for several reasons. First, since the leader and the individual members were to independently calculate the interest earned by the group, the equal deposits would facilitate the accounting process and encourage self-sustainability. Also, the equality among deposits would minimize the potential for conflict, if suspicions arose about the total savings of one individual member. There would be no scope for such confusion if everyone had the same amount invested in the group account. Lastly, with each member depositing the same amount, no one member could dominate the savings group by virtue of having a larger share of the investment.

The individual account would be kept in the respective member's passbook. She could keep it with herself or leave it with the leader or any trusted friend if she feared that, for example, her husband would demand access to the account once he knew it existed. The group leader would also maintain the group account in one large ledger.

From SEWA's organizational side, they found that it was easiest for the SEWA Bank to cooperatively manage the rural funds through the respective district-level organizations. In the case of Banaskantha, this was the DWCRA program, and eventually the BDMSA. Since it is impractical for the women to hold individual accounts in the SEWA Bank in Ahmedabad, a four-hour bus ride away, their individual accounts are maintained through their village savings and loan group. The group then holds its account with the district and the district maintains a single account with the SEWA Bank. Though the chain of three different levels may sound complex, it was far more convenient than having 35,000 individual accounts in a bank 200 kilometers away.

Ultimately, this structure would more easily facilitate the eventual transition to a decentralized association, capable of remaining independent of the sister organization in Ahmedabad. With the district-level organizations assuming many of the roles that SEWA Bank fulfills for its urban members, those organizations gradually become capable of assuming greater responsibilities. In the case of Banaskantha, the BDMSA has now grown to fulfill many functions within the savings and loan program. The BDMSA and the leaders of the individual savings groups are responsible for collecting the savings each month, as well as distributing the loaned funds and collecting the loan payments. Accounting for individual deposits are, as always, kept in a passbook for the account-holder, as well as in a group account kept and maintained by the group leader. Also, accounts for all groups are kept at the BDMSA office.

Applications for loans are accepted at the group level and reviewed at the district association level. Under most circumstances, the SEWA Bank merely responds to the loan recommendations and requests from the BDMSA. Under this highly evolved system, the bank now serves primarily as a resource of funding while the execution and administration of the program take places independently at the district level.

Since the first meetings in a handful of villages, over a decade ago, the savings program has proved to be one of the most popular activities among SEWA members. Since then, many more groups have formed, and those before them have established the saving habit to the satisfaction of the other members. They have since developed enough confidence in themselves and each other to begin taking loans.

Historically, in recent history at least, many micro-credit programs in India were funded by the government and funneled through NGOs. Unfortunately, such programs had many flaws. First of all, many were too focused on targets: a target for the number of total loans given out or a target community to receive the loans. In the rush to get the loans distributed, little attention was paid to conveying any appreciation for the responsibilities that come with a loan. In fact, by neglecting to emphasize these responsibilities, these micro-credit programs, in essence, discouraged repayment, similar to the nationalized banks, mentioned earlier, that were obligated to loan to the poor. The underlying assumption was that the poor were incapable of paying, so no attention was paid to fostering any financial discipline.

SEWA sought to establish a credit program that resembled its savings program in its utilization of the group strategy and all the benefits that came with it, such as communal discipline, minimal use of human resources, and sustainability. Also, though saving was perhaps initially more important to the organizers and the members, the stigma of defaulting on a loan was greater than that of missing a deposit in a savings account. Therefore, the intimidatory pressure of taking a loan was greater and the confidence and support offered by a group was all the more crucial. Fortunately, with the strength of at least a year's experience in saving for each of these groups, the structure was already in place for a viable credit program.

The first step in taking a loan is stating its purpose and assessing how much money is needed to achieve the investment's goal. Micro-credit programs traditionally encourage the recipients to invest in their own small-scale entrepreneurship. Artisans take loans to purchase sewing machines. Cattle-breeders take loans to increase their stock. By utilizing their resources to increase their income, they are better able to repay their loans, in addition to being able to improve their standard of living. The idea is to start with smaller loans, and build your capacity to the point where you can take increasingly larger loans or finance your progress independently.

The major portion of the application review process takes place at the group level. The applications are prepared at the group level, with the successful applicant earning the trust and approval of the rest of the group and the group leader. The group leaders attend training sessions and exposure trips that teach them about the daily functioning of a savings and credit group, like accounting, but they also learn about different ways in which loans can be used and how much money it takes to achieve a certain end. These leaders then become resources for the members of their group, encouraging them and guiding them.

Once the application is prepared, it is submitted and reviewed at the district level. The district associations have a loan committee that then considers the application in the light of the support of the other members, the applicant's account status and the practicality of the loan. If there are any questions, such as whether the level of funds requested is consistent with the intended use, a member of the committee visits the village and discusses it further with the applicant. Then, once a loan is approved, the requests for funds are submitted to the SEWA Bank in Ahmedabad.

The bank then loans the funds to the district associations at 17 percent per annum. The district associations then loan the funds to the groups at 21 percent per annum. Finally, the groups loan the funds to the members at 24 percent per annum. In the case of the SEWA Bank and the district associations, the added interest is used to cover administrative costs. The interest added by the groups is added to the group savings account and distributed equally among the members, adding further incentive to borrow.

Because the application process is so clear and defined for each member, very few applications are made that are not worthy of approval.

Therefore, the vast majority does receive approval, though some are turned down. The definition of a productive purpose for a loan is expanded in the case of the SEWA savings and credit groups, as opposed to conventional banks, but there are still limitations. For example, funerals and weddings are not considered productive purposes. Some members have withdrawn their savings in frustration as a result, while others do so though they see the reasons why loans are denied for these functions, and later rejoin a savings group once they can afford it again. However, spending on both funerals and weddings has escalated almost exponentially in recent decades among the poor, as they emulate the lavish practices of those of greater means. Every savings group has discussed this phenomenon, and agreed to discourage such practices and forbid loans that perpetuate them. This shift in attitude, in addition to the fact that such loans achieve nothing in the direction of improving one's ability to pay off debts, has led all the groups to decide not to grant loans for weddings or funerals before the first deposits are even made.

One final reason why a loan may be turned down is that members from the applicant's group have outstanding loan payments. In these cases, as with a missed deposit, the group can act as a support network if the reasons for defaulting are compellingly legitimate, or a source of motivation if the reason has more to do with poor self-discipline. Since each member has a vested interest in each other members' successful loan repayment, this support network is active. The success of this program is reflected by the over 95 percent recovery rate on loans taken.

Finding a Better Way

This SEWA credit system has been functioning since the early 1990s and provided a great many loans for a diverse number of purposes. In particular, small-scale entrepreneurship has been heavily supported. This support has increased incomes and, therefore, improved health, nutrition, homes and savings accounts, among other things. However, the time required to receive a loan can be as long as three months. While this time period may work in long-term business planning, there is still a great need for short-term, unplanned expenses, such as medical emergencies and food shortages.

The shortcomings on the delivery of credit are mirrored on the savings side. In Murthy's comprehensive study of savings groups in Kheda and Banaskantha districts, mentioned earlier, it was found that only 24 percent of the SEWA savings group members kept all of their savings with the group. A total of 58 percent kept the savings in one other place, and 17 percent in two other places, while another 1 percent had more than two places where they kept their money. Of those who saved money in other places, 68 percent kept their money at home, 17 percent in a local bank, 5 percent at the post office, and 4 percent with their employer. At least some of those who kept money in a local bank can be assumed to have made that option in part because of their participation in the savings groups. But, the fact that the majority of the members use other resources indicates that the savings program, like the credit program, has limitations. In general, the numbers indicate that SEWA has increased the saving trend, but has not replaced traditional methods. Furthermore, in determining whether the glass is half-empty or half-full, SEWA has most likely spread knowledge more conducive to the use of other financial resources.

As the group members become more familiar and comfortable with the savings and then the credit system, and as its limitations become more apparent, a further advance is beginning to be made. The services and support provided by the rural banking system are necessary in the early stages of the program, but these add to the costs for the members and the SEWA Bank. For example, working as a group means that some members who have more savable money are still limited to saving only at a level feasible to the poorest members. And the credit system is too time-consuming to serve a great many crucial uses. Although the rural system is not nearly as costly as a system of branch offices throughout the districts would have been, the multi-level structure has its price.

As mentioned before, in order to maintain the system, interest rates on loans are raised to 24 percent per annum by the time they reach the individual borrower. While this is the normal commercial interest rate in India, the SEWA Bank can offer loans to Ahmedabad members at an interest rate of 18 percent per annum. This difference between urban and rural members is required to fund the extra personnel and travel necessary in order to keep the system working. SEWA is working on a method of to avoiding such costs.

In 15 groups across Banaskantha, a new system is being tested. With these groups, the group account is transferred to cooperative local banks in Banaskantha. Now that the women have acquired the saving habit, and learnt how the banking system functions, they are more capable and less intimidated by conventional banks. Each month, the group leader collects the deposits and puts them into the group account at the bank. While the women are more familiar with banking practices, the single deposit made to the teller is large enough to avoid annoyance or processing costs in excess of the deposit.

As for credit, the district association acts as the guarantor on loans given directly by the bank to the groups. The loan committee still reviews the applications, since it is accountable as the guarantor, but the rest of the process is between the bank and the borrowers. This system is simple, sustainable and made possible because of the years of capacity-building under the older process.

Because the members of the credit groups qualify for subsidized loans, which were disastrous for the nationalized banks in the 1970s, they still get such loans. The difference is that they pay them back. Both the bank and the groups appreciate this change, but all the groups have also decided to maintain the group interest rate at 24 percent on loans from the local banks. For example, if the local bank loans funds to the groups at 12 percent, the groups will charge themselves an additional 12 percent. This extra interest will be added to the groups' savings accounts and contribute to the further expansion of saved funds.

This last point has added relevance, because most banks loan to a group in proportion to the amount the group has accumulated in its savings account. The bank normally loans up to three times the amount that the group has in its savings account. Thus, a group that has accumulated Rs. 9,000 will have Rs. 27,000 at its disposal. In real terms, this is the difference between buying a bullock cart or making the down payment on a tractor. The implications for entrepreneurial potential are significant.

The main benefit of the new system is the shift in the location of the group accounts. This change will provide even more rapid accessibility of funds than maintaining an account in the SEWA Bank. The sudden need for funds is most acutely felt in emergencies. Medical emergencies are the most common, but others, such as natural disasters, occur with some frequency as well. The sudden and unforeseeable nature of these events inevitably forces the women to turn to moneylenders. This institution is the only source of immediate funds available to these women. Though the loaning process through any bank is not as quick as with the moneylender, the new system can fit into the picture. Where the previous system, with accounts in the SEWA Bank, took as long as three months for a loan to be processed, the new system takes one week.

The women may still be forced to turn to the moneylender in the heat of the moment. Although the interest is high, the money is immediately available. But, in a matter of weeks or days, they can apply for and receive a loan at their local bank. This way, the women can quickly refinance their loans, replacing the high rate of interest of the moneylenders with the more reasonable rate of a bank.

Biography: Investing in Leadership

Subhadraben, from the village of Datrana, used to regularly take loans from a moneylender at an interest rate of well over 100 percent a year. She used the money to buy seeds and rent a field. In good years, she could easily pay back the loan. But, in bad years, she often found herself deep in debt. It always turned out to be a tremendous gamble. One year, she would take a loan of Rs. 3,000 for cumin seeds and make as much as Rs.15,000 on the harvest. The next year, she would borrow the same amount and, with no rains, find herself more than Rs. 6,000 in debt. By the time SEWA organizers first came to Datrana, at the end of a drought, she had lost the gamble for three straight years.

Datrana has been very active in several SEWA programs. Savings are no exception. The enthusiasm for forming a savings group brought together 65 women initially. The group started by saving Rs. 10 a month. Recognized for her innate intelligence, Subhadraben was chosen as a leader in this group. The intention of the group was to learn how to save regularly before starting with loans. However, Subhadraben recalls, she was reluctant to lead the group into a loan scheme even after they had proved to themselves they could save. She was afraid of the prospect of managing the interest calculations and other responsibilities for the 65 members, even with the help of a SEWA organizer. Besides, most women were content with their savings activity and reluctant to take loans.

But, Subhadraben had earned a spot on the savings spearhead team. As a member of the spearhead team, she made monthly trips to the SEWA Bank and elsewhere to build on her training. As her confidence in her management and accounting abilities grew, she went on an exposure trip to visit the MYRADA, a micro-credit group in Bangalore. There, she saw women rotating their savings, using the loaned funds in creative ways. Subhadraben started thinking of how Datrana could use loans for cattle, housing and even seeds.

On her return, she told her group about what she had seen. Together, they decided to divide into three smaller, more manageable groups. Two of those groups have since decided to rotate their funds in the form of loans. Subhadraben used her first group loan of Rs. 2,000 to buy seeds again. Her subsequent cumin crop, she estimates, earned between Rs. 35,000 to Rs. 40,000. Through grass-roots capitalization, she has realized a rate of return that would make any Ahmedabad industrialist's head turn. With that money, she has bought a well pump and made improvements on her house, the latter aided by a BDMSA housing loan.

The next crop was not as good, but the stakes of the gamble were not as high since she had enough accumulated capital to exclude the moneylender.

She still has enough left to start again next year. Besides, she can always take a loan from her group at a fair rate of interest. She is now in a secure position and can consistently build her income and her assets. She is confident about her entrepreneurial skills. She knows how to budget and manage finances. Through unconventional banking, she has proven herself bankable by any standard.

Subhadraben has also worked hard to make sure others get access to the same resources. Her responsibilities as a spearhead team member include direct supervision of savings and loan activity in seven ·different villages. Madhutra is one of these villages and has run into difficulties. One of the women who took a loan refused to pay it back. Subhadraben met with the members of the group, and then confronted the woman. When Subhadraben's efforts at persuasion failed, she helped the group devise strategies by which the recalcitrant woman would be moved to relent. Most importantly, no further loans would be given to any member of the group until the loan was repaid. This ultimately strengthened the determination of the whole group to put pressure on the defaulter, who recently paid back her loan. The Madhutra group is now functioning once again.

As with other SEWA members, Subhadraben's participation is a balance between receiving benefits and extending benefits back to the collective organization. And Subhadraben feels that this synergy is at the heart of what is becoming an increasingly self-sustaining process.

Micro-finance: Beyond Micro-credit

Since its inception, the concept of micro-credit has changed the lives of thousands of people. Access to capital on a scale appropriate to the needs of the poor has simply been revolutionary. Around the world, micro-credit has challenged many long-held misconceptions, such as the financial irresponsibility of the poor, especially women. Loans to the poor (considered too risky an investment earlier), in amounts that enabled them to start modest businesses or improve their lives in other ways, have been a widely recognized success. It has unlocked entrepreneurial potential and liberated many from the recurring costs of poverty, such as debt, wells that go dry or houses that fall because they cannot stand up to the elements.

SEWA and the SEWA Bank recognized the strength of micro-credit early on, and quickly began to act on the lessons of its success elsewhere. Over a period of time, however, the SEWA members have also recognized the necessity for other financial tools. They wanted to go beyond micro-credit and envisioned a broader scope of resources that could be utilized, even though they were only poor women. What they envisioned can best be described as micro-finance.

Micro-finance goes well beyond savings and loans. Micro-finance also means access to social security, healthcare, housing and even the more fundamental needs such as employment and education. True economic empowerment means that one has the ability and opportunity to earn money, options for using that money, and mechanisms by which one can ensure that that money is used in the most useful manner possible. Micro-finance is a multi-faceted concept, with the facets fused together in a synergistic relationship engendering stability. SEWA has endeavored to bring all of those resources to its members in order to help create a degree of empowerment that is more comprehensive and sustainable.

First among the extended micro-finance tools is a social security and insurance program. Poor nutrition and hard work take their toll on the rural women's overall health. Medical emergencies, as mentioned before, are one of the most common reasons why they have to turn to moneylenders. To address this problem, SEWA has devised a social security scheme. Through a plan consisting of components from two companies, the Life Insurance Company of India and United Insurance, the members can have coverage that is appropriate to their individual situations.

The women pay a monthly premium of Rs. 30 over a period of three years and receive several practical benefits for life. Any hospital stay, medicine, test, surgery, or doctors fee is covered for up to Rs. 3,000. A sum is given upon the death of the woman or her husband, which could be financially devastating to a family struggling to get above the poverty line, and in need of every income-earner. If the death is from natural causes, the family receives Rs. 3,000. If the death is the result of an accident, the family receives Rs. 35,000. In the case of the loss of the woman's house, or any of the tools of her trade due to a natural disaster, such as flood or cyclone, or an unnatural disaster such as a riot or communal violence, they can receive up to Rs. 5,000.

Special emphasis has been placed on issues of women's health and occupational health. Because the insurance industry is predominantly a male domain, subtle discrimination can neglect issues specific to women. Because the policy sought by SEWA is specifically for women, it has been free from such flaws. For example, regular prenatal check-ups are covered under the policy. Then, after the birth, the woman receives Rs. 300 to cover the loss of wages and ensure that the new mother is not forced back to work before her recovery is complete.

Under normal circumstances, to have such coverage would cost between Rs. 1,200 to Rs. 5,000 per year. However, through SEWA, both companies offer policies to the poor for a one-time payment of Rs. 750. Unfortunately, this is still beyond the reach of many people, many of whom are SEWA members. To accommodate their needs, the SEWA Bank has arranged to pay the lumpsum payment on their behalf, allowing the members to reimburse the SEWA Bank over a three-year period. In some cases, the installments for the insurance policy are simply deducted from the accumulating interest in a member's savings account. Many members are now using the insurance policy and getting a lot of mileage out of it. Though there have been major advances in the living conditions of these women, health and nutrition take time to improve. As they do, the women and their families have the support needed to ensure survival.

Many members in many districts have utilized the insurance program since the scheme was established. However, in Kutch and Banaskantha, the women were, until recently, still working to secure public acknowledgment of social security as a priority. The cyclone of June 1998 served to awaken the demand for protection. Over 10,000 human lives were estimated to have been lost in that storm. The damage to property was also severe. Since then, 500 members in Kutch alone have invested in the insurance policy and put it to beneficial use.

A more in-depth description of the cyclone and the evolution of the social security program is provided in a later chapter. The experience illuminated another aspect of the micro-finance program, housing. The mud and dung huts that dominate the typical village landscape are another symptom of the vicious cycle that can push the poor into a spiraling deterioration of their way of life. For example, when a violent cyclone comes, as it did in June of 1998, time becomes precious. Outbreaks of dysentery and malaria then loom as a great threat to the entire community. Immediate attention must be given to sanitation and other preventative measures in order to be protected from these diseases. However, when one's home literally melts away in the rain of the storm, the difficulties become exacerbated. Time spent on maintaining health now has to be spent on rebuilding shelter.

In 1995, the BDMSA initiated a program that specifically provided loans for housing improvements and repairs. Leaky thatched roofs could be replaced with impermeable tiles. Dirt floors could be covered with concrete. And, as noted before, soluble mud and dung walls could be replaced with weather-resistant plaster. These benefits were augmented by the fact that the women's homes were not only where they lived, but also where they worked.

In the case of an artisan, she and her family were protected from the elements, as were the tools of her trade, raw materials and finished work.

Since the program's inception, from 1995 to 1999, as many as 190 women have been loaned a total of over Rs. 160,000 for housing. Furthermore, after the cyclone in June of 1998, funds for 200 additional houses have been allocated by the BDMSA. The loans are interest-free, and the women pay on an installment schedule that makes the repayment complete after 20 months.

Here, it must also be noted that giving this type of loan on the BDMSA's scale is no simple matter. Despite the good intentions of the vast majority of participants, there have been a few cases where the loans were not used for their intended purpose. Without the added discipline imposed by the group lending system, and the complications of betraying the trust of the members of one's community, a few recipients of the housing loans, not tied to the savings groups, made errors in judgment. Upon discovering this, the BDMSA quickly adjusted the program to eliminate such activity. Now, the loans are given to the participants, not in the form of cash, but rather in credit. The women purchase the materials they need, such as lumber and cement, from the respective merchant on credit. The receipt is then brought to the BDMSA office, where the staff sees to it that the bill is paid. Also, the BDMSA staff goes to the houses under the program to observe the progress in relation to the expenses. Since the introduction of this method, there have been no difficulties like the inappropriate use of funds.

As an added dynamic to the housing program, in most cases, the women have the title to the house in which they have invested so much and which stand in their own name. The association is hesitant to loan money to a member unless she is willing to take full accountability for the loan. This means that she must be responsible for the house to be invested in. Under these circumstances, many husbands have found the transfer of title highly practical, since the improvements come to constitute a significant portion of the final value of the house.

The importance of the women assuming responsibility for the titles to their houses cannot be underestimated. In her book, A Field of One's Own, Bina Agarwal cites many of the gains achieved when a woman has her land and house registered in her own name. First, it closes the gender gap that influences the allocation of household resources, such as food, medicine and education. As evidenced by markedly higher rates of malnutrition, morbidity, mortality, and lower rates of literacy among women in Gujarat and throughout India, as opposed to men in the same families, gender plays a significant role in the unequal distribution of household resources.

However, women's ownership of their houses counteracts this trend, empowering women to enforce a more equitable system of resource allocation.

This seems even more important when one considers that women, especially in poor rural households, are more likely to use their assets to the benefit of the entire family, especially the children. As noted before, men are more likely to spend at least part of their resources on alcohol, tobacco, or food and drinks with friends. In a study cited by Agarwal, it was found that 90 to 100 percent of a woman's earnings are normally used to benefit the family, while men rarely contributed over 75 percent of their earnings to the family (Agarwal 1994: 29). By the registration of the house in the woman's name, her more fortuitous and balanced influence on household finance is further strengthened.

Furthermore, the house in the woman's name reflects a new social reality. The fact is that women are increasingly becoming the actual heads of the households. They are increasingly entering the workforce, or their participation is at least finally being recognized, and the degree of their monetary contribution to the household is often in excess of that of the males. It must also be considered that recent social changes include erosion of the kinship support system. This change is not only especially important for women in terms of aging and widowhood, but also in the face of more recent occurrences of male migration and marital breakdown. Women are, in many respects, now faced with more difficulties and less familial support in facing them. Again, registration of the house in the women's name protects them and their children from such sources of destitution.

Lastly, beyond the politics of the household, the politics of the village depends greatly upon ownership of the land. More specifically, land is the basis for political power and social status, and for obvious reasons. With land as the foundation of the rural economy, it is natural that its importance is reflected in other realms. If women have ownership of the land, their social power and political status are more duly reflected.

In many ways, SEWA's micro-finance program as a whole, including savings, credit, insurance and housing activities, are adaptations that have relied heavily on the experiences of other successful NGOs and community-based organizations. In particular, the group approach to savings and micro-credit were trails blazed by organizations such as the Working Women's Forum in Chennai, India, and Grameen Bank in Bangladesh.

However, SEWA's approach also differs from most other organizations in many ways. First of all, the SEWA Bank does not accept any outside grants or subsidized loans to be used as capital for loans to members. The concern has always been that such practices encourage dependence on those outside institutions. Instead, the SEWA Bank has always demanded the same self-sustainability from itself as it does with its account-holders and borrowers.

Most importantly, SEWA and the SEWA Bank have distinguished themselves in the area of micro-finance through the comprehensive range of financial tools offered to its members. In the end, the savings groups and the rest of the micro-finance programs offer a support structure that allows the women to rely upon each other for advice, encouragement, discipline when needed, and understanding. Along the way, the women gain stability, confidence, and not only ownership of assets, but also ownership of their own lives.

Biography: Saved from Death and Debt

Fatmabai, from the village of Khadak, was a talented embroiderer. However, the recurring pain in her stomach was at times so severe that she could not work. The pain had been present for several months and was increasing in frequency and intensity. However, it was not until she went to an association meeting at the Naliya sub-center that she had her stomach looked at by a doctor. When she came to the sub-center, the pain was at a peak. The organizers at Naliya immediately took her to the hospital, taking care of all the paperwork for her and making sure she was cared for.

The doctor there said it was a stomach infection, gave Fatmabai a prescription for antibiotics and sent her on her way. But her pain did not go away. Since the new SEWA health insurance plan covered the costs of her hospital visit and any subsequent visits, she had the luxury of a second opinion when the first did not satisfy. This time, she went to a private clinic and her problem was diagnosed as appendicitis. An operation was immediately scheduled and again the insurance covered most of the expenses.

As Fatmabai now recovers from the operation that took place a few days ago, she is already feeling much better. Without the support of the organizers and the insurance scheme, Fatmabai knows she would have hesitated before going to a doctor, let alone getting a second opinion. In addition to indebtedness to merchants for food, medical emergencies are a major contributor to rural indebtedness. In emergency situations, the rural poor are often forced to accept highly exploitative loan terms from moneylenders.

If her children are ill, that is one thing. But her acquired tolerance of pain and her concern for cost have always been prohibiting factors in her decisions about whether or not to seek medical attention. Yet, in the case of appendicitis, if she had hesitated much longer, it would have meant her life. Fortunately, something allowed her to reconsider her previous reluctance. Fatmabai's insurance not only saved her family from a life of debt. It saved her life.

Chapter 6
HEALTH AND NUTRITION

The link between health and nutrition is close and crucial. Our diet is the single greatest controllable factor in determining our physical well-being. Access to nutrition affords us the building blocks needed to develop normally, and the energy to work, play, and ward off sickness. Conversely, poor access to nutrition stunts our growth, drains us of energy and leaves us vulnerable to ill-health and disease. No public health strategy, particularly in a nation with a large number of undernourished people, can ignore the importance of the issue of nutrition.

Since India's independence, the country's total food output has grown at a substantial rate. But the increased food production has been paralleled by an equally substantial growth in population. The result is that per capita food production levels have barely increased at all. Considering the threat of famine that constantly loomed over pre-Independence India, the efficient distribution of the food resources has always been a necessity for the survival of the state and its citizens. In view of the importance of nutrition in terms of health and productivity, particularly for the poor who are at the greatest risk and constitute a third of the Indian populace, a mechanism for supplying food to that vulnerable group is crucial.

An efficient system of healthcare delivery, important in itself, becomes even more important in the light of the poor nutritional status of large sections of the population. The effects of a meager food supply on a large scale simply manifest the symptoms of the undernourished individual to an alarmingly large proportion of the population. In the 1999 United Nations Human Development Index, which takes into account GDP, as well as health, education and other social indicators, India ranked 132nd out of the 174 countries studied. This implied that India's people were worse off than those of Sri Lanka (90th), China (98th), and Indonesia (105th), to name a few countries that share some characteristics with India (UNDP 1999: 135).

The factors contributing to India's low status in comparison with the rest of the global community include an estimated life expectancy of 62.6 years (Sri Lanka: 73.1 years). The maternal mortality rate was reported to be 570 women per 100,000 live births (China: 95 per 100,000). India's infant mortality rate was 71 per 1,000 births (Indonesia: 45 per 1,000). An estimated 53 percent of the children, between the ages of zero and five years during 1990–97 were underweight. In the same time period, 71 percent of the Indian population lacked access to proper sanitation.

Fortunately, some of the early architects of the Indian state had a great degree of foresight on these issues, and aspired to establish the healthcare and food distribution systems required to confront the challenges. Unfortunately, despite their vision, efforts of the government have had a hard time catching up with the harsh reality.

Health for Few by 2000

The blueprint for the Indian healthcare system was drawn up by the 'Health Survey and Development Committee,' popularly known as the Bhore Committee, after Sir Joseph Bhore, the chairman of the panel. This committee was established in 1943, and presented its final recommendations for a healthcare system in 1946. The committee's recommendations focused on the importance of preventive health, particularly in rural communities. It generally reflected a practical and progressive way of thinking, seeing past the symptoms and getting at the root-causes of poor public health. Poor water supply and sanitation, nutrition and general health awareness were identified as the main obstacles (Kamalamma 1996: 64). The subsequent policy recommendations avoided the pitfall of emphasizing the more high-profile, curative medicine as the panacea.

The proposed instrument for addressing the public health concerns was to be an extensive network of primary health centers (PHCs), spread throughout the country. More specifically, the plan to evolve was that each development block was to have one community health center (CHC), supported by several PHCs, to be supported, in turn, by several sub-centers. Each facility would be staffed by doctors, nurses, pharmacists and other trained health care providers; the size of the staff depending on the relative level of the facility. Furthermore, the level of diagnostic and treatment resources would also reflect the level of the facility, with the CHCs having the greatest size and sophistication.

In the first Five-Year Plan (1951–56), the Bhore Committee's recommendations were taken heavily into consideration. The PHCs were established and rhetorical attention was paid to sanitation, awareness, services specifically for mothers and children, and family planning. In total, 3.3 percent of the budget for the first Five-Year Plan was allocated for health.

Later Five-Year Plans continued to try and expand upon the PHC system, but several issues hindered the overall success of the policy. First of all, later expenditure on health did not reach the initial 3.3 percent allocation. By the Seventh Five-Year Plan (1985–1990), only 1.9 percent of total government expenditure was devoted to health. Of those funds, over a half ended up being spent on large urban hospitals with the latest equipment, academic institutions for training surgeons and physicians, and other curative and clinical medicine (Bhat 1990: 128). Furthermore, of those trained doctors, a significant portion left India after their training and practiced in the West, particularly in the United States. Meanwhile, a shortage of trained nurses exacerbated the situation. In 1990, there were 381,000 registered doctors in India, but only 111,235 registered nurses (Sainath 1996: 25). Considering that the bulk of health care work, under normal circumstances, is performed by nurses, this is a troubling statistic. To make matters worse, by the Fourth Five-Year Plan (1969–74), family planning program targets ate up much of whatever staff and resources there were, while engendering fear among the poorer populace of the government in general, and the health system in particular.

Several other well-intentioned, inspired concepts attempted to fill the gaps left by the failing system. But, like much of the system as a whole, these great ideas did not quite fulfill their intended goals. Village health workers and auxiliary nurse midwives were both proposed solutions, which provided for trained individuals, on a large scale, to be based in each and every village. These were primarily people from the villages themselves, with an educational background that could be reasonably expected from such origins. These people underwent training in basic diagnostics, with the ability to recognize and treat mild aches and pains, as well as dehydration, one of the main killers of infants and babies suffering from diarrhea and any of its numerous sources. Ultimately, however, these people were poorly supported, and their roles and responsibilities were not clearly defined. Their training was not on a continual basis. Some became drunk with the power of their vast and vital knowledge, in comparison with those they treated, and became quack doctors, charging for the services. Also, when the good ones made referrals for the maladies they were not qualified to treat, the patients were still confronted with the same old shortcomings of the rest of the system.

At the grass-roots level, many other problems have become apparent. First of all, relatively few doctors have actually shown any desire to practice medicine in rural areas. In order to pursue the medical profession, in most cases, one must possess significant educational and financial resources. With most of the wealth concentrated in the cities, and a struggling rural educational system to match the health system, most doctors come from, and are partial to, an urban life. This situation has left a shortage of doctors particularly in rural areas, and many PHCs have vacancies for this key position. In these cases, the clinic compounder often diagnoses the patients' illnesses and prescribes the drugs, in addition to distributing the medicine, his originally mandated duty.

A rise in quackery has also filled the vacuum where the erosion of access to traditional forms of medicine, such as ayurvedic, and the limits of allopathic, Western medicine have left a void. In some cases, warped hybrids of ayurvedic and allopathic medicine translate into odd, voodoo-esque rituals with sacrificed chickens, chanted incantations and high fees (Sainath 1996: 33).

Over the course of time, of those doctors willingly posted to PHCs, many set up nearby private clinics simultaneously. Often, this dual practice leads them to neglect their government post, where they are full-time employees, in favor of their more profitable enterprise. In other cases, the doctors actually charge fees for services rendered in the PHC facilities, where everything but the medicine is supposed to be covered by tax rupees.

As a result of all its shortcomings, much of the population is hesitant, even scared, to go to the public health centers. Despite the much higher costs, mothers go to the private clinics when they feel the lives of their family members are in danger. Often, these private clinics are run by the very same doctors who are obligated to provide the same services at the PHC. But, because the PHC may be a few villages away, and only visited infrequently, the patients are unaware that they have a right to the same services, often from the same person, free of charge. They simply go to the private clinic in a natural response to the circumstances.

As the system stands, there is no demand for improvement of the government health system, since the people have turned, albeit without another choice, to private clinics. Many of the rural poor are unaware of the magnitude of the failure of the system and the doctors' failure to fulfill their obligations. Even when the patients are aware, they only confront the issue in an emergency. In such circumstances, those in need of help are in no position to demand their due. Common sense indicates that it would be unwise to challenge the person who holds the lives of yourself and your loved ones in his hands.

SEWA has gradually begun to address issues of health in Banaskantha and the other rural areas where it is active. Much of the SEWA strategy focuses on getting better healthcare from an improved government health-care system. The infrastructure and expertise required to maintain an effec-tive health care system excludes SEWA from setting up an independent alternative. Nor would SEWA want to.

Where government programs exist, SEWA avoids establishing parallel structures. Instead, SEWA has striven to complement and improve access to government resources. The provision of public health is no different. SEWA members, impoverished women, represent the portion of the popu-lation that is in the greatest need of health care. Therefore, much of SEWA's efforts relate to matching demand and supply together.

SEWA and its members have made an effort to look to the PHC system as the first option. One weakness of the system is that, because of its poor record, many have looked elsewhere for healthcare, either because the PHC option is less desirable or because it is simply unavailable. This trend has given the impression of a minimal demand for government health services. Truant PHC doctors can manipulate this reality to argue that people inherently avoid government services, justifying their private practices. When decisions relat-ing to government health care expenditure come up, the under-utilization of the services influences the decisions of those who hold the purse-strings in a negative direction. In general, without patients, the public health centers can suffer the same decline in health as the population they fail to serve.

By turning to the PHC, SEWA members are advocating for the improvement of the system in the best way possible. In the case of poorly run PHCs, the shortcomings are confronted rather than avoided. This is the first step in healing the system. In the case of PHCs making sincere efforts to meet the needs of the community, the increased demand becomes an asset to the system.

In the district of Kutch, for example, the PHC system's General Hospital in the main town, Bhuj, has given priority to DWCRA referrals, under-standing that access to their facilities can be difficult for poor rural women. The paperwork and persistence required to gain access to care in this hos-pital can be prohibitive to women who are illiterate and unaccustomed to such circumstances. The SEWA organizers are familiar with the routine of the government hospital and expedite the process for the ailing member. Furthermore, the hospital staff gives priority to the DWCRA members where possible.

Some PHC doctors and other district health workers are also aware of the referral option with the DWCRA members, and can utilize it in the case of more severe illnesses. If the health worker is not aware, the DWCRA members can inform them. In a system where genuinely concerned health care professionals may be hesitant to refer potentially serious illnesses to the central hospital because of the fatal delays in the process, the priority referral gives them the confidence to act.

At first glance, the priority given to DWCRA members may smack of preferential treatment. However, when one considers the population that makes up the DWCRA program, rural women living below the poverty line, the fairness of giving an otherwise excluded community access to health care is evident.

SEWA has also built upon other government programs that may not have reached some isolated rural communities. Dais play a crucial role in rural communities, where both regular and emergency access to medical care is difficult. The knowledge these midwives possess, handed down form generation to generation, saves lives every day in India. Though this knowledge is often extensive, and reinforced with experience, it has its limits. Many dais are capable of detecting the signs of potential complications in childbirth, such as breach births, anemia, and the dangers presented to underage expectant mothers. These are problems many of them encounter frequently enough and they are adept at handling them.

However, a few practices among dais can be ill-conceived. Among some, it is a tradition to cut the umbilical cord with household or field implements, unsterilized and in some cases covered with rust. Some dais also respond to delayed labor by pushing on the stomach of the pregnant mother, unknowingly risking the rupture of the uterus and the death of both the mother and the child.

The government has made efforts in the past to reach these dais and build upon their knowledge and experience. A few of the dais in the rural villages where SEWA is active have had training from government sources, though the vast majority has not. Utilizing SEWA's access to these women who trust it, training has been extended to the dais on several occasions. These women have joined SEWA members who are also dais from other districts on exposure trips, visiting PHCs and hospitals and talking with medical professionals, as well as other women like themselves. They have been given the opportunity to gain knowledge from people other than the dais who were their mentors, and to become acquainted with members of the PHC's staff devoted enough to take the time to pass information along to them.

Most importantly, the dais have become more familiar with the PHC system and have, perhaps, developed greater confidence in the system. As they recognize signs of potentially risky deliveries, they are more likely to encourage the expectant mother to seek help from the local PHC or sub-center. Also, as empowered, knowledgeable women who deal with health issues on a regular basis, they become strong candidates to advocate for improvements. If they find that their local PHC does not help those they refer, they discuss this matter with the other dais from the surrounding villages, who may well be SEWA members, too. They can also bring it up at the district association level and perhaps foment concerted action.

In the case of PHCs that provide quality care to the women the dais refer, the community's confidence will grow. The advice of the dais in the area of prenatal care opens the door for greater utilization of the PHCs in other areas, and expanded use of the government system's resources.

Other SEWA efforts in the area of health care are more extensively mentioned elsewhere in this book, within the contexts of the area of income generation to which they apply. SEWA has supported a mobile health van that travels to the more remote areas of Banaskantha and Kutch, where there is less access to the PHC system. In particular, the van targets communities largely employed in salt farming, a high health-risk occupation, due to its generally poor sanitary conditions, and to the fact that it necessitates living on the edge of the desert, far from most public services, including health.

SEWA has also helped provide eye clinics for its members in Banaskantha and Kutch, where there are a large number of craftswomen, whose occupation requires good eyesight, but contributes to its decline. The SEWA members' efforts at water provision, and its implications for improved sanitation, as well as the insurance program, which makes health care affordable, are also more extensively described elsewhere, though they deserve mention here.

There is a good reason for choosing to describe many of these health-related interventions on the part of SEWA more extensively in the other sections. It is intended to be illustrative of an aspect of SEWA's overall philosophy. Employment and income security have always been the first priority for SEWA members. Those who advocate health and education above all else in community development may fail to realize the severity of the deprivation existing in some places. Though the solutions they advocate are essential to the betterment of society, they are only getting part of the answer. Sending a child to school is, sadly, not an option when it means a loss in income and less food for the family. The occasional health clinic will have little impact when basic nutrition is not available to the population. When mere survival is still an issue, little else can be achieved until the fear of starvation is gone.

SEWA does make an effort at improving their members' and their communities' access to health care. But, in SEWA's collective view, the best way of achieving this goal is empowering them to make and pursue their demands. The movement's goal is not to provide healthcare, but to improve access to it. As a labor union for the self-employed, the best way for SEWA to achieve this goal is through income generation, the improved access to nutrition it affords, and organized advocacy. This strategy is reflected in SEWA's actions, and hopefully in the content and organization of this book.

Biography: Feeling Better about Herself

At first glance, Mankorba of Kharadia village is an afflicted woman, and perhaps a bit of a hypochondriac. Her life till now has been filled with one malady after another, and she describes them in a dramatic manner. By the time the first SEWA organizer came to her village, in order to discuss craftwork, Mankorba was suffering from nosebleeds, headaches and general anxiety. In particular, anytime she had to leave her home or her village, the symptoms would all appear simultaneously. Though her family and community traditions strictly limited her travel options anyway, her other troubles forbade such ventures.

However, Mankorba immediately caught the attention of the organizers who came to Kharadia because of her exceptional skill as an embroiderer. She also immediately confided to the SEWA organizers about her chronic nosebleeds, and they offered to take her to a hospital. Though this meant travel, she figured it would be worth it. A few weeks later, around the same time that a craft group was formed in her village, she had an operation on her sinuses. The nosebleeds ended almost completely just as she assumed a leadership position in her DWCRA group. Her initial responsibility was leading the skill upgradation training of the other women to improve the quality of their work.

However, the focus and strain of her new job increased the frequency of her headaches to the point where she could not work. This time, a SEWA eye clinic was arranged near her village and she had an eye examination. It turned out that her vision was very poor and that she required glasses. She got prescription glasses on the spot, and since then her headaches have significantly decreased.

Yet, her headaches have not disappeared. On a recent trip to Ahmedabad, for a meeting with the Chief Minister of Gujarat, Mankorba was stricken with an unnerving headache. The anxiety of the travel was too much, and she started regretting her decision to attend the meeting. Soon, however, her health turned for the better. The meeting lasted over two hours and several important issues were discussed and many pledges made by the Chief Minister. These promises, if fulfilled, would have a great impact on the women present, and a guarded excitement spread through many of them. When the meeting was over, Mankorba confided in Reemaben, SEWA's General Secretary, that she was feeling much better. She exclaimed: 'My head is so full of ideas that the pain has gone!'

In the end, it appears that Mankorba is perhaps not a hypochondriac at all. Other than a possible migraine condition, her real malady may be that she has a strong physical reaction to the world around her. When she has concerns they not only stay in her head, but also manifest themselves in the form of physical ailments. In that case, a sense of hope, self-awareness and purpose seem to be the best cure.

The Public Distribution System and Shakti Packet

Like the healthcare system, the early architects of the Indian state also envisioned an extensive food distribution system to meet the needs of the nation. However, while the health care system was in many ways at least well-conceived, the food distribution system had significant flaws in conception as well as execution.

The public distribution system (PDS) began as a World War II rationing scheme, restricted to urban areas. In India, as in most other countries involved in the war during that time, ration cards were distributed among the general populace and used to regulate consumption in a time of scarcity. At the time, the rationing scheme made sense, tempering the growing urban demand that may have otherwise drawn resources like a vacuum from the rural areas that were less able to afford access to food.

However, in the 1960s, the PDS became a permanent mechanism for distributing foodgrains received as international aid by the Indian government. Since this aid was free, the government of India made a profit, even at reduced prices, from the PDS sales. This money was then used to support various development schemes. In particular, at that time, industrial development was the focus of national attention, so the PDS, and the schemes it helped fund, reflected a noticeable tilt toward urban issues.

In theory, the PDS is implemented via fair price shops (FPS). These shops, supposed to be dispersed and so accessible to the entire population, provide essential foods, kerosene, and other necessities at controlled prices. However, the reality in rural areas is that these shops are often too far from some of the villages to be accessible. Then, if the women from the more remote villages make the journey to the nearest FPS, there is no guarantee that the shop will be stocked with all of the required items, or even be open at all.

In some cases, the failure of the public distribution system leads some women to resort to moneylenders in order to get food. Because the food in the FPS is subsidized, it is more affordable to the poor. But, affordable or not, when the food is not available, the people have to turn to the non-subsidized private merchants for the necessities of survival. One of the greatest sources of debt among the poor is the money owed by villagers to those who run the provision shops, FPS and otherwise. Often, the person running the FPS is one of the better-off in the village. That merchant, therefore, has the resources to loan money to the villagers in the form of store credit. These loans are then often extended at exorbitant rates of interest.

Lastly, much of the food found in an FPS is substandard in several ways. Purchased centrally, the products stocked are not reflective of regional tastes. The Banaskantha diet, for example, traditionally includes much coarser grains than are normally provided by FPS. Items such as millet, and pulses, not common in other parts of India, constitute the major source of nutrition in this region. The FPS shops are generally insensitive to these variations in tastes and do not normally carry such items. Also, the quality of the subsidized produce is notoriously poor. In many cases, women will pay the extra money for the non-subsidized rice because the alternative is filled with too many stones to make the saved expense worthwhile. As with the health care system, the shortcomings of PDS often push the poor to the costlier alternatives.

"Shakti" (a Sanskrit-based word meaning "strength") is often lacking in Banaskantha, for several reasons. Regional shortages, fluctuating prices and natural disasters are only some of the problems that can compromise a rural community's ability to feed itself. These difficulties then become even more acute in a particularly remote, arid, disaster-prone area, such as Banaskantha. The Shakti Packet program was originally initiated in

1993 by the BDMSA in five drought-prone villages. The participants included 2,400 women and their households, and the program has since expanded.

The Shakti Packet program addresses all of the issues of food quality, availability, and affordability. The participating SEWA members meet monthly to determine their food needs for the next 30 days. Once this is determined, a budget is submitted to the association. The BDMSA then loans the group the money required to purchase the necessary items. The group food is then bought wholesale at a local agricultural produce yard, or, if not available there, directly from local farmers. Transportation of the purchases and the woman who runs the program are budgeted for 1 percent of the total costs. The food is then kept in the village, its distribution strictly accounted for. The initial loan is subsequently returned to the BDMSA, using funds from the Shakti Packet sales.

The overall benefits are many. The money saved by buying the food wholesale makes up for the interest on the loan. The women gain experience in resource and financial management. The purchase of the food also directly benefits the local economy. As opposed to being purchased at the national level, the food is purchased and usually produced locally. Also, the food purchased is more accommodating to the local tastes. Other unique touches include the supply of items such as soap and contraceptives, otherwise not available at the FPS.

Asset in Emergency

An unexpected benefit of the Shakti Packet program became apparent during the severe floods of 1997. Roads had been made impassable and supply lines cut. At the same time, diseases began to spread while medical resources were cut off. Even when the waters subsided, there were not enough supplies available, nor any system of distribution set up to see that they got to where they were most needed.

The effects of any disaster can be devastating, and these are most harshly reflected in terms of food. First of all, supply lines are cut off and the immediate availability of food declines sharply. Furthermore, what food is available is susceptible to severe increases in price due to the inevitable scarcity. Simultaneously, loss of work due to the disaster often inhibits a household's ability to pay such prices. It is in under these desperate circumstances and exploitative conditions that debt is incurred. Through it all, it is the women who suffer the most. As the household becomes less and less able to feed itself, it is often the women who suffer the greatest proportional loss of access to food and medical attention.

In the long run after a disaster, such as a flood, the issues are no different than in the short run. In anticipation of future shortages due to loss in crops and a decrease in supply, food prices remain inflated. The decrease in opportunities for income from agricultural labor remains: as the crops had long since been washed away, so there is nothing to tend or harvest. Debt increases, household nutrition worsens and, again, it is the women who feel the brunt of the difficulties.

The Shakti Packet, by virtue of its system of buying in bulk, and in advance, is prepared to deal with the short-term shortages caused by severed supply lines. With a large stock acquired before the flood, there is ample margin for survival. In the long run, buying in bulk and in advance offers a leverage in bargaining down or waiting out inflated prices. Also, seeds and other means of recouping the losses caused by the flood become available. Ultimately, as other sections point out, other employment opportunities, not specifically agriculturally related, as well as reasonable loan resources are available through the BDMSA, all in the name of women. Their empowerment ensures that there is more to go around, no matter what the circumstances, and that there is more equitable distribution of what there is.

In the face of dire circumstances, the Shakti Packet system proved to be a vital lifeline for the supply and distribution of food and medicines, including those that stemmed the tide of a severe malaria epidemic. The government was deeply divided over the facts of an epidemic resulting from the flood and was, therefore, largely ineffective in many ways. As cases of fever in Banaskantha began to rise into the thousands, different government agencies gave out conflicting reports. The most blatant contradictions arose between the State Ministry of Health and the Chief Minister of Gujarat. Two weeks after the start of the epidemic became known, the Ministry of Health was reporting 22,230 suspected cases of malaria and over 100 resultant deaths (*The Times of India:* 1). However, the Chief Minister, and those allied with him, claimed that only one death had been caused by malaria, which warranted no unusual concern.

The Chief Minister was ultimately proved tragically wrong. His miscalculation delayed a concerted effort on the part of the government. Without his consent, many resources were held up. By the time it was all over, more than 25,000 cases of malaria were reported, 500 of which resulted in deaths. When the government finally did sort out its internal problems, the epidemic had grown out of control. Realizing this, SEWA and some other NGOs, including the Indian Red Cross, were recruited to assist the government in getting the situation under control. Ration levels for the essential foods were increased to help the victims build enough strength to combat the illness. Anti-malaria pills were distributed, as were chlorine tablets for infected water. Also, since the flood washed away the freshly planted seeds in the fields, seeds were distributed so that the harvest could be restored.

These items were quickly and effectively distributed through the Shakti Packet channels, reaching over 8,500 people in their time of need. The strengths of the program persist throughout the year. However, in the time of emergency, they became more apparent. By being more responsive to local needs and more inclusive of local participation, the program has proven itself an improvement upon the FPS system. The Government of India's public distribution system is known for its shortcomings, particularly in rural areas. In addition, with a program that has such basic shortcomings, its performance in a time of crisis can hardly be counted upon to be effective.

Nobel laureate in Economics Amartya Sen has observed that the public distribution system, "routinely falls below target in its supply of food to the rural population during droughts" (Drèze and Sen 1989: 125). The Shakti Packet has broadened the scope and enhanced the quality of the theme of this government program and proved what new things can be done with an old idea to meet the targets in flood, drought or otherwise. Again, SEWA's aim is not to produce parallel structures to government programs. In this case, SEWA's Shakti Packet has proven to be a useful experiment in how to improve the PDS.

As part of the 1999 budget proposals of the Government of India, increases in the PDS prices of rice, wheat, sugar, urea and cooking gas were hotly debated. The opposition parties managed to force the ruling coalition to back down on the increases for the below-poverty line ration-card-holders. The political process has, in this manner, helped adjust the system so that it serves more efficiently the portion of the population in greatest need.

The significance of such a change should not be overlooked. Food distribution is a political maze, with everyone's self-interest at stake. The fact that a change was made, though minor, indicates that there is a chance for progress.

In the debate process, the Finance Secretary painted a grim picture of the 'unsustainable' subsidies that justified the ruling party's proposed hike. According to him, the inefficiency of the PDS could collapse the entire budget. The fact of the matter is that the subsidies, in comparison with what the government pays for the rations, are high. However, this can be attributed to several factors, one of which is the inefficient method by which the government acquires and distributes those rations. In addition to being top-heavy bureaucratically, it is also susceptible to corruption, since the commodities have to travel through so many channels.

It is time to adjust and streamline the PDS so that it is more clearly an instrument of poverty alleviation. This means focusing on poorer recipients, and decentralizing, perhaps even making it an entrepreneurial tool rather than a bureaucratic burden. Increased emphasis should also be placed on rural distribution, where the purchasing power is lower and physical accessibility more of a challenge. A comparison of the Shakti Packet with the PDS system will bring many of these issues to light. As the Shakti Packet program progresses, its success could have an impact at the policy level. As the push for decentralization gains momentum, the Shakti Packet can serve to provide a few lessons in developing a system of locally managed food distribution that addresses the needs and tastes of the poor, while eschewing corruption, poor quality and poor accessibility in rural areas.

Biography: Thinking Differently

Ranbai lives in Anternesh village, and is President of the BDMSA. In that capacity, she has participated in a great deal of training for leadership and management. It has all been quite useful, too, in other ways. Ranbai runs the Shakti Packet in Anternesh, which serves as a vital lifeline for her village during the monsoon season.

Even under normal conditions, Anternesh is an isolated village. The lone bus that comes to the village makes only one round trip per day. But, when the rains come, the tenuous connection that Anternesh's only road provides to the outside world is submerged, and the village's connection is severed. The road is flooded and travel to any other village can be dangerous, time-consuming and highly impractical.

In 1993, the flooding was particularly severe and prolonged. When the available food in the village ran out, Ranbai's husband and brothers were among those who had to cross the river, raging where the road once was, and walk several more kilometers to get food. Then, of course, they had to return and repeat the treacherous crossing, this time loaded down with what they had bought.

When the floods subsided and Ranbai could once again travel out of her village to attend to her responsibilities with the BDMSA, she brought up Anternesh's circumstances with fellow-members. This was ultimately what brought the Shakti Packet to her village and gave it the special mission of preparing for floods and other emergencies.

Now, when the rains cut off the road, the Anternesh Shakti Packet has to serve 150 families in Anternesh and neighboring villages. Ranbai has to do a lot of planning and record-keeping in order to make this work. Fortunately, over the years, she has learnt to do this well. In her own words, planning purchases for 150 households has forced her to 'think differently' as compared with the days when she only bought for one household, her own.

The food and supplies in the Shakti Packet shop are less expensive than at the regular merchants' shops and of a better quality than the items at the FPS. Good-quality rice from a merchant is Rs. 12 per kilogram. Rice from an FPS is only Rs. 8.50 per kilogram. Included in that FPS kilogram, however, are stones and many inferior grains. The Shakti Packet is sup-plied with good-quality rice for Rs. 11 per kilogram, offering the best of both of the other options. Other products follow the same trend.

Most importantly, the credit offered through the Shakti Packet to SEWA members is interest-free. When the merchants extend credit, it is often at very high rates of interest. In fact, indebtedness to these merchants is the most common form of rural debt. For example, 5 kilograms of rice has to be paid back with either 15 kilograms of rice later (produce is a common form of pay-ment for agricultural labor), or in rupees at an interest rate of 10–15 percent per month. The Shakti Packet offers relief from this form of oppression.

It is a very difficult program to run. Ranbai has to keep strict accounts and make informed purchases months in advance, especially before the monsoon season. Furthermore, she has to collect payments, diplomatically and sympathetically, from fellow-members and friends. The tact and management capacity required are all skills that she has developed as a BDMSA leader.

Chapter 7

KUTCH AND DWCRA

The efforts of SEWA in Banaskantha did not go unnoticed. One of the many groups that were pleased with the results was the Government of Gujarat's Rural Development Department. Throughout the state, this department was broken down into several District Rural Development Agencies (DRDA), that oversaw the implementation of the DWCRA program. The department was not only pleased with the success the Banaskantha DRDA enjoyed, but also saw that its strategics could be applied elsewhere as well. After all, Banaskantha was not the only arid, impoverished district in the state.

Kutch is a district that borders Banaskantha and consists largely of desert land. Hence the name Kutch, since it is the Rann of Kutch desert that fills the district's boundaries. The physical conditions of Kutch can be said to be even more extreme than Banaskantha's. Like Banaskantha, much of the land is sandy, saline soil in a drought-prone region. However, a greater proportion is sheer desert. There are also green areas in Kutch, supported by an underground aquifer, but they are very few, and they are not the areas in which SEWA operates. With the determination to work with the poorest of the poor, SEWA bases its activities in three western blocks of Kutch which are among the least hospitable in the district: Lakhpat, Nakhatrana, and Abadasa.

The conditions in these three blocks present a formidable challenge to economic prosperity. Kutch is geographically the single largest district in all of India, with a population that is widely and sparsely dispersed. The distances between habitable grounds that are capable of supporting a community, if only barely, are great. One town can be separated from the next by as much as 50 kilometers of bumpy, sometimes washed-out roads. For SEWA, these conditions meant that getting involved in the area would be difficult. All this distance would have to be frequently covered by organizers in the beginning, and later by leaders from the villages as well. Strategies would have to be planned accordingly and the appropriate resources sought.

However, Kutch has one advantage over other regions, despite its climatic shortcomings. Its craft tradition — in embroidery, mirror work, and tie-dyeing — is renowned in India. As in Banaskantha, over the centuries, the women of Kutch developed their unique style to fulfill the needs of their families. The pieces they produce are considered instruments of wealth and indicators of identity. Also, as in Banaskantha, the crafts the women produce are sought by traders, who offer terms of trade that exploit the craftswomen's lack of awareness about the actual market value of their work. However, the difference between the two districts is that, while they have similar styles, it is Kutch that is normally associated with this distinct type of craftwork.

In 1993, the State Rural Development Department approached SEWA to get involved in Kutch. Immediately, the need for more information was apparent. The initial action research done by SEWA and the FPI brought the craft situation to light. It also revealed a startling situation in the overall labor economy for the craftswomen of the region. Out of 463 responses to a survey of total employment among craftswomen in the villages of Kutch, 163 (35 percent) respondents worked between 21 and 30 days a year, 197 (43 percent) respondents only worked 11 to 20 days a year, and 100 (22 percent) respondents worked between one day and 10 days a year. Only three respondents worked more than one month out of a year! Similarly, in a survey of women's income, 675 out of 788 (86 percent) respondents indicated that their income was less than Rs. 500 per month.

As in Banaskantha, what work there was depended largely on the seasonal rains. People were not working because there was no work to be had. Ironically, this lack of employment opportunity meant that the women had to work harder, finding other ways in which the family could survive. With an average income well below the poverty line and a gross lack of employment opportunity as the source, the need for improvement was tremendous.

Considering SEWA's experience in organizing artisans for income-generating opportunities, as well as the Kutch artisans' special abilities, structuring the development activities of the district around craft production groups was a logical beginning. At the invitation of the State Rural Development Department, SEWA undertook the task of building what was to become the Kutch Craft Association.

This association has its roots in the groundbreaking efforts of Professor Ramesh Bhatt of the FPI. It was his investigation into the poor living conditions of the district, and his confidence that SEWA could make a difference, that planted the seed for what is now beginning to bloom in Kutch. After the survey cited, undertaken by FPI and partly funded by the Royal Netherlands Embassy, it became very clear that the craft tradition would provide an effective entry point into the development of Kutch. Furthermore, the survey was conducted with a specific plan of action as its goal. The starting point was to understand what needs were present as well as what skills were available to address those needs. From this, a strategy could begin to form.

The proposal for the development program, which Professor Bhatt played an instrumental role in drafting, envisioned a comprehensive effort. It was to be a multi-partner program, including financial support from the UNICEF, the Government of India, the Government of Gujarat, and the National Bank for Agriculture and Rural Development (NABARD). SEWA was to provide additional financial support, as well as be the project-implementing agency. Once drawn up, all of these entities agreed to the plan and work got underway.

The first step was to organize the community around the needs and skills of the community. SEWA organizers would initiate discussions with the craftswomen in the villages and try to generate interest in the betterment of their communities. Those interested could join together and form groups around artisan production as an income-generating activity. Employment was the primary need, only after which could the other improvements follow.

After the groups were formed, a skill assessment was to be performed. This was to give the groups and the organizers a better idea of how intensive the training needed to be. Also, by observing the raw talent of the craftswomen, a better idea could be formed about the potential markets and product lines.

With an idea about the available skills, skill upgradation could be undertaken effectively. The individual women possessed the necessary skills to varying degrees. Some were masters while others were less advanced in their development. The proposed system could bring women of all skill levels together to build communal abilities.

As the implementing agency, SEWA was promised the use of funds for staff, such as the organizers. Furthermore, because of the large size of the district, a main center and three sub-centers were to be arranged. These were to be management centers, training facilities, storage places for production, and shelters for the night.

The group members and their families were to rise above the official poverty line, become economically self-sufficient, and gain access to better basic health and social security. The goals were similar to those formulated in Banaskantha in 1989. However, the goals as well as the means to be used to achieve them were also influenced by the experience of years since SEWA's first foray into rural development.

SEWA and Development of Women and Children in Rural Areas

By 1993, SEWA was an established labor union with over two decades of experience and well-recognized success. In particular, SEWA's most recent success had been in the rural arena. Originally an urban labor union for informal sector workers, SEWA had begun to broaden the scope of its activities in the early 1990s. From the slums of Ahmedabad, SEWA was now moving to the arid, drought-stricken, rural areas in the northern part of Gujarat. Banaskantha had offered many lessons to SEWA, and the hope was to build from them. First of all, it was found that a primary vehicle for this move to the rural arena was the Development of Women and Children in Rural Areas (DWCRA) program.

In the late 1980s, the Government of India initiated the DWCRA program. It was, at that time, jointly funded by the Government of India, the individual states, and UNICEF. However, it met with mixed results. In fact, in most cases, it failed to make the impact it aspired to: improving the socio-economic status of women and children by supporting income-generating activities for rural women living below the poverty line. Yet, SEWA's partnership with the DWCRA was an exception. In Banaskantha, with saline soil and water, spreading desertification, unpredictable rainfall and widespread poverty, SEWA was effectively implementing the government program. Thousands of women had been organized into craft groups, dairy cooperatives, and tree nursery and plantation cooperatives, to name just a few.

The DWCRA program grew out of a special commission formed by the Government of India in 1979. Their charge was to develop a program that would specifically target rural poor women and children, the most neglected section of the Indian population. A prominent member of that commission was Ela Bhatt, founder of SEWA. The program of their design sought to make an immediate and direct impact by improving the employment situation of the women.

Unemployment and underemployment in the rural areas is immeasurably high. Without employment, there is no income. Without income, there is no food, healthcare, education or any other commodity or service needed for survival. The DWCRA program sought to provide groups of rural poor women with the means to support themselves with income through their own underutilized skills and entrepreneurial potential.

The DWCRA further focused its aim by concentrating on women who lived below the poverty line (BPL). In rural areas, the official BPL level is Rs. 12,000 per year, an amount barely conducive to survival. By narrowing its scope, the DWCRA intensified its purpose. Only the poorest of the poor could register for the DWCRA program, that would hopefully annul the applicability of that very title.

Through a DWCRA fund of Rs. 15,000, these groups, consisting of up to 20 women each, were provided with start-up capital. The money was used as a rotating fund for the women to purchase raw materials for their crafts, fodder for their cattle, or seedlings for their nurseries. The hope was that these groups, once provided the resources to establish themselves, would become self-sustaining. With an initial investment by the DWCRA, the returns would be immediate and continue to accumulate in the long term.

Furthermore, because it was the women who were the entrepreneurs, it was the women who were in control of the gains. As mentioned before, it was common knowledge in many circles that the woman's income was far more likely to be utilized to the benefit of the family, especially the children. Both academic research and practical experience point to the fact that, while poor women most often use all of their income for things such as food, clothing, and healthcare for the whole family, men are more likely to spend a large portion of their earnings on food and drinks with friends, tobacco products, alcohol and, often, even gambling. Thus, improvement in the lives of women more directly translates into improvement in the lives of their families and communities.

The lessons SEWA learned from the challenges and successes in Banaskantha were many. First, it learned that the conventional labor union approach, which was SEWA's traditional method, was not applicable to a rural area where the issue was not improving the terms of employment, but rather the provision of employment itself. With a sizeable surplus in the labor market, employment opportunities were scarce in proportion to the population, and not well-paying. A labor union had no leverage where there were no jobs, so SEWA had to learn how to help generate employment. Only when the members had sustainable work would they have bargaining power like their urban sisters.

Realizing the importance of sustainable employment, SEWA learned how to use the DWCRA as a tool to achieve the goals for which the program was intended. Previously, cooperatives were the apparatus used to generate employment opportunities, and this apparatus worked well. Since 1972, SEWA members have formed numerous cooperatives around head-loading, construction work, dairy, craft, and childcare, among others. However, the process of forming these cooperatives is often tedious and complicated. An elaborate application process sometimes makes the registration of the cooperative an ordeal that lasts several years. Then, once the cooperative is registered, they face rigid regulations and an austere auditing structure. Since some officials estimate[1] that 80 percent of India's NGOs exist only on paper, these formalities are quite justified. But, for SEWA, widely recognized as part of the other 20 percent, the process was often an impediment to real progress. The DWCRA offers a flexible alternative. Since the groups were in a rural area, unaccustomed to formal organization, time was needed for the learning process. This need was then not only true for the groups, but for SEWA as well. Rural development, in the manner that they were practicing it, was still a relatively new phenomenon. Since 1972, SEWA as an institution has always been learning and adapting. The DWCRA made an allowance for this. The registration process, for a well-established and proven organization like SEWA, was timely and efficient. Regulations were helpful guidelines rather than restrictive demands. Most significantly, there was room for trial and error. Within the conventional cooperative system, if it was seen in the course of an audit that a cooperative was not functioning well, it was often punished or simply disbanded. The DWCRA acknowledged that the concept of rural development was still itself in the process of development. The best way to improve the methods was to judiciously experiment. The activities described in this book are examples of this experimentation. The sincere devotion to investing in human capital and building the capacity of the members for a more sustainable development is a process fostered by SEWA and largely facilitated by the DWCRA.

Any attempt at community development at the grass-roots level will only be successful if the people work not as individuals, but as a group. At a disadvantage because of the lack of employment opportunity in a saturated labor market, it is imperative that the community works collectively. The

DWCRA offered SEWA members a flexible means of cooperative work, without the constraints of a cooperative. By focusing on building the capacity of the participants, and paying deliberate attention to developing markets for the products, the DWCRA and SEWA worked well together.

The DWCRA program had actually already been implemented in Kutch in 1989 by the Kutch District Rural Development Agency (KDRDA), and had also specifically targeted the craftswomen. By 1993, when SEWA became involved, approximately 20 groups had already been registered. Without exception, however, all the groups were inactive. Beyond signing the women up and registering them into cooperatives, little was done to foster their progress. Some paper was shuffled and money 'doled' out, but little else was done. No training. No advising. No support network. The result was that the Rs. 15,000 that the DWCRA had provided was wasted and the women still had no real means of income.

Recognizing the mistakes of detached involvement, SEWA set up a long-term strategy by which the DWCRA groups would become strong enough to pull their members up from below the poverty line and become self-sustaining as individuals and as a group. The process of what has become known as capacity-building takes a long time, and SEWA was aware of this fact. However, others involved in development efforts, such as the government and other national and international funding agencies, often operate on different time scales. The level of commitment required and the amount of time needed to achieve the goals that outsiders set for these communities was still in the process of being fully appreciated. The government was ultimately accountable to the voters and the other funding agencies were accountable to their own constituencies, with the bottom line that they all wanted results where they had supplied the funds. SEWA, as the implementing agency whose role was to direct the funds, was therefore the one under pressure from the various donors to get the results.

This pressure had its value, as it directly and indirectly kept SEWA on the task. However, it often forced unrealistic and impractical constraints on SEWA and the communities with which they were working. By way of example, although capacity-building was the new buzzword, few agencies wanted to invest in training the local population. Projects like water pipelines, roads, and irrigation infrastructure were popular funding targets, but there was little enthusiasm for teaching the local population how to use and maintain these things. Certainly, there was no need to consult with the local population to learn of their needs directly, or to learn from the methods that they traditionally used to address them.

SEWA had struggled in other districts to overcome this obstacle, as was described in the part of the book dealing with Banaskantha. It had tried to establish a precedent by which local abilities were respected, their inputs valued and investment in human capital at the grass-roots level seen as a necessity. Because SEWA had been invited by a state government agency, an invitation prompted by appreciation for past work, there was hope that more credence would be given to SEWA's ideology in Kutch, to respond to community demand rather than to demand of the community.

Indeed, this hope of understanding seemed a viable prospect. The KDRDA offered valuable support in the early stages by organizing the artisans. Although, by 1993, all the 20 previously formed DWCRA groups were inactive, they had been registered and the names of the craftswomen recorded. This gave SEWA a starting point from which they could contact the village women and begin working with them. The SEWA organizers began by going to the villages that already had registered groups. They also brought along the KDRDA Assistant Project Officer, who worked specifically with the DWCRA groups.

In addition, the initial action research done by SEWA and the FPI, that listed the aggregate employment in the craft sector quoted before, also came in handy. The research had been done village by village, so records remained that gave a good profile of each one. With good help and good information, SEWA was well prepared for the next step.

Refining the Organization Process

Kutch resembled Banaskantha in so many ways, but it was also significantly different. As SEWA began its activity, it was conscious of improving upon its experience in Banaskantha, avoiding the same old pitfalls while adapting to the new conditions. This focus was particularly intense with the craft program. In Banaskantha, crafts constituted one of several interventions. With the somewhat more limited land-based resources in Kutch, and the particularly strong tradition in crafts, the work in Kutch would have a narrower scope. But, what it lost in diversity could be compensated for in intensity. SEWA could deeply scrutinize its craft experience in Banaskantha, improve and streamline.

With limited resources to start with, SEWA had to be selective about the craft groups they would help organize. The criteria were simple: the groups whose members were in the greatest need were the groups to be organized first. In addition, some groups had become entangled in political complexities. For example, some of the previously registered groups were under the 'leadership' of the most powerful village landowner's wife, often only a proxy for her husband. In such instances, the prospects for progress had limitations.

Out of the original 20 groups, SEWA decided to work with four. In addition, SEWA organized 17 new groups, focusing on villages that were more remote and isolated geographically and economically. At this point, the necessary registration of these groups went very smoothly, relative to SEWA's experiences elsewhere. This success was largely due to the full support of the KDRDA office and the foresight of the earlier action research.

After and during the initial selection of the groups, the SEWA organizers conducted meetings in the villages. Each meeting would consti- tute a dialogue about the present conditions in the village and the possibili- ties of the DWCRA program. This dialogue was a crucial stage and presented many difficulties. As in most cases, none of the women had traveled beyond the boundaries of their own block, let alone district. They had no real standard by which to measure their own condition, and felt less of a keen need to improve their lives. Thus, the organizers had to spend a great deal of time discussing the possibilities for improvement.

Group formation began once the organizers conveyed a sense of the need for improvement in the community. The interested women, as a group, selected leaders and collected the names of the other members. To get to this point took several meetings with the organizers, but the commit- ment on the part of both the craftswomen and the organizers became estab- lished. Once the names were collected, and it was confirmed that they were BPL, the application was submitted to the DRDA. Then the group was officially registered.

At that point, the group set a date for an in-depth skill assessment. On the appointed day, the skill assessment followed this pattern: the SEWA organizers, and, in the early stages, the same Dastkar expert who had helped in Banaskantha, arrived in a village in the morning. They distribu- ted plain cloth, needles, and different colors of thread to the women in the new group. These women then had until the afternoon to embroider a design of their own onto the cloth. Meanwhile, one by one, the SEWA

Plate 7.1: Embroidery in progress under the auspices of the DWCRA Program

organizers recorded the names and addresses of the craftswomen. A picture of each individual woman was taken, her village was noted, and other basic information gathered.

Lastly, when these tasks were completed, the day's embroidery work was collected and later assessed. This is where the Kutch system began to improve upon what was done previously, learning from the lessons provided in Banaskantha. On the basis of the speed and quality of the work done that day, a master craftswoman from the Gujarat State Handicraft Development Corporation rated each village craftswoman as either an 'A,' 'B,' or 'C.' The A-level craftswomen were those whose skills were proficient and required no training to be able to make a saleable product. Women who could produce at that level, at that time, were very few. Many were of the B-level, which meant they required some training, be it either in design, color arrangement, overall quality, or some combination of the three. However, their skills were sufficient.

The vast majority of the craftswomen were placed at the C-level. This meant that they would require a lot of training before being able to make a saleable product. Although these women were making clothing for their families, it had to be understood that the demands of creating products for market were much greater. The prices offered for their work were significant, but the crafts had to be of good quality to attract buyers. Also, tastes were different. Rural Kutch tastes tended towards loud color combinations, which grated with the tastes of both the middle-class, urban, domestic market as well as the international market.

Each craftswoman would soon get an identification card with basic information about her, a photograph, and her classification. With this card, her membership in both SEWA and the DWCRA was recorded and she was ready to begin work with fellow craftswomen of her village. Once the registration of the groups was complete, each group was given the DWCRA fund of Rs. 15,000. Out of this, a sum of Rs. 2,500 was contributed to a district-level fund for purchasing raw materials. A sum of Rs. 10,000 was then contributed to a fund for purchasing finished products. By setting aside this amount, the groups allowed for spot payment for their finished goods. The products were rarely sold the moment the goods were produced, but the artisans still needed income. Thus, when the finished goods were completed, money was taken from this fund, and then replenished once the goods were sold. Lastly, a sum of Rs. 1,100 was put in a SEWA (and later Kutch Craft Association) account and used to cover operational costs, including marketing and transportation of the goods.

Even the four previously registered DWCRA groups needed the funds and the training. Although they had been provided with the money when they were originally registered, all these groups had left it in the bank account where it was deposited. They were afraid to use the money, unaware of the terms of the DWCRA program and unsure of how to use the funds. Thus, all groups were starting out on an equal footing.

Next, a comprehensive training program was initiated. To alleviate the burdens of the women, and their time lost to other activities, a training-cum-production approach was adopted. For the training period of six to nine months, the women were compensated with a stipend of Rs. 350 per month. During that period, the women were closely monitored by other craftswomen classified earlier in the A-level during the previous skill-testing. These trainers stressed the quality of the women's work and suggested ways to improve.

First, a woman from each village in the A-level was given a two-day orientation on how to pass her skills along and monitor the other women's work. The women of this category learned to manage the training and distinguish between good work and poor-quality work. They further strengthened their understanding of color combinations, design, and quality of execution. They also learned to take attendance and record individual progress.

The training of the leaders, conducted in their own villages, lasted three months for B-level craftswomen and nine months for C-level craftswomen. To facilitate the training, each group individually set up its program to suit the schedules of the members. For five hours a day, the whole group would sit down together and work. That way, they could compare each other's work, jointly learn from the trainer's assistance, and discuss the recent developments together. Nor did their training stop there.

One snag was that when the women finished the training, their production quality quickly declined to its previous state. Thus, many of the initial post-training consignments were turned down by the quality inspectors at the SEWA office. Though the women's capabilities had increased, some remained under the impression that quantity was the best way to make money. Just as it was with the traders, the craftswomen thought that taking the time to produce crafts of superior quality was unnecessary. Also, with their experience of government drought-work schemes in craft, as also in areas such as road and irrigation construction, the women felt that the earlier stipend would simply continue regardless of output. Earlier charity-like programs had left their imprint. However, those delusions were quickly shattered when the poor-quality production was rejected. The organizers were initially confused and concerned with the turn of events. But the craftswomen quickly understood the issue and the workwomanship immediately improved again.

There were also those women who simply did not have the experience to even qualify for the C-level. These women lacked the capacity, but were nevertheless in need of income. The craft that Kutch was perhaps most famous for, was tie-dyeing. A cut above the hippie-popularized style of tie-dyeing, the region had a tradition of intricate designs, expertly executed with vivid colors. But traders had their influence on this craft too, and eventually left their damaging mark. Dividing the process, the traders paid the village women to do the tying, but took the worked fabric elsewhere to be dyed. The result was that, over a period, many women became unaware of the second part of the process. They senselessly tied the fabric into the required patterns, but had little idea why. When SEWA organizers showed them the tie-dyed fabrics, the craftswomen refused to believe that it was the end-result of their labor.

To address this issue, SEWA members from Ahmedabad, most notably Rehematben, a master craftswoman, went to Kutch and taught the complete process to those women who had previously only been tiers, as well as to others with no experience of tie-dyeing or embroidery but who needed employment. Subsequently, these women began to get full rewards for their full work, reclaiming their community's lost skill.

The most significant difference between the establishment of the groups in Banaskantha and that of the groups in Kutch was that the program initially envisioned and described to the Kutch craftswomen was the exact strategy that was implemented. In Banaskantha, however, a series of trial-and-error methods had been used, to begin with, as the organizers took on most of the training and work assessment. Eventually, in Banaskantha, too, the craftswomen assumed more and more of such responsibilities. Ultimately, the systems used in both the places were similar, but the changes required in Banaskantha impeded the flow of progress. Much of the confusion and the slower pace of the capacity-building process were avoided in Kutch, thanks to the pioneering efforts in Banaskantha.

In the end, SEWA learned that the process that placed more confidence in the abilities of the women, most notably in their ability (if given the resources and opportunity) to learn quickly and assume greater responsibilities, was the better strategy.

Kutch Craft Association

By 1994, the 21 groups formed till then felt the need to further strengthen the organizational structure. Two leaders from each group went to Bhuj, the main city in Kutch district, and discussed the issue. By the end of that meeting, the consensus among the 42 leaders was strongly in favor of forming a district association — independent of, but still in partnership with SEWA. After discussing the functions of such an association, they prepared an application to the Charity Commissioner of the district. After a year of further questions and answers, the women took the next step towards self-sustainability.

On 24 May 1995, SEWA handed the project implementation responsibilities over to Kutch Craft Association. As a labor union, SEWA's role is to intervene on behalf of the informal sector and, in the case of most rural areas, build upon demand for employment opportunity. However, to maintain its focus as a labor union, SEWA abstains from making its role the direct provision of those employment opportunities. Instead, the Kutch Craft Association takes on the role of administrating the income-generating schemes, and SEWA continues to empower those same women to further utilize their progress. Like the BDMSA in Banaskantha, the Kutch Craft Association became the project implementation agency that continues to directly tap SEWA's experience and resources.

While continuing to provide the resources for developing the skills of the craftswomen, the Kutch Craft Association also worked to reduce the cost of production by buying raw materials in bulk. In the early stages of the program, the funds were deposited in a joint bank account, with the Kutch Craft Association and the group leaders as the co-signatories. Out of the original DWCRA fund of Rs. 15,000, as mentioned before, a sum of Rs. 2,500 was allotted for the purchase of raw materials. After each group submitted a production plan, outlining their proposed costs and material needs, the Kutch Craft Association would purchase the raw materials in bulk, lowering the total cost of production.

Each time the group picked up raw materials, the money was deducted from their account of Rs. 2,500. When they came back after two weeks to deposit the finished work, and were paid on the spot, they were then able to replenish their account. As for the other money in their account, it was used to pay wages in the initial stages, before sales caught up with production. In some cases, it was also used for other forms of capital investment, such as a sewing machine to stitch the garments together after the embroidery had been done.

As part of the original proposal, drawn up by Professor Bhatt, the main outlet for the Kutch Craft Association's products was to be an emporium in Ahmedabad. SEWA already had two outlets in the city, housed in the SEWA offices there. Also, the craftswomen in Banaskantha had the Banas Craft on C.G. Road, an upscale shopping district in Ahmedabad. With the success in sales at these outlets, it was felt that a Kutch Craft store could also secure a portion of the market.

Funding was set aside for the emporium, but other obstacles remained. Retail space was at a premium in Ahmedabad at the time, and a suitable location at a suitable price was hard to find. Also, constructing a new building would have involved a long-drawn-out process, requiring a tender period for contractors, with little guarantee of satisfactory work.

Meanwhile, SEWA and the Kutch Craft Association came to realize that Kutch required a different marketing strategy. The larger distances between the villages, the fewer resources for the bigger area, and the greater separation from Ahmedabad required of the Association and its members an enhanced degree of independence. While the emphasis on an

Ahmedabad outlet promised many sales, the driving force behind those sales inevitably had to be an Ahmedabad-based sales staff. None of the Kutch women were willing to fill such a role, and this meant that with such a system they could assume little responsibility in selling their products. This drawback did not bode well for self-sustainability. Instead of expending energy in applying the necessary pressure on the government donors, the Association made the bold choice to develop a more appropriate market strategy.

Developing market linkages was to prove a complex matter. But, again, the Banaskantha experience came in useful. The Banas Craft had recently been established and was aggressively building market contacts. Exhibition appearances were arranged, orders solicited and, as mentioned, a retail shop opened in the upscale shopping district of Ahmedabad.

Since both the Banas Craft and the fledgling Kutch Craft were based on similar programs, principles, and membership bases, there was much room for collaboration. The Kutch artisans did decide to utilize the Banas Craft shop as an outlet for some of their goods. But, emphasis was placed on numerous exhibitions shared with the Banas Craft, and with Oxfam and other organizations with which Banas Craft had already established relationships. This gave the Kutch Craft a solid beginning.

However, the key to the Kutch Craft's success would be the extent to which it could build upon, rather than rely on, the previous work of their Banaskantha sisters. First, care was taken to differentiate between the products from the two districts. Rather than compete with each other, the two craft organizations were to complement each other, mutually developing market interest that would shape the demand for their crafts.

To begin with, the styles were different. In the process of skill testing in Kutch for registration, six distinct sub-styles of embroidery were identified among the pieces made. Each of those designs was also distinct from anything produced in Banaskantha. Not only were the specific shapes and colors different, but materials varied, as did overall design schemes. Some were compact and some spread out. Some had a sharp form line and some, rounded corners. In practical terms, there was enough variation to appeal to a wide range of tastes without detracting from the popularity of other Banas Craft or Kutch Craft products. To deal with all these styles, a catalogue of designs was prepared, that continues to incorporate traditional and new designs. This documentation simultaneously provided a means of preservation as well as a resource for creating a multitude of innovative products.

Furthermore, a concerted effort has been made by the Banas Craft and the Kutch Craft to differentiate their products. The Banas Craft produces shawls, while the Kutch Craft produces saris. The Banas Craft produces door ornaments, while Kutch Craft produces file folders. The list goes on and offers a diverse line of products to the market.

Kutch Craft also made a more direct effort to cultivate the local market. Although Kutch district is poor land for agriculture, the tourist industry is relatively strong. Despite its harsh edge, the desert possesses a starkly elegant beauty that is increasingly attracting tourists. An added attraction is the 'authentic' Indian culture preserved through centuries of isolation from mainstream society. Thus, the breed of tourist that makes the effort to go to Kutch is often interested in the traditional, colorful life, and crafts of the region.

The Kutch Craft Association has been attempting to develop the local market. Placards have been placed in some of the hotels in the area and even a few taxi drivers have been personally enlightened about the splendor of the women's work, by many of the women themselves. All this is in line with a lower-cost advertising strategy. The Banas Craft, when it started, undertook an aggressive advertising campaign in newspapers and other media. The results were positive, but the costs exceeded anything the Kutch Craft Association could afford. Instead, the Kutch Craft Association has taken a less costly route, as these examples show.

Similarly, more energy has been focused on larger-scale, institutional orders. This will hopefully prove a more cost-effective strategy, in addition to complementing the Banas Craft's efforts in retail-oriented marketing. It is also hoped that the Kutch Craft Association's forthcoming Internet web page will help develop a stronger export market. What they lack in financial resources, they make up in creativity and effort.

The Operational Infrastructure Difficulties

To facilitate the network of income-generating activity by training, purchasing raw materials in bulk, marketing, and later making savings accessible to women in remote villages, a certain degree of efficiently utilized infrastructure was necessary. In the original proposal to the Gujarat State Rural Development Agency, SEWA called for a main center and three sub-centers in each of the three blocks in which they were working. Before it began working in Kutch, SEWA was promised that these resources would be available.

The large size of the area and the distances between the villages pose one of the greatest challenges in Kutch. Every time a group finishes with its work for the period, the leader has to collect the goods and deliver them to the association. If there were only one center, in Bhuj, the main population center in the area, some of these women would have to travel over 150 kilometers to get there. Considering road conditions and the bus system, that one-way trip could itself take up an entire day. This was simply impractical and unreasonable.

The need for a main center and three strategically distributed sub-centers was clear from the beginning. Organizers needed a space where they could meet with each other and the other members, base communications with SEWA in Ahmedabad, government officials in Bhuj and Gandhinagar, and even eat, rest, and sleep. It is amazing that, in the early days of the program, the work carried on although the establishment of just a main center was grossly delayed.

From the beginning, the KDRDA insisted on a permanent space rather than a rented one. In response to this insistence, SEWA quickly selected 32 sites that could potentially be purchased. Out of these, 20 were shown to the government officials and, out of them, three were selected. Unfortunately, taxes on the sale of property in India can be exorbitant, so people often choose several means to bypass the taxes. Black money is one common method of achieving this. The sale price is under-reported and the difference made up in the form of an unreported exchange of cash. Thus, the amount taxed is significantly less. Yet, when the government is doing the purchasing, as was the case with the main center, black market money is not an option. The result was an impasse where no sale could be achieved.

To compensate, the District Collector's office offered three district government buildings. By the time the first of these offers was made, the Kutch Craft Association had already been formed, so they had submitted the necessary application. Unfortunately, because rural Kutch is not a favorite posting for Indian Administrative Service officers, six District Collectors had come and gone in Kutch over a six-year period. Each time, the applicant had to begin again and the Association's District Coordinator had to re-explain the situation to the new Collector. Meanwhile, the Kutch Craft Association survived by renting and converting an office in a residential district. Negotiations continue to this day with the current District Collector, and a permanent space will hopefully soon materialize.

Because of the great size of the area covered in the Association's activities, it was also decided that there would be one sub-center in each of the three blocks where the Kutch Craft Association was operating: in Naliya town in Abadasa block, Nakhatrana in Nakhatrana block, and Dayapar in Lakhpat block. These sub-centers would serve as training centers, storage facilities for raw materials and finished goods, distribution centers for the finished goods, meeting locations and living space for staff.

Site selection was the first step, and the taluka panchayat dragged its feet in presenting the options. Naliya was to be the first sub-center and it took a year to set aside some land. Construction began in 1994, but was delayed by rains, and remained slow after the rains were over. After two and a half years, the building was nearly completed, but still lacked water, electricity, telephone lines, and window frames. By that time, the government had already exceeded its budget, so work had to stop. Desperate for a space to work, the Kutch Craft Association moved in anyway. Water and electricity, and most recently a telephone, have subsequently been provided A fax machine and computer resources — the staples of modern organizations — are eagerly awaited.

This is the best-case scenario. The other two sub-centers are still looking for land. To make do, the Kutch Craft Association has been forced to rent small spaces available in the other two blocks. The root of the problem is political. Though the KDRDA invited SEWA to get involved and pledged their support, like the District Collectors, there have been six KDRDA Directors in as many years. With each Director, the Kutch Craft Association has been obliged to describe the program and explain the supporting role the KDRDA had committed itself to. Kutch, as a remote and sparsely populated district, is not a popular posting for an officer in the Indian Administrative Service, and sometimes the KDRDA Directors only accept their duties grudgingly. Some have also been supportive but, like the others, they only remain for a year.

To compensate for this inconsistency, the UNICEF stepped in and provided a vehicle for the Kutch Craft Association's use. With the lack of a well-established sub-center system, travel throughout the three blocks has become even more important. It has filled many roles, transporting trainers and organizers to and from the villages, as well as medical staff and supplies. At the same time, raw materials and finished goods are shared between the groups and the association, saving time and money for all involved.

Independence for the
Members and the Organization

Despite the difficulties in getting resources, the membership in the Kutch Craft Association has been increasing at a healthy pace. After the first year of actual operation, there were 21 groups, with a total of 700 members. The next year, 1996, saw a rise to 1,100 members, slightly below the target set in the original proposal. At this point, the Kutch Craft Association came to realize more fully the difficulties that the great size and relative isolation of the region presented. Rather than rush ahead and fulfill an arbitrary quota, the Kutch Craft Association made the brave choice of sacrificing the target in favor of more substantive work.

As the provision of infrastructure was delayed, and a relatively small staff had to cover a large area, the Kutch Craft Association focused on consolidation rather than expansion. The staff of both SEWA and the Kutch Craft Association were going through a period where each person had multiple responsibilities. They did not have time to focus on one issue, nor did they have time to keep up with the broader issue of where the organizations, as a whole, were headed. Instead, they found themselves frantically trying to cope with their hectic workload.

Similarly, there was concern that the Kutch Craft Association's growth in numbers was to the detriment of the members' growth in individual capacity. In the face of these difficulties, the Kutch Craft Association froze membership expansion for 1997–98.

The years were instead spent focusing on the use of what resources they had to improve the skills and income of the current members.

One strategy for achieving their goals of increased skills and income, and preparing the members for the 21st century, was an initiative on member education called 'Lateral Learning.' This strategy set up a system where members from among the leadership in SEWA would meet monthly or bimonthly, changing the location of the meeting each time so that they could get a stronger idea of what other members and programs in the SEWA family were doing. The meetings were organized around several topics and included various leaders, but they all shared one thing in common. They stressed the sharing of information within the organization.

One such group of meetings was the spearhead team meetings. As mentioned earlier, there are spearhead teams in every district for the different program activities. In Kutch, there is a spearhead team for crafts, savings and credit, capacity-building, campaigning, health and research. Each of these teams comprises two organizers and eight leaders from among the village groups. It is these teams that coordinate and implement the recruitment, training, and monitoring of the groups in their respective areas. In short, they are the engines driving the programs.

It is crucial for the leaders to be well aware of SEWA's activities and developments. Every month, each of these Kutch spearhead teams gets together with its counterparts from other districts and shares experiences and ideas. For example, the Kutch savings spearhead team may travel to Banaskantha district where they would meet with other districts' savings leaders. In fact, it was at one of these meetings that the Kutch team learned about the internal lending system, mentioned in the chapter on micro-finance with reference to Banaskantha, which is now beginning to be used in Kutch.

In addition to learning about new programs, these leaders learn about better ways to do the same programs. Likewise, the Kutch leaders share their experiences with others to help them build better programs. Also, the monthly meeting of the Executive Committee of SEWA, of whom one member is from the Kutch Craft, rotates its meeting from district to district.

The agendas to the meetings are not limited to specific topics. Nor are they limited to formal committees. The topics range from setting up a business plan or production plan to marketing and record-keeping. Also, leaders from the different groups attend exposure trips, visiting other districts' successful programs, as well as successful organizations in other parts of India. Within their own community, they have a lot to learn from each other.

As a result of all these decisions, the members are more independent and will require less and less support from the association. In fact, they will be able to offer training and guidance as the new groups form. The decision to halt expansion and focus on consolidation is a strong indication of the commitment of SEWA and the Kutch Craft Association to build the capacity of their members. After two years of internal growth, they are now ready to begin to accept more women as members. The result will be seen as the association proficiently incorporates its new members into the fold.

From the perspective of the craftswomen, the early stages of the program development were a unique experience. Considering the strength of character evident in many of the women today, and the system of production they have established, it is hard to imagine them having the fears and inhibitions they first had. When the SEWA organizers first came to the villages, the women were anxious for the opportunity for income. In some villages, where the traders had been active, the promise of better returns was the point of interest. For villages not visited by the traders, the promise of returns alone was the reason for interest. Talk of ownership of the means of production, training, leadership, and capacity-building was ignored by the women, in a rush for employment opportunity.

As mentioned while discussing group selection and registration, it became clear to the organizers that the women had rarely left the confines of their village. The prevailing attitude became further apparent to the organizers when they spoke to the women about leaving the village to perform the duties of the groups. Most of the organizers in that early stage were educated women of the middle class, from towns or urban areas. Since educated women were non-existent in the villages, the organizers were not as consciously aware of the village women's fear of the world beyond their village.

It was not only considered taboo for the women to leave their villages but, in some cases, it was against the well-defined laws of the community. Sodha women, for example, were not even allowed to leave their homes, in most cases. In addition, false stories about women leaving the village only to be sold as maidservants, or worse, compounded a fear that was hard to overcome.

There was also the general impression that there was no reason to leave the village. If the traders could come to the village to distribute the work, why could these new SEWA 'traders' not do the same? Ideas of empowerment, capacity-building and self-sustainability, even when explained and re-explained in terms consistent with rural culture, simply made no sense to the women. They saw SEWA as a new trader who would continue to provide work for them, perhaps on somewhat better terms. Along the same lines, what need was there to undergo training? Embroidery work and tie-dyeing were leisure activities that occasionally provided a source of income. If the quality of the work was sufficient for the old traders, it ought to be good enough for the new as well.

SEWA organizers had run into the same sentiments in other places as well. However, the greater degree of cultural isolation, stemming from the large distances from village to village, from the surrounding desert area that cut off interaction with other regions, and even from the noticeable absence of television, had its effect. Even in remote villages in Banaskantha, one would find the occasional TV and satellite dish. Kutch was different.

In the eyes of an organizer, there were many things lacking in the lives of these women, from accessible healthcare to simple employment. But, to these women who knew no other standard by which to measure their condition, there was no conspicuous need for change. They were not aware that they had a right to a better life.

SEWA had greater ambitions in mind and sought to share their vision with these women. Aware of how difficult it would be to convince these women of the need for experience in the 'outside world', the SEWA organizers chose an indirect path. If these groups were ever going to be independent and self-sustaining, every member, especially anyone who would take a leadership role, needed to be confident and capable enough to go beyond their village. To accomplish this feat, the SEWA organizers agreed to bring the work to the women in the village. Although it was a heavy burden for a small staff with limited resources, the work provided to the craftswomen began to be seen at its face value. Over six months, the craftswomen were getting far greater returns than ever in their experience with the traders.

With the initial training in the villages, the quality was improving and the market paid a much higher price for the product. At that point, SEWA organizers explained to the women that they would no longer be able to come to the villages. The organizers had to focus on their primary job, which was to go to new villages to organize new groups. By this time, leaders had emerged in the first groups, and they all recognized the value of the new program. If it meant continued income, the craftswomen would find the strength to leave their village to go to the sub-center, when needed.

Many of the craftswomen were even bold enough to travel to Ahmedabad in those first few months. What they found there changed their whole perspective on their own work. Hitherto selling to traders, or not selling at all, the women had never realized what prices their goods could attract in the open market. Nor had their quality of production been as high as it had now become. In the city, these women went to the Banas Craft, other shops, exhibitions, and Law Garden, where in the evenings, the sidewalks are packed with merchants selling crafts from the rural areas, including Kutch. Also, the craftswomen toured the Calico Museum, one of the finest museums in the world devoted to crafts and textiles, in Ahmedabad. As a result, a greater appreciation for the value of their work began to drive their further progress.

Since then, the women's independence has grown. Most of the women have journeyed as far as Ahmedabad, where they have attended craft exhibitions and SEWA meetings, or articulated their needs to the likes of the Chief Minister of the state of Gujarat or the First Lady of the United States of America. Some have even traveled to other parts of India and beyond. But, the most important achievement is that all of the women have learnt what possibilities lie out there and have developed a hunger for them. They have learnt that every community has the right of access to potable water, to medical care and to education. They have learned of other ways in which they can generate income, such as dairy cooperatives or social forestry.

Since the beginning, it has not been only the income that has drawn the women to their groups, the association, and SEWA, though income has been a major factor. It is also the process of achieving those goals that has provided a multitude of less tangible consequences and contributed to the women's success. They have the confidence to leave the confines of their village and explore the world that surrounds them. Though they had always contributed a great deal to their families, they had not previously acknowledged their own contributions. Now, they were contributing even more, taking credit where credit was due, asserting their wills in accordance with their efforts. They found strength in themselves and strength in their numbers. Having learned these things, they are beginning to demand more of themselves, their neighbors and their government.

National Consultation on DWCRA

SEWA's efforts in Kutch began partly because the Government of Gujarat had been so impressed with the success of the DWCRA program in Banaskantha. The enthusiasm, which had inspired the government to invite SEWA's involvement in Kutch, did not dwindle. In 1996, the state hosted the National Consultation on the DWCRA. This was the first time this important meeting was held in Gujarat, and it included such high-level officials as India's Minister of Development. During this meeting, the Government of Gujarat proudly asserted the efforts of SEWA, particularly in Kutch and Banaskantha.

Rising to the occasion, SEWA used the opportunity to make an impact at the policy level. With the respect earned from its work, SEWA presented several issues that, they felt, would improve the program. First, the spirit of consultation was to be taken further. Once a year was not enough. Nor were the most important people in the program in attendance. SEWA proposed that district-level DWCRA meetings be held once a month, with specific attention being paid to including the members of the DWCRA groups themselves. The difficulties in acquiring the promised resources on time, could be greatly reduced if communication were improved. The practicability of those resources as well as the delivery would also be improved if the voices of the women members were heard.

Also among the list of proposed improvements was the availability of more funds. The amount of Rs. 15,000 was sufficient for starting a group, but for the full benefit of the possibilities, more was needed. Specifically, marketing and production needed to be further supported. The original focus of the DWCRA was training and production. Marketing was one of the remaining areas of the program that had to be enhanced. The women were organized, devoted, and their skills were sharp. But, without a market to sell their goods, all their work would go to waste.

In the same manner, the women were limited in their production capacity by external factors. Their working capital was not sufficient to match their abilities. The sum of Rs. 10,000 that the group received for raw materials, when divided between 15 women, was not enough to purchase all the necessary materials for production. Instead, the women had to work in small installments because they could only afford to buy limited amounts of raw material.

Officials from the National Consultation on DWCRA have taken some of SEWA's recommendations to heart. Since the meeting, an additional sum of Rs. 4,000 has been provided to each group to be used for marketing, and another of Rs. 10,000 supplied to each group for increased production through expanded working capital. Grass-roots success has made a difference at the policy level.

The government has also taken up other practical recommendations. In its list of recommendations for change, SEWA stressed the importance of ensuring the availability of raw materials, skills and markets before the DWCRA group's activity began. Many DWCRA efforts in other parts of the country were failing and developing nothing except a bad name for the program. Part of the difficulty was that there was not enough groundwork being done before the groups were started. This drawback led to delays and disappointment when the DWCRA system failed. Without the three necessary ingredients of raw materials, skills, and markets from the start, an uncertain beginning was usually followed by an untimely end.

Second, if raw materials, skills, and markets were in place, the groups would still need 'settling time' to adjust to the program. Any person entering a new job would require a period of adjustment to understand their new role. Impoverished rural women were no exception. Organization and empowerment were potentially revolutionary concepts to these women. They needed time to adjust without accelerated expectations being put upon them. If the program was to have its intended impact, time was an additional input.

One reason for the required time investment was the need to build the leadership skills and self-sufficiency of all the women, not just a handful. To achieve this end, SEWA recommended a system of rotating leadership within the groups. The different leaders would have a positive impact on the group dynamic. Rotating leadership would allow for different women to develop their leadership skills. It would tap the various strengths of the different leaders, whose rotating tenures would diversify the goals and direction of the whole group. Also, if needed, it would check the potential abuses of a leader, since she would have to be concerned with the repercussions when her term was over. In general, the multiple leaders would add strength and balance to the groups.

SEWA also recommended that a greater degree of experience-sharing and transparency be adopted by the program. The size to which the program had grown meant that there were a multitude of experiences that could be shared. The flexibility of the program allowed for a greater degree of creativity. The result was that there was a whole spectrum of possibilities to be explored. If there were a way by which the different groups could share those experiences, it could make a great contribution to the success of the collective groups.

The other category of recommendations were related to broadening the scope of the DWCRA in order to intensify its effect. SEWA's emphasis on employment opportunity as the key to rural development and empowerment was well incorporated into the DWCRA. However, employment was only the first, not the sole priority. For development to be successful, it has to be multi-dimensional. Once employment was secured, the DWCRA could also be a tool for delivering support services.

SEWA discovered that once its members were organized and functioning as DWCRA groups, there was a great deal of potential in their collective strength. As groups, they were not only effective in raising their incomes, but also in collectively demanding and acquiring increased access to savings resources, water, healthcare, and education. The groups provided a delivery system and managerial body that was already in place.

Furthermore, their spirit of empowerment was an effective means of monitoring the quality of the services. For example, the public health centers are in place, but they do not function properly. Significant investments have been made, but the system still breaks down. If the DWCRA groups were mandated to monitor the PHCs, the women would take responsibility for alerting the proper authorities when the health system failed. Education and other public services could, likewise, be more efficiently delivered.

The government has taken this recommendation to heart and looks to both the Kutch Craft Association and the BDMSA as models. The Kutch and Banaskantha Associations' federation of the DWCRA groups is a tried and tested example of good organizational structure. They are cohesive, democratic, multi-level federations of many groups. The organization has been built from the bottom up and the results are reflected in the associations' responsiveness to the members' demands.

Through a process of convergence, the government is hoping to deliver a variety of resources, from income-generating activity, to health, education, and even old-age pensions through DWCRA federations. The process is now entering the initial stages of implementation with the SEWA programs in Kutch, Banaskantha and Surendranagar. The initiative has been given the title 'community-based convergence services'. The primary implementing agent will be 'community mobilization teams', similar to the organizers and spearhead teams that are the backbone of SEWA's efforts.

On the basis of the success in Banaskantha and Kutch, convergence may be the next step towards community empowerment in India. If that is the case, the importance of what has taken place so far in Kutch and Banaskantha will become doubly important.

Biography: Breaking Community Barriers

Deyuba, from the village of Vedhar Orida, is from the Sodha community. All her life, Deyuba has been strictly confined to her house and her village. She was never allowed to work outside her home and so had limited options. The same restrictions were imposed on her women ancestors, but they had developed a rich craft tradition to compensate for their restricted lifestyle. Deyuba has inherited that tradition and now makes most of her family's income from this work.

Work is particularly important for Deyuba because she will have to increasingly rely upon herself to support her whole family. Another tradition in the Sodha community is that the women marry men who are many years their senior. Deyuba is in the middle of her life, but her husband has already had to retire from any form of strenuous work, which means just about any form of employment available to the rural poor.

Yet, economically unproductive men still do not often lose dominating influence over the lives of their women. When Deyuba first joined the DWCRA group, she was selected as the skill upgradation trainer and group leader. For most DWCRA leaders in other villages, this required a certain degree of travel. However, Deyuba's husband and community strictly forbade it. The Kutch Craft Association organizers accommodated the group in their difficulty. For three years, the work was brought to the women without their ever having to leave their village.

The main resistance to the women leaving the village surprisingly came from a teacher from Vedhar Orida, the most educated man in the village. Rather than enlightening him about the benefits of women's independence, education had led him to foresee a potential challenge to the established patriarchy, and so he staunchly resisted it. He counter-organized the men of the village into a body solidly opposed to the women's empowerment.

Yet, time is an educator, and the teacher learned a lesson. After a few years of productive work in the village, the SEWA organizers gave an ultimatum to the men: either let the women travel, or the work will discontinue. The organizers' resources were strained by the constant attention Vedhar Orida required. But, they also knew that the full value of the women's work was now more widely appreciated.

The men relented. The teacher himself commented that he could see the economic gains from the craft activity and supported the women's independence. Since then, Deyuba has made her first trip to Ahmedabad and even to Bangalore, where she attended a craft exhibition, and plans to continue to do so on a regular basis.

Note

1. An estimate based on a statement made by a high-level UN official who wishes to remain anonymous.

Chapter 8

WOMEN AND
THE PANCHAYAT

Village-based government on the Indian subcontinent is far older than the Indian nation itself. Gandhi was a strong advocate for local governance and saw it as the foundation for the new nation. However, by the time India became independent and the Constitution was written and ratified, there was no significant role delineated for local government. At the time, it was felt that the only way to harness the energy and enthusiasm for the nation's development would be through a strong and centralized government. Delhi would drive the development and the rest of the country would follow.

By the late 1950s, it became apparent that efforts at rural development were failing to achieve their intended goals. It further became clear that this was not due to a lack of effort. Many resources and much rhetoric were devoted to rural development. It seemed, rather, that the problem was due to a poor implementation structure. As a result, the sentiment for local rule had gained strength, as had the argument that it would be a more efficient way to manage development resources. Thus, the Team for the Study of Community Projects and National Extension Service, better known as the Balwantrai Mehta Committee, named after its chairman, was mandated by the central government to look into better ways to utilize the national resources devoted to improving rural life. The committee recommended what came to be known as the Panchayati Raj.

In the form of a directive from the central government to the states, a three-tier system of village-level, block-level, and district-level institutions was recommended. Decisions would be made and direction given at the village-level upon approval by block- and district-level officials. At the village-level would be the gram panchayat, an institution that had already existed informally in many parts of the country for centuries. Then, at the block-level would be the panchayat samiti with the zila parishad at the district-level. The emphasis was on bottom-up democracy and management of resources rather than top-down governance. By adopting a traditional Indian system of local rule and extending it beyond the village-level, the Mehta Committee introduced one of the most significant reforms ever undertaken by the Indian government.

Gujarat was one of the few states that made a sincere effort to implement the Panchayati Raj. In 1961, the national legislation was accepted and ratified at the state-level and became part of Gujarat's government structure. Yet, over a period of time, even in Gujarat, the system in some ways remained center-oriented and never changed, while the aspects that had been localized by the legislation eventually reverted to the pre-Panchayati Raj status quo. By the 1980s, Gujarat was one of the strongest states as far as support for local government went. However, it still depended little on the panchayat system for either planning or implementation. This situation was specifically and, perhaps most inappropriately, the case with development oriented programs. Such programs were largely subsumed by the District Collector's office.

Problems with Achieving Local Government

The reasons for the failure of government to reach the hands of the people were many. One of the largest contributing factors involved the state-level bureaucrats and politicians, who feared the loss of power and purpose at the hands of an empowered panchayat. Similarly, at the national level in the 1970s, politics became less an issue of parties and ideas and more an issue of personalities, with the head of government becoming the central figure. One symptom of this trend was the specifically targeted welfare programs, aimed at the Scheduled Castes, women, or minorities, for example. The manner of the delivery of the programs suggested to the recipients that these were the charitable gifts of the government, and, more specifically, the Prime Minister. The dispersion of developmental funds became a form of political largesse, and the control of the resources a powerful political asset.

On the flip side, perceptions of the capacities of village politics were, sometimes deservedly and sometimes not, tainted with skepticism. Rural politicians were seen as too conservative, especially in the 1970s, at a time when leftish politics were in ascendance. Furthermore, stories of severe and occasionally violent political conflict filled the pages of the country's newspapers. All these factors contributed to a view largely held by the powerful urban classes that village politics were infected with corruption, ignorance, and inability.

Regardless of the validity or invalidity of the perceptions towards local governance, certain facts were indisputable. In most cases, the panchayat system was easily manipulated by the traditional elite and used to legitimize their continued dominance over their communities. Similarly, if somewhat less surreptitiously than some higher-level politicians, those in control of the panchayats often used development resources for their own personal political and economic gains. Favors were exchanged for loyalty or cash. Funds meant for community development were embezzled. In many cases, this was simply accepted as the norm.

Synchronous with these corrupt practices was the need to keep the general community ignorant of the opportunities actually available for them. The sarpanch, for example, could procure the funds for a well in his village, dig the well near his fields and claim it for himself, and maybe even charge the public for using it, despite the fact that it was intended for the public and built with public funds. If the community was unaware of where the funding came from, they would not complain. This form of corruption was allowed to continue undetected and unchecked.

No country is immune to such abuses, but the relatively large number of development programs in India has allowed for an exceptionally high degree of these difficulties. The sum of all these factors was that government decisions, and particularly development programs, were increasingly controlled at the central level. By the late 1980s, the Panchayati Raj directive was largely ignored or forgotten. During this time, large-scale programs such as the 'Remove Poverty' campaign and the Green Revolution were undertaken and did perhaps as much damage to the rural poor as they helped them. Without any input from those people whom these programs were meant to affect, the results were predictably disappointing.

The 73rd Amendment

Despite widespread and deep reluctance to entrust power to the panchayat system, there were those who felt that the answer was not to neglect the rural communities, but rather to prepare them better for self-governance. This revived support, in 1989 and again in 1990, found expression in a proposed constitutional amendment. However, it failed to pass on both occasions, for many of the reasons previously mentioned, namely mistrust of the village leadership and the bureaucracy's reluctance to cede power.

Finally, in 1992, the 73rd Amendment to the Constitution of the Republic of India was passed. This amendment made it compulsory, not just recommended as in the 1959 Panchayati Raj Directive, for states to establish and support panchayats. The amendment, now under implementation, is large in scope. The four major themes are as follows: one-third of the total panchayat seats are to be reserved for women; the practice of direct elections is to be increased; panchayat elections are to be compulsory every five years; and an enhanced number of responsibilities are to be transferred to the panchayats. The following are among the new responsibilities:

- Land improvement and soil conservation
- Minor irrigation, water management, and watershed development
- Animal husbandry and dairying
- Social forestry and minor forest produce
- Cottage industry
- Rural housing
- Roads, electrification, and communication
- Health, including primary health centers and dispensaries
- Education, including primary, and secondary schools
- Public distribution system
- Poverty alleviation
- Women and development

For those familiar with SEWA-related activities in Banaskantha, and the potential future activities in Kutch, the parallels with this list are striking. The panchayat has suddenly become, on paper, a principal factor in almost every conceivable aspect of the development of rural India. The formidable challenge is now to make that a productive reality.

Women in Power

In the local elections of 1994, in the three districts of Kutch where the Kutch Craft Association is active, 61 women sarpanches were elected. Yet, underneath this number lie some deeper issues. Certainly, some of these women were elected because they were assertive, dynamic women who struggled and won their way into the position. However, it is likely that a larger number of these women were selected by no impetus of their own, but by the powerful men in their villages.

The Gujarat law specifically reserved certain sarpanch seats for women and lower castes. Ironically, that is exactly the type of person many of these men wanted to choose. They were confident that such vulnerable people could be controlled. In many cases, the rural elite would handpick the candidates whom, they felt, they could most easily manipulate. To some, it seemed their traditional hold on the local population was immune from meddling reform.

Despite a rosy veneer, deeper issues surrounded the election of these women. Left to the devices of the traditional elite, it was hard to tell whether the 73rd Amendment was going to improve the situation. Which was worse, the dozens of reserved panchayat seats that remained empty for lack of women candidates, or some of the women sarpanches who were proxies for the powers that be and always have been? In such circumstances, perhaps it was better the old way.

Recognizing this dilemma, SEWA organized several training sessions for its numerous members who were newly elected panchayat members and sarpanches. Since all of SEWA's members were women, and many of them were from impoverished, lower-caste backgrounds, they were prime targets for proxy seats. However, as empowered women with a growing understanding of their potential, many SEWA members were also among the assertive and dynamic women who struggled and independently won their positions. Women of both of these categories, and the spectrum in between, first gathered in Ahmedabad to understand their new roles better.

Three training sessions have taken place, the first and the third in Ahmedabad, and the second in Naliya. Despite the different venues, they all followed a similar format. The first training, in 1997, was broadcast via closed circuit satellite to all nine districts in Gujarat where SEWA was working. A presentation, given to the women, explained the history of the panchayat and the details of the 73rd Amendment. The women then became familiar with their responsibilities. They learned that the power was in their hands to build roads, improve housing and develop the economy in general. They saw that, as elected officials, they not only had the responsibility, but the mandate to improve the conditions in their communities.

In addition, and perhaps most importantly, the women learned of the different resources they had at their disposal to fulfill their duties most effectively. If it was an irrigation project that their community wanted, the women learned what government department would be the contact point. They became familiar with the seeming maze of government officials at the district level, and how they could be helpful.

Next, the women were trained in how to formulate a budget. Fundamental issues such as visualizing plans over a year period, prioritizing goals, and estimating costs were covered. The women had to learn how to articulate these ideas on the government-provided budget form. This last task was harder than it sounded. The trainers, such as those from the Ahmedabad Study Action Group (ASAG), had a strong background in the subject and were experienced and well-educated, but had to admit befuddlement in the face of the government budget forms. Whether intentionally or unintentionally, the budget forms had been made so confusing that only the government bureaucrats could easily translate their meaning. Perhaps, it was meant as a way to check corruption by creating an elaborate system that defied manipulation. Perhaps, it was a method by which the bureaucracy could maintain the real control over the purse-strings and, therefore, the power. Either way, the budget form was an obstacle to effective local government if the women could not understand it. Great care was taken by ASAG and SEWA to simplify and clarify the process in their training.

Also discussed were ways in which to conduct gram sabhas (village meetings). The village meetings were, by law, to be held twice a year. During these meetings, all registered voters in the village gathered and conferred with their elected representatives. These representatives, namely the sarpanch and the other members of the panchayat, had to share their plans and information about their progress with the village. The voters then had the chance to question, support, and voice their opinions. In essence, the gram sabha was meant to be the foundation of Indian democracy.

In reality, gram sabha meetings rarely took place. Some panchayats simply lacked the initiative. Some lacked the ability. Others yet lacked the desire and purposely neglected their legal responsibility. They preferred to keep the voters in the dark, where they were powerless to interfere. SEWA helped train these women how to conduct a meeting of that size, and gave them the confidence to conduct them.

First, the importance of the meeting was discussed in the training session. Though democracy may be an ancient idea, it has taken several forms, many of which fall short of its prescribed goal. It is less so the case today, but still not rare, that the poor and women, for example, can be excluded from the democratic process while that governing entity can still be labeled democratic. Experience is the main teacher, especially for those without the privilege of an education (i.e., poor women). Thus, if a system of government is exclusionary, but is still called democratic, those excluded accept the limited definition of democracy, to their own exclusion. Discussing the more inclusive idea of democracy was an eye-opening experience for some of the newly elected sarpanches, who had never attended a gram sabha meeting, either because they were not allowed to attend or because the meetings did not take place.

In gaining a better appreciation of the democratic process, the newly elected village representatives were moved to not only hold the meetings, but to encourage all to attend. The nuts and bolts of holding such a meeting were then covered, such as creating an agenda and adding a structure to the meeting. With a sense of purpose and empowerment, it was hoped, the newly elected officials would perform this important duty, and perform it well.

Lastly, the training addressed a common form of corruption at the panchayat level. In many instances, particularly when the sarpanch is only semi-literate or illiterate, as is the case with many of the SEWA women, the secretary of the panchayat is a central figure. Not an elected position, a secretary is nonetheless in a position of power. One secretary is assigned to every panchayat, and is responsible for recording the minutes, keeping accounts and seeing to the other functionary details. As a government employee, the secretaries are educated at least up to the 10th standard, and paid a salary comparable to that of a police officer with complete job security. In the rural areas, this position is to be envied.

Many secretaries fulfill their duties well, playing a crucial role in facilitating local government. However, there are some who take advantage of their position. The ASAG/SEWA trainings addressed these issues, alerting the sarpanches and panchayat members to beware of signing (or thumbprinting in instances of illiteracy) documents of unknown contents. The women also learned how to identify discrepancies in the accounting and how to either confront or bypass the secretary if there were problems.

The women elected to the panchayats, as sarpanches or members, have exceeded their own expectations, in most cases. To the disappointment of some in the traditional elite, who saw the women as proxies to be controlled, the women have found strength in their positions and have appropriated what was rightfully theirs. To the delight of their neighbors, the women have learned to be effective leaders, contributing substantially to the improvement of their villages. They know how to formulate and share a vision for a better future. They know how to curb corruption and get the most benefit out of the resources offered.

As elections came up again in 2000, some of these women lost and some retained their seats. As a rule, a seat reserved for a woman in one election is not reserved in the next election, since the reservations are on a rotational basis. But, the women elected to reserved seats have now accumulated the knowledge and experience that could translate into more votes in the next election, and perhaps a victory regardless of reservation. In addition, new women will inevitably take seats in other villages in future elections, and women's leadership will continue to grow.

In the process, the women are learning to lead on a larger and larger scale. They are learning to defeat corruption and get results. They know who is responsible for what government function and they know how to hold those officials to their responsibilities. Best of all, they are learning to lead the development of their own communities.

Biography: A Legitimated Leader

Basrabai, the sarpanch of the village of Mohadi, has a surprising yet common story behind her rise to her position. However, her use of that position will hopefully in the future be an equally common story. In the 1994 district elections, the sarpanch seat for Mohadi was reserved for women candidates. The men in the village had a meeting to discuss this and decided that none of the women wanted to run. They presented their conclusion to the officials at the taluka panchayat office, but were dismayed to learn they had no choice in the matter: either the sarpanch was a woman or there was to be no sarpanch.

Basrabai's uncle was given the task of finding the suitable woman. He first asked his wife, but she refused. He then asked his daughter, but got the same result. Finally, he came to Basrabai, who herself refused to run on three separate occasions. But, in the face of her uncle's continuing pressure, Basrabai finally relented. She went with her uncle to the taluka panchayat office, put her thumbprint signature in some book and left.

Several weeks later, Basrabai learned that she had been elected sarpanch when someone read her name to her from a list in the newspaper. After that, according to her duties, she attended the panchayat meetings and thumbprinted the documents put before her by the secretary.

Then Basrabai attended a ASAG/SEWA-organized training session on the roles and responsibilities of panchayat members. There she learned how to prepare a budget, lead a meeting and check corrupt practices by panchayat secretaries, among other things. She would soon be able to put this training to good use.

After the training, Basrabai was attending a SEWA meeting at the Abadasa sub-center. This sub-center shared a campus with the taluka panchayat, where Basrabai had noticed her panchayat's secretary's presence. She entered the building and discovered that the secretary was receiving funds for the construction of a road in her village. While such circumstances would normally be considered good, Basrabai knew that no such road was planned by the Mohadi panchayat, nor was it apparent that the road was going to materialize. This money was going straight into the pocket of the secretary and whoever helped him secure the funds.

Basrabai and Monaben, the district coordinator of the Kutch Craft Association, confronted the secretary and threatened to expose his corruption if he did not return the money. The money was promptly returned and Basrabai eventually got an apology from the secretary, who has performed well ever since.

But Basrabai did not stop there. First of all, the road funds were used to actually build the road. Basrabai's next mission was to get water for her village. Knowing that there was a water pipeline near-by, Basrabai went to the local GWSSB office and asked for either a connection to the pipeline or a reason, in writing, why her village could not be connected. She got her water. Next was a bus stop. Then, she pushed for, and received interest-free housing loans for her village. Now, after she used the same tactics as she did for water, electricity is reportedly on the way.

Basrabai hoped her record in office would be taken into consideration in the next elections. She had achieved more for her village than any sarpanch before. However, in the next elections, she had to contend for an unreserved seat. The competition was stiff, but her platform of previous success served her well. In the 1999 elections, Basrabai retained her seat with a resounding electoral victory.

Chapter 9

THE CYCLONE OF 1998

The morning of 9 June 1998 began like most other days for the fishermen, salt farmers and day laborers of Kutch. The winds were slightly stronger than usual, but the monsoon season was approaching. There was no reason to apprehend what was to come and people went to work as usual. However, what came in just a few short hours later were winds of over 180 kilometers per hour. Driven by the high winds was a storm surging up to 20 meters above the normal sea level on the coast and two tidal waves. It was a cyclone more destructive than any that could be recalled or imagined by even the oldest survivors.

Kandla, the second largest port in India, suffered the most extensive devastation. Official estimates were 1,000 people dead and 1,500 missing. In retrospect, the more widely accepted figures from the press and NGOs, estimating 10,000 deaths, seem more accurate. Kandla was hit so hard partly because of its location, and partly because of its condition. Or, rather, because of the condition of the working poor who made up the majority of the city's population. The day-laborers who worked the docks and related industries were paid barely a subsistence wage and forced to set up makeshift houses on the margins of the harbor, amid the industrial waste and polluted water. Their homes were constructed from whatever scrap materials were available. Sticks, mud, dung, scrap wood, and metal did not provide much shelter from a storm of this magnitude.

The shantytowns that the workers and their families lived in were the first to be swallowed by the surging waters. Women and children were swept away in the torrent, or buried and drowned under collapsed houses, waiting for husbands and fathers to return home before abandoning the premises. What seemed like a logical decision, intended to keep the family united, ended up as a fatal mistake, separating families forever, as the surprising speed and force of the cyclone left no means of escape. Estimates of the deaths vary so widely because so few bodies could be found, either buried under the debris or washed out to sea in the violent storm.

Though the cyclone took less of a toll on human lives in other places, it still caused severe destruction. In the coastal villages of Kutch, fisherman who left their houses that morning never returned. Inland, crops were destroyed, precious trees, in a struggle to reforest and reverse desertification, were uprooted, fodder was destroyed, and cattle killed. Furthermore, salt workers' harvests, often their only income of the year was washed away, and many houses were destroyed. The last two points were significant, because they were among the many examples of how disaster was more destructive towards the poor. Salt farming is notoriously a trade of the poorest of the poor, because its discomforts, risks and meager reward make it intolerable for any but those who have no choice. As the cyclone painfully illustrated, one of the risks is untimely rain, which can wash away all the salt that has been laboriously extracted from the desert sands. Similarly, strong rain can wash away a kuchcha house, dissolving it back into the ground from which it came. In both cases, it is the poor, the ones who can least afford to lose a home or a livelihood, that lose the most. This is exactly what happened in the cyclone of 1998.

SEWA's Immediate Response

On the morning of 9 June, when the cyclone struck, several SEWA organizers in Kutch were in the villages. Many others were at the sub-centers with many of the members, holding meetings. Unlike most of the poor in the region, most of these people were aware that the cyclone was going to strike, but they had no idea that it was going to be as intense as it was. By the time the storm subsided, the organizers at the sub-centers went with the members, anxious to find out their families and villages had fared through the storm. Some found that their houses were damaged or destroyed, and other assets lost. However, in the interior regions, where most of SEWA's activity took place, there was minimal loss of human life. At least, none that was realized until those who had migrated to the coast returned to their native villages, or did not return in some cases.

Because they were on the spot when it happened, the SEWA organizers were among the first to begin to comprehend and communicate back to Ahmedabad the extent of the damage that had been done. These people covered as much ground as possible, coming into contact with many people, trying to ascertain what was needed and where it was most in need. By the day after the cyclone, although SEWA had not been active in the Kandla area, they had discovered first-hand the devastation there. So, on the second day, with communication back and forth between Kutch and Ahmedabad, SEWA decided to center its emergency response in Kandla.

By 11 June, the organizers already in Kutch were joined by more organizers from Ahmedabad and Banaskantha who were there to help start the process of recovering from the disaster. The new arrivals brought with them packets of cooked food, grains, clothes, medicines and plastic sheets. Through contact and exchanges of information with the victims, SEWA knew that most people not only lacked food, but also the resources necessary for preparing the food. Therefore, SEWA avoided the mistake of many of the early relief groups by providing food that was already prepared, or easy to prepare with limited resources.

While these organizers were at work, others in Ahmedabad, from SEWA academy and all the districts where SEWA is active, got together and prepared to go to Kutch. SEWA also sought the help of the Disaster Mitigation Institute (DMI), a part of the Foundation for Public Interest, so closely involved with SEWA's past efforts in both Banaskantha, Kutch and elsewhere. Together, SEWA and DMI expeditiously compiled a survey to find out what relief, both short and long-term, would be of the greatest use to the victims. By 12 June, these people, armed with the survey findings, left for Kutch.

The scene that the organizers encountered in Kandla was disturbing. By all accounts, the smell of the bodies being burned by the army and police was almost as overpowering as the smell of those decomposing bodies that were not yet taken care of. Rumors of a gas leak had forced many people to flee before recovering all the bodies of their loved ones. Some had lost more family members than could be counted on one hand and so the search was particularly difficult for them. The completeness of the destruction, the confusion of the clean-up and the anguish of the survivors presented a harrowing scene for the organizers, many of whom were young women who were new to SEWA.

The chaos that ensued from the destruction infected other relief agencies at work. Some would just pull their trucks, loaded with donated supplies, to the side of the road and unload the food, clothing and other resources to anyone in the vicinity, without making any effort to learn where the greatest need was, or whether the people needed the things at all. In some cases, SEWA organizers recall, they saw relief workers from other agencies accepting the supplies for themselves.

SEWA had long been recognized as a reliable and effective NGO and so, when individuals and groups wanted to contribute to the relief effort, many trusted SEWA with the duty of getting their contribution to those who were most in need. Therefore, SEWA became a temporary depository for a great many resources. SEWA took these expectations seriously and made every effort to use the resources as effectively as possible.

An early issue was that of donated clothing. Much of the donated clothing came from urban areas where the clothing of choice for women was the salwar kameez. However, in the rural areas, women were accustomed to the sari. SEWA was well aware of this difference, as well as the serious obstacle it would present in such a strongly traditional society as Kutch. Though many relief agencies disregarded this difference, or failed to consider it altogether, SEWA knew that wearing a salwar-kameez would be a very uncomfortable experience for the women who had already suffered a great deal. In response, SEWA moved quickly to negotiate with used-clothes vendors, many of whom are SEWA members, a fair price for the donated salwar-kameezes, the proceeds of which were used to purchase saris.

However, as the survey progressed, it became clear that neither clothing nor food was the first concern of the victims. These people were hungry, above all, for information: 'Where is my family? How can I get home? What do I do now?' Amid the chaos, many people were unaware of where their family members were, or whether they were still alive, though most had come to assume the worst. Those who had found the bodies of their loved ones did not know what to do with them.

To make matters worse, the gas-leak rumor had forced many people to flee the area, leaving whatever was left, dead or alive, behind. Furthermore, rumors outside Kutch about the police and army commandeering vehicles in order to transport dead bodies made the owners and drivers of those vehicles reluctant to transport relief items into Kutch. On the other side, the government had offered free rail transport back home to migrants, and compensation was available to those who had lost family members. But, few knew of the availability of such support or the procedures required to gain access to them. In general, information was not disseminated well. Indeed, few knew the cyclone was coming, in the first place!

SEWA tried to improve the situation through the house-to-house survey. Rather than requiring those in need of help to come to them, SEWA organizers went to those in need. They asked them questions about what they needed, but also told them of what was already available. In the days immediately after the cyclone, SEWA undertook this activity in Kandla until the government and other relief agencies began to mobilize more thoroughly.

The government was reporting that only 1,000 people had died in the cyclone and 1,500 were missing. These figures were compiled, using the number of deaths that had been registered, meaning that only the bodies presented and identified to the authorities by the family members were counted. However, many of the bodies had been washed out to sea, while others had either been hastily burned by the authorities for fear of an epidemic, or were unidentifiable due to the violence of the storm or the process of decomposition. Similarly, the 'missing' people were only those about whom their surviving families had reported to the authorities. Few families bothered to go through this bureaucratic procedure, seeing little value in it in the face of their grief and efforts to recover (the failure to register the 'missing' would later prove an obstacle as will be discussed below). Even the term 'missing' seemed a misnomer, as the reality of their deaths became clearer.

On 13 June, four days after the cyclone, SEWA held a press conference in Ahmedabad. With the support of the DMI and Oxfam, SEWA urged the press to reconsider the statistics that the government was reporting, point-ing to the source of error relating to the registration of the official deaths. Similarly, SEWA pointed to the destruction of things other than human life and emphasized the need for long-term recovery as well. To that effect, the rural areas were in just as much need as Kandla, which was receiving the only attention from the media. However, many of the deaths were of migrants from the rural areas within Kutch and beyond. The surviving migrants would be returning to destroyed houses and economies, making themselves even more vulnerable to the next disaster.

SEWA's Long-term Response

The knowledge of the destruction outside of Kandla was minimal, and, therefore, so was the response to it. In Banaskantha and rural Kutch, SEWA was largely alone in its efforts towards long-term recovery. Many of those who survived Kandla returned to these areas, to destroyed homes and destroyed economies. As with the emergency relief effort in the days immediately after the cyclone, SEWA began with a house-to-house survey.

By then, most victims' main concern was the financial recovery that would allow them to rebuild their lives. Many had learnt of the disaster compensation the government had offered to those who had lost family members. They had also learnt that, in order to be eligible for that com-pensation, they had to have their deceased relatives registered as 'dead' with the local authorities. The only way to accomplish this was to present the bodies to those authorities. Yet, the bodies were either buried under debris, washed out to sea, decomposed beyond recognition, or burned by those same authorities who demanded physical proof. Under the circumstances, not many of the people SEWA covered in the survey were in a position to receive what the government was offering.

SEWA approached the state officials administering the funds allotted for the disaster relief compensation. For obvious reasons, the government would be reluctant to distribute the funds when they had no physical evidence of the deaths. Manipulation of the system would be fairly easy if the state government, with no way of verifying the thousands reported dead, had to accept the applications without such convincing evidence. However, it was simply impossible to expect those who had lost family members to meet the government requirements.

SEWA advocated a logical solution to the problem of registering those who had been killed by the cyclone. It proposed that the local government undertake the process of verifying the deaths. Village panchayat members would know who had been lost from their villages. These were people from their own community and, in some cases, their own families. These panchayat members could compile the lists of the dead and submit them to the taluka panchayat for verification. Then, from the taluka panchayat, the names could be submitted to the state government. This process would provide a structure that would limit the potential for abuse and overcome the problem posed by the impossible requirements of the government's system.

SEWA also had problems with its own system of compensation to the affected SEWA members. The SEWA social security scheme had already showed a need for reform in the face of the previous floods in other districts. The original disaster policy, with the United India Insurance Company, proved impractical for the impoverished SEWA members. When the floods had destroyed the homes of the SEWA members in 1997, leaving them without any shelter, the women needed to repair their homes as quickly as possible. They then took loans, often from moneylenders, purchased the necessary materials and undertook the repairs, assuming they would be compensated by the insurance scheme.

However, the United India Insurance was slow in processing the claims and was reluctant to compensate the women for damage that, due to the urgent repairs, was no longer apparent by the time the claim assessors had got around to inspecting the sites. Meanwhile, the interest on the loans began to accumulate, and the women found themselves in deeper debt than they would have otherwise been in because they had expected compensation that was either slow in coming or not coming at all. When the United India Insurance did finally distribute the compensation, the amounts were insulting. The figures ranged from Rs. 35 to Rs. 125 for destroyed houses and lost tools of trade.

In fairness to the insurance company, as mentioned before, much of the damage had been repaired before the company assessors had time to verify the claims. Furthermore, many of the houses were disaster-prone, and would be traditionally considered uninsurable. Though the pittance extended was a weak compromise, SEWA recognized that the issue was not the insurance company's failure to fulfill its obligations, but rather the failure of the entire insurance industry to address the unique conditions of the poor. While SEWA began to advocate the improvement of this situation, they also had to find a solution to the unresolved issues still faced by the victims of the cyclone.

When the devastation of the cyclone started to become apparent, and it became clear that the compensation from the insurance scheme was insufficient, SEWA realized that it had to decentralize the disaster relief scheme. To be prepared for the urgent needs of disaster recovery, SEWA members discontinued the disaster portion of their policy with the insurance company, and instead shifted that portion of the dues to independent disaster funds in the different districts. For example, the funds contributed by the Kutch members would be compiled into a Kutch disaster relief fund maintained by SEWA. That way, when and if disaster struck, it would be the SEWA members and organizers who would manage the disbursement of the funds. Their knowledge, experience and positions would enable them to fulfill the duties delineated by the fund more quickly, fairly and competently than any current insurance company could do. SEWA has also continued to encourage the nationalized insurance companies to consider formulating specific policies more conducive to addressing the conditions of the poor.

However, decentralized disaster-fund reform was instigated by the damage apparent after the cyclone, and thus not in place before the storm. Out of 3,000 policy-holders in the insurance scheme, 600 submitted claims for damage after the cyclone. With the United Insurance of India demurring, SEWA knew it had to act independently. Because it had been the repository of many resources from donors desirous of a dependable organization involved in the relief work, SEWA had a significant pool of funds allocated for the recovery effort. In light of the failure of the insurance policy, SEWA allocated some of these funds for the costs of repairing and replacing the damaged or destroyed homes and assets of those who had already paid their dues.

Despite the scheme's tribulations, SEWA found increasing demand from the movement's members for access to insurance. However, the Rs. 65 required per year to participate in the disaster insurance scheme was an amount rarely available in a household where such funds were not accumulated before an urgent use for the money arose. Whatever the case, money was hard to hold on to money, especially for the poor. In response, SEWA devised alternative payment plans that made the scheme more feasible. One alternative allowed the members to pay a monthly fee of Rs. 20 per month for two years. This was handed over to SEWA Bank, with the bank covering the cost of the dues until the accumulated principle generated enough interest to pay the yearly dues.

A second alternative was a one-time payment of Rs. 500, the principal amount required to generate interest accumulation equal to the insurance scheme dues. This alternative was more viable for members who had received compensation from the government for the deaths of their close family members. In their case, they had cash but, with one income-earner less, the demands on that cash were increasing. They had to quickly prioritize their needs before the money evaporated. The second scheme allowed for this.

Government Policy
and SEWA Advocacy

In 'Rebuilding Our Lives', an account of SEWA's activities in the aftermath of the cyclone, the author of the study, Tara Polzer, stated her opinion of the importance of SEWA's efforts thus: 'The most important work related to long-term rehabilitation which SEWA has carried out in Kutch to date is the pressure it has put on the government to accept this [death and damage toll] data and provide timely compensation to the families affected'. The government guarantees compensation to the surviving family members of those killed in natural disasters. These funds are meant to give families the ability to rebuild their lives after the loss and mollify the destruction of the economy of a disaster-struck region. The hope is that early intervention will stem the deterioration of socio-economic factors and reduce the inputs needed from the government in the recovery process further down the road.

As a result of the cyclone, the need for intervention of this kind was great, yet the government was not even willing to accept the true extent of the damage. As mentioned before, the government was not willing to declare a person 'officially dead' unless the body was physically presented to the proper authorities. SEWA's first confrontation with this policy took place while conveying an accurate account of the death toll to the public. In that case, the media readily accepted the higher numbers, perhaps in part out of their own sensationalist motives. However, when the time came for the government to consider the higher figures, when families were asking the government to fulfill its obligations, the motivation led to the other direction.

The amount of money the government promised was Rs. 240,000 for families of those who died in a disaster. With the 1,000 people declared officially dead, this would mean a lot of money. For the 10,000 people who actually died, this would mean a figure that was more than a district government's yearly budget. Hence, the government was reluctant to accept the more realistic figures.

Though the funds were to be dispersed at the district level, the policy that dictated the determination of the recipients was to be made at the state level. Thus, SEWA focused attention on the Gujarat State Relief Commissioner. Understanding the government's concern for potential abuse of the system without the availability of the ultimate evidence, SEWA proposed the system by which local panchayats would compile the lists of the deceased and submit them to the taluka panchayat. Then, the taluka panchayat would investigate and verify the claims and forward them to the District Collector's office, where the funds were distributed. The Relief Commissioner was satisfied with the proposal and worked for and achieved its approval.

The process initiated after the government's approval followed that which SEWA proposed. In Kutch and all the surrounding districts, where migrants to Kandla had originated, gram panchayats submitted the names to the taluka panchayats, which investigated their validity. The taluka panchayats, regardless of their district, sent these lists to the Kutch District Collector's Office. Through this system, an increasing number of families have received the funds promised by the government.

Cyclone's Impact on the Salt Workers

Though deaths were by far the worst effect of the cyclone, some of the living expressed their feeling that such a fate would have been more merciful.

Such was the case of the salt workers. Of all the employment groups, salt workers were the worst-affected. Their numbers figured large in the death toll, since many had come to Kandla to sell their early salt harvest at the port and found additional work as laborers, loading the salt onto ships. Those who had not yet completed their harvest saw the fruits of their labor dissolve and wash away in the rains and tide that accompanied the monsoon. In the latter case, it was a difficult fate in itself. It meant the loss of a year's income, debt and a great deal of suffering in the future.

The government had justified a tax on the salt trade with promises of social services to the salt workers in return. Theirs was notoriously hard labor with little profit. Even more notorious, if it were noticed, were the especially hard demands put upon the women involved with the trade. Salt workers worked their crop in the harshest of conditions, in the middle of the desert, in the middle of the dry season. For the men, this meant tolerating the heat while monitoring the temperature of the brine water evaporating and leaving the salt behind. For the women, this meant digging trenches in the heat and wading knee deep in the brine, which induced skin diseases and discomfort. Both men and women have to perform these tasks while living on the work-site, with the nearest sources of potable water and food many kilometers away in the nearest village, maybe. Also, it was the women who normally had to walk these distances and carry back the supplies when the family was in need.

Because the work was known to be difficult, and the profit margin marginal, none but the poorest would accept the job. In some cases, they undertook the work independently. In others, they were recruited by larger salt industrialists who extended loans to the salt workers for equipment and supplies during the work. In either case, the salt workers assumed all the risks if the crop was a bust or washed away in untimely rains. But, it was the hope of a good harvest and safe delivery to market that kept the impoverished salt farmers returning to the desert every season.

When the government levied the taxes on the trade, it targeted salt producers with over 100 acres of productive land. However, the impact of the tax was passed on to the weakest member of the salt-production community, the salt worker. In return, the government promised health care, childcare, and other benefits from the tax revenues. Yet none of these promises had materialized into action. The State Salt Commissioner often collected over Rs. 12 million per year from its tax on the salt trade. Out of these funds, Rs. 2 million were supposedly committed to the welfare of the salt workers. After the cyclone, SEWA redoubled its efforts to encourage the government to meet its obligations to the salt workers. Trying to turn disaster into opportunity, SEWA and its salt-worker members tried to highlight the impact of the cyclone on the salt workers as leverage.

In the aftermath of the cyclone, SEWA and the DMI formulated a proposal that was submitted to the Salt Commissioner. The proposal called for establishment of healthcare, childcare, housing resources and social security, and suggested ways to deliver them. This elicited little response from the government and the issues remains unresolved. It is hoped that, in the near future, the combined efforts of the SEWA members and the DMI will produce results. Meanwhile, the lobbying effort continues.

Government Response

The government response to the cyclone was better than could be expected in terms of a commitment of resources. Many branches contributed to the effort. The army and the police prevented an epidemic by leading the way with a rapid clean-up, including the unenviable task of disposing of bodies, rancid and gruesome from decomposition in the high temperatures. SEWA organizers commented that the smell, even from a distance, was unbearable. The Indian Railways, sensitive to the needs of the thousands of migrants affected, promptly offered free return passage home for the victims. Government hospitals were overwhelmed but coping. Government supplies were reaching the scene.

However, the information and coordination involved in these government efforts was a limiting factor. The government consists of a large bureaucracy, as anywhere else, and this hindered the coordination between the different branches and made the availability of information a scattered affair. Though some photographs were taken, the army and the police disposed of the corpses without knowing of the Collector's requirements for registering someone as officially dead. It took time for the community to learn that free rail passage was available, since the Indian Railways specialized in mass movement of the population and not mass dissemination of information. People who were ill or wishing to bring their deceased relatives to morgue facilities often had to travel from hospital to hospital until they could find the one designated for that specific purpose. The government resources made available were not always getting to those who needed them most because there was no efficient mechanism to bring supply to meet demand: namely, information.

As the recovery effort progressed, it became apparent that even the government's generosity in terms of resources had its premature limits. In this case, the limit was one of geography. The government efforts were centered on Kandla, to the exclusion of the surrounding areas, which had been less affected, but severely affected nonetheless. Banaskantha, Surendranagar, and other areas of Kutch were all regions where SEWA had deep and extensive roots in the community. Many SEWA members lost family or property as a result of the cyclone, but none of these three district governments acknowledged this reality.

The district officials in Kutch, questioned by SEWA organizers about the conditions in the villages outside of Kandla, responded that they had not been 'instructed' to go to the villages and so were not interested in going. Similarly, district officials in the other districts were apprehensive about acknowledging the existence of damage outside of Kandla, dominating the state and national governments' and media's attention. Fighting the tide of popular attention, SEWA tried to draw support for rehabilitation in the more neglected regions.

The primary damage done in the inland areas was the partial damage or complete destruction of houses. SEWA fought for compensation for those who had subscribed to the insurance scheme; however, that was still a minority of the members. Many more had suffered the loss of or damage to their homes and had not even any promises of support to fall back on. In this case, SEWA intervened directly where the difficulties had been for the other aspects of the recovery. SEWA gathered information about the damage done in these neglected areas and articulated the demand to the government. The government, subsequently, replied with the supply. In Banaskantha, the national Awas Yojni Housing Fund had allocated funds to the district, but political knots had interminably delayed the distribution of the funds at the district level. When the urgency of the need for housing in the district was presented to the authorities, the knots were quickly untied and resources for 1,000 houses were put in the hands of those who most needed them.

At the national level, the Development Commission for Handicrafts, at SEWA's urging, recognized the importance of the house for craftswomen. It is a home, a workplace and a storage area. In response, the commission diversified their activities and funded the reconstruction of 200 houses for artisans affected by the cyclone. In each case, the housing repairs and reconstructions produced houses that were far more capable of standing up to the elements, no matter how severe.

The government response to the cyclone was a mixed affair. In many ways, the government showed its concern for the victims and, without a doubt, made the largest material contribution to both the short-term relief and long-term recovery efforts. Both SEWA and the government learned a lot from the work that took place after 9 June 1998. In addition to learning more about how to manage their own individual resources, they learned how to work together. SEWA learned that the most effective method for working with the government in such situations was to bring the government officials out of their offices and to the villages. Likewise, the government learned to go with SEWA to the villages and place more trust in their judgment.

The best indication of the lessons learnt came the very next year. In May 1999, another cyclone hit the coast of Kutch. This cyclone turned out to be less severe than the one of the previous year. However, it did cause a great deal of damage. This time, the government, SEWA and their members in Kutch were prepared. Warnings were extended throughout the district, and these reached even the remotest villages. Buses were sent to all the villages in the anticipated path of danger, and people were brought to concrete structures on high ground, where food, blankets and safety were available.

In the end, there was no loss of human life due to poor preparedness. However, there was significant loss of life to cattle and damage to houses. Here, the government response has also been improved. For example, the Housing Development Finance Corporation loaned funds to the SEWA Bank, which were then distributed among the members in loan amounts of Rs. 34,000 each. In return for concrete walls and solid roofs, the members pay Rs. 150 a month, while the government covers Rs. 280 of the monthly installment. This combination not only aids in the recovery from the previous two cyclones, but also protects against the threat of the next one.

Chapter 10
SEWA IN THE NEW MILLENNIUM

SEWA began in Banaskantha with clear, steadfast goals and a flexible attitude regarding their attainment. Part of the flexibility stemmed from the fact that many of the goals were synonymous with the strategy used to attain them. Organization-building, capacity-building, building bargaining power and awareness were all parts of the ends as well as the means. Thus, every achievement was a double achievement, and freedom came from the strength of that inter-relatedness.

The flexibility of the SEWA intervention in Banaskantha broadened the implications of those ideas and actions beyond the borders of this one district, as evidenced by the events in Kutch. At the initiation of the work in Banaskantha, flexibility meant a broader scope of activities SEWA could potentially undertake, depending on the need-based demand of the future members. Now that the Banaskantha experience has progressed to the point where conclusions about its success can be drawn, that same flexibility means a broader scope of other environments in which a similar strategy can be applied. The lessons learnt have been many, and their implications do not end with Banaskantha, or Kutch or even with SEWA.

The use made of the DWCRA program in Banaskantha and Kutch is one implication. The DWCRA was meant to be a different kind of government development initiative. It was different because it focused on women and children living below the poverty line, the most neglected in the Indian population. It was different because it sought to give a hand-up rather than a hand-out. However, the DWCRA program had largely proven a failure in other parts of India. These failures have led many to condemn the entire program.

The events in Banaskantha and Kutch indicate that perhaps the failure of the DWCRA in other places was less due to inherent problems with the program, and at least partly due to the way in which it was applied. Despite all the different approaches that DWCRA offered, the result would be no different if it were applied in the same manner of detached development. The groups formed by SEWA members received the same amount as other groups in other parts of India. The difference was that the SEWA groups were also given a support network. They received training, they developed access to markets and, meanwhile, they were simultaneously working to improve their lives through other means — for example, by developing access to water resources or fighting to change harmful government policies.

SEWA's success with the DWCRA has shown that the program can work. But, it has to be applied in a manner that builds upon, rather than limits itself to, the resources that the government scheme itself has to offer. Simply organizing craftswomen into groups and putting the scheme's funds into bank accounts in their name, as had taken place in Banaskantha and Kutch before SEWA became involved, is not a proper use of the scheme's resources. In fact, it is abuse of those resources. SEWA's experience illustrates that the DWCRA is a worthy program, but that it has to be implemented in a manner worthy of its intent.

Similarly, SEWA's success with the savings and credit program also emphasizes the importance of factors beyond the basic application of a program. As with its micro-finance activities in urban Ahmedabad, SEWA offered micro-finance in concert with its other programs in rural Banaskantha and Kutch as well. By 1989, SEWA had already come to feel strongly about the importance of integrating financial services with other development initiatives in order to be most successful. At the same time, however, there were several quite well recognized micro-credit programs both in India and elsewhere that assumed that micro-credit alone was sufficient to enable impoverished would-be entrepreneurs to overcome the obstacles of poverty.

The SEWA Bank's approach is somewhat different. First of all, SEWA members take part in micro-finance rather than micro-credit. The difference is that micro-finance diversifies the ways in which the members can manage their finances beyond micro-loans. Savings, safety deposits, insurance, access to health care, housing loans and entrepreneurial loans, in addition to training in how best to utilize and manage these opportunities, are all available to the SEWA members. Then, of course, the members have the option of using their resources in conjunction with their fellow-members in income-generating schemes such as craftwork, milk cooperatives, and tree nurseries, for example, where the collective effort translates into enhanced marketing resources, among other advantages.

The implications at the more general level of what SEWA has achieved in Banaskantha and Kutch are equally broad. For example, the success of the "Water as a Regenerative Input" program highlights not only the value of traditional water-harvesting techniques, but also the value of the many little solutions where the big solution is less applicable. Many of the other programs make this point as well.

However, the little solution is no panacea. It is not always the right solution, just the one that is more likely to be managed efficiently since it is managed at the grass-roots level. It is possible to adopt some of the advantages of the little solution into the planning and implementation of the big solution. Again, the "Water as a Regenerative Input" program illustrates how this possibility might work. The pani panchayats, in addition to plastic-lined ponds and contour bunding, have made the effort to assume the responsibilities of pipeline maintenance. Though the pani panchayats ran into difficulties in trying to assume this responsibility, such a role might have been successful, if they had been involved in the planning stages of the whole project. It might have been as successful as the smaller-scale, traditional techniques are proving to be.

The general strategies of organization building, capacity-building, as well as building bargaining power and awareness were synthesized by employment. SEWA began in Banaskantha with an ideology that already embraced these ideas. Its subsequent involvement has served to develop these ideas even further. Other aspects were added to this SEWA ideology in the course of the next decade, and many of these were first revealed in Banaskantha. The importance of water, taken for granted where available, was realized in the first weeks during the action research done in conjunction with the FPI. This idea became a pillar of the SEWA strategy, affecting programs ranging from "Water as a Regenerative Input" and other land-based programs such as tree nurseries and dairy cooperatives to the intentional encouragement of non-land-based, non-water-dependent activities such as craftwork. SEWA discovered for itself the importance of water in everyday life for everyone, but especially the women. Because it had been such a common part of life, it took a discerning perspective to realize the wasteful amount of time women had to spend 'fetching' water. This time took away from productivity, among other things.

The devastating impact of migration was another lesson that became truly apparent to SEWA members for the first time in Banaskantha. In Ahmedabad, migration meant overcrowding, makeshift housing and a desperate need for work, as in-migration was the issue. It was in Banaskantha that SEWA first confronted the other side of the issue. The disruption caused by migration to communal life, the drain on the economy and the waste of resources presented difficulties similar to those in urban areas, but unique in their own right. The impact of these problems was severe enough in the rural areas to cause SEWA to take note and make it a focus of the program.

Many other problems are pandemic to the poor, regardless of whether they live in a city slum or a rural village. The problems may take different forms or have impacts of differing severity, but they are symptoms of the same affliction. Thus, many of the issues SEWA faced in Banaskantha were issues they had faced before. Banaskantha simply forced SEWA to take a deeper look at these challenges and reassess their strategies for overcoming them.

SEWA has always seen employment as the key to liberating the poor from poverty. Charity means the necessity for more charity from the same or other donors later on, just as charity also means only temporary relief for the recipients. This cycle is unnecessary, since most among the poor have the ability and desire to lift themselves out of their condition without the repetitious crutch of charity. SEWA was founded on the principle that protecting the means of income of impoverished people allows them to devote more resources to fight against oppression. As SEWA progresses, the members have added other instruments to their arsenal, such as banking, childcare and health care.

SEWA's evolution in Banaskantha and Kutch has followed the doctrine of the importance of employment, and added meaning to it. Employment is the key, but its protection would be futile when there is no employment to protect. Such was the case when SEWA began in Banaskantha and later in Kutch. In response, SEWA learned to directly address the issue of unemployment in addition to poor employment conditions. This shift was significant, and SEWA explicitly resisted the impetus to consider itself, or be considered, an employer. This policy was particularly difficult in the beginning, as the new members, unaccustomed to belonging to anything but their parents and subsequently their husbands, as essentially property, perceived their relationship with SEWA as an employer-employee one. To understand the meaning of 'belonging' to an organization would take time for these women. But, during that time they learned a great deal and began to realize their own potential, not as employees, but as the organized self-employed. With that status came more responsibility. But, the ability to take on those responsibilities was also part of the process.

To unlock the employment-generating potential of the members, SEWA invests a great deal in capacity-building. Though it is mentioned many times in the SEWA context, to the point where it may begin to seem clichéd, capacity-building finds such frequent mention because it is so sincerely applied. Its prominence in principle and practice is based in the SEWA members' recognition of the power within themselves and the value of developing it. This value should not be underestimated. How significant is it for an unemployed woman to learn a new skill that can be used to support a family? How significant is the change when a woman who, 10 years ago, rarely left her village, finds herself taking part in a craft exhibition in a city a several days journey from her home? How significant is it for an illiterate or semi-literate woman to learn to keep accounts and maintain a budget? The answer to all these questions is that it is not only important, but also essential for truly effective and self-sustainable progress.

Organization building is both the cause and the effect of the individual capacity-building of the members. As the members gain strength from their SEWA involvement, so too do they give strength to their village group, local organization and the larger SEWA movement. The strength that each member contributes to the organization does not begin or end merely with the sum that they add to the membership role, though the final tally does gain one's attention. The over 140,000 members are more than a number for SEWA. Each one is an individual, with skills, experience, ideas and a voice. Each of those members has a multitude of opportunities throughout the year to express that individuality. Whether it is a democratic process, such as Executive Committee elections for all of SEWA, or a more fundamental process such as decision by consensus in a small group, the structure of the organization not only allows, but also elicits the participation of all its members. At times, this structure generates a cacophony of ideas and opinions from a membership that spans over different regions and different livelihoods. However, it is the diversity of those voices that gives strength to SEWA. That is organization-building.

The ultimate result to individual and organizational capacity-building is the acquisition of bargaining power. As evidenced by the support won from the Chief Minister, the SEWA members gain attention by virtue of their numbers. Once they have that attention, they maintain and utilize it. They advocate changes that reflect the thoughts and experiences of those most directly involved and traditionally the least heard. Through the processes of capacity-building and organization-building, they achieve bargaining power. So, the cycle continues as the SEWA members head into the next millennium.

The Millennium Campaign

'So long as the poor remain powerless, poverty cannot be alleviated.' This SEWA mantra captures a spirit that is gaining momentum. But, it also describes an idea that often proves difficult to put into practice. The SEWA members are not immune to challenges. In fact, they are even more vulnerable to the risks of change. They are poor. They are illiterate. They are women. But, they are also persevering. They are informed. And they are organized.

A recent extension of this ideology has begun to shape the SEWA movement's progress beyond the year 2000. It is SEWA's Millennium Campaign. It is not a radically different strategy from what SEWA has acted upon before. In fact, there is nothing it contains that is new to SEWA. Rather, it is a distillation of past ideas and experiences, refined to face the new challenges of the future. As always, the best expression of its principles can be seen in its practice.

SEWA's Millennium Campaign focuses on the four basic needs of the poor: capital formation at the household level, capacity-building, social security, and collective strength through organization. All these needs are interdependent for self-sustainability and so must be integrated. The simultaneous pursuit of all the four basic needs of the poor ensures the accomplishment of each individual goal as well as the ability to achieve the others. A brief discussion of the nature and significance of each of the four needs illustrates their interrelationship.

Capital Formation at the Grass-roots Level

Capital formation at the household level is essential to unlocking the productive potential of those who are denied access to resources. The poor have skills. The poor have abilities. But, the poor do not have the freedom to exercise those virtues, chained to an abject existence in a struggle for survival. To have their own field, their own tools of production, or their own bank account is to have an independence that liberates them from the vulnerability of poverty. Energies spent on haplessly avoiding starvation or spiraling debt can then be devoted to actively pursuing productive abilities and a better life.

SEWA members have overcome many obstacles to gain access to capital resources. The traditional system of moneylenders often included exploitative interest rates, but was the only system available. Despite national legislation obligating state banks to offer loans to the poor, illiterate, impoverished women were universally rejected as 'unbankable'. The primary objection was that the women had no assets for collateral, the very condition the loan was meant to address. If the family had a house, or was fortunate enough to have some land, it was not in the woman's name. Her income was devoted to the family's needs: food, clothing, shelter, with little opportunity to save.

The SEWA members first address the situation by establishing the saving habit, as discussed before. As groups, usually of about 20, the women individually contribute Rs. 10 or Rs. 15 per month. It is a notable amount for the women, but would be considered an annoyance to most bank personnel who would have to facilitate the deposit. Instead, the women contribute their deposit into a group account that is itself deposited in the SEWA Bank.

For a minimum of one year, the women steadfastly make their deposits, cultivating the saving habit. Temptations as well as emergencies arise, and the women can face these with the support of the group. As the savings accumulate, many of the usual financial drains dissipate. The members appreciate the value of financial management as the interest appreciates. Ultimately, they become capable of taking loans, small at first, but growing with their experience.

Loans have ranged in size from Rs. 100 to Rs. 100,000 as they have also ranged in their purposes. Women have purchased cattle, tools of their trades, raw materials, and land. They have refinanced debts to moneylenders with sources offering more reasonable interest rates, among other things. SEWA members have also arranged for women to take special housing loans, for both improvements and new construction, on the condition that the houses are put in the women's names.

As the women have proven themselves bankable, other sources have opened up to them. The National Bank for Agriculture and Rural Development (NABARD) has incorporated the specific needs of the impoverished women and expanded opportunities available to them. As the members were still becoming accustomed to the loan process, loans were limited to the funds accumulated as a group. Now, as they enter the new millennium, they have achieved access to the conventional banking system as bankable people.

Capacity-building

Building the capacities of the poor is not only a means of utilizing the capital they have access to. It also allows them to continue to evolve on pace with an increasingly changing environment. Access to capital is far less valuable without access to technology, information, education, and skills. India is facing significant structural changes in its economy: shifts that traditionally have the greatest negative impact on the most vulnerable sectors in the market. However, capacity-building enables the poor to minimize their vulnerabilities and maximize their capabilities.

SEWA has invested a great deal in human capital. Members in Kutch and Banaskantha have further developed their traditional embroidery and patchwork and made it an occupation. Formerly innumerate savings group leaders have learnt advanced accounting procedures. Some members have learnt how to run tree nurseries. Others have learnt how to run a gram sabha. All the members have learnt to demand their rights.

SEWA members have acquired their skills and knowledge through many different means. Some members have traveled far to attend training programs. Some training programs have come to the members. The establishment of spearhead teams, which get especially intensive training and train others in return, has further enhanced the training. These teams consist of eight village leaders in their respective activities, as well as two organizers. There is a spearhead team for each activity in each district. The savings spearhead team from Kheda, one of the other rural districts where SEWA is active, goes to the SEWA Bank most weekends, or on a field visit to a district where SEWA is active. There, the Kheda savings spearhead team meets with the other savings spearhead teams from other districts. They discuss the others' difficulties and expand upon their training. The women then take these lessons back to their villages and put them into practice, sharing them with the members of their respective savings groups.

The SEWA members have learnt lessons through training as well as expanded experiences. The courage they take from the group enables the women to travel beyond their villages, which they were not previously allowed to do. They take loans and endeavor into income-generating ventures, showing a remarkable aptitude for entrepreneurial activity. In all these processes, they are building their own capacities to face the future challenges to their future success.

Access to Social Security

Access to social security allows the poor to focus on progress without having to be preoccupied with disaster. The vulnerabilities of the poor are inextricably linked to the fundamental necessities of life, health, home and occupation. With inadequate nutrition, substandard building materials, and little opportunity, the risks to life's necessities are chronic, and poverty is a continuous cycle. Social security reduces the severity of these risks and allows people to move forward rather than remain paralyzed by fear.

SEWA has addressed this issue from several directions. The most common source of debt to moneylenders is medical emergencies. In an unexpected and critical situation, many poor women are forced to turn to the money-lender to pay for a doctor's bill or medicines. Under these circumstances, the women are desperate and vulnerable to exploitative loan terms. Health insurance either enables these women to pay off these loans quickly, before interest piles up, or allows them to bypass the loan process all together.

The poor are also more vulnerable to natural disasters. Their homes are on marginal land, more prone to flood or drought, and sometimes both. The building materials are also marginal and prone to disintegration in high winds or rains. With their homes often go the vast majority of their assets and the tools of their trade, besides their shelter. Housing insurance, as well as access to resources for disaster-proofing homes, allows the SEWA members to weather the storms they face.

Insurance for damage from riots and insurance for the tools of trade are further examples of adapting an otherwise exclusionary institution to fit the needs of the poor. In addition, the implementation of these policies is unique. For some things, such as housing, SEWA organizers act as damage assessors, utilizing their familiarity with and proximity to the people affected in order to expedite an urgent process. In other ways, the organiz-ers also help the women navigate a process that requires a certain degree of literacy and familiarity with systems that have little precedent in the lives of the rural poor.

Collective Strength
through Organization

The SEWA organization brings a collective strength to the SEWA members and to the SEWA movement. This organization is the key to the whole process. Individually, the poor are often at the mercy of others and others' willingness to intervene on their behalf. Despite, and in many ways because of, the herculean efforts of most impoverished individuals to ensure their families' survival, they do not have the strength to struggle beyond the sub-sistence level. Yet, collectively, they have the ability to intervene on their own behalf. Organization gives them this perspective, power and leverage to struggle. Together, it is easier to find the solutions and fight for them.

Similarly, as a group, people can bring their diverse ideas and abilities together to simultaneously address the many problems they face, rather than mustering the strength to address only one at a time. The simultane-ous implementation of all the four aspects of the Millennium Campaign is essential for true achievement of their common goals. The lives of impov-erished rural women are complex. It follows that any effort to improve those lives has to be multi-dimensional to be effective. Addressing only one hardship at a time leaves the multitude of others to fill the void. Conversely, the separate initiatives of the Millennium Campaign support each other in their efforts.

However, the Millennium Campaign does not contain any elements that are new to SEWA. The campaign is an elaboration on the theme of the Ten Points, highlighted in the introduction to this book. In fact, per-haps the best way to measure the effects of SEWA's efforts in Banaskantha and Kutch is by SEWA's own standards. Listed below, these Ten Points are the strategic objectives that SEWA seeks to achieve for all its members. Listed below, these Ten Points are comprehensive in scope and provide a demanding standard by which to measure the progress described in this volume.

1. Increased Employment Opportunities

Since its inception, SEWA has identified the need for employment as the primary need of its members. Every other goal listed below can only be achieved to a sustainable level when access to employment is assured. In rural areas, this need has been emphasized even more due to the initial lack of employment opportunities. The rural economy is too often mono-dimensional, with agriculture as the sole sector of significance. Poor land and water resources, combined with drought, translate into mass under-employment and unemployment.

The lack of employment leaves little opportunity for income. Without income, there is poor nutrition, health care is unaffordable, childcare impossible, housing options marginal, with no asset, no organization and no leadership, and no place for self-reliance in their lexicon. Employment is not only the foundation of the economy, but the society as well.

Since 1989 (in Banaskantha) and 1993 (in Kutch), the women of SEWA have made tremendous strides in generating income opportunities for themselves and their communities. They have literally revived rural industries, such as dairy production, that had previously succumbed to the harsh circumstances. A further example is agricultural production, steadily increased by prudently building up the water-harvesting capacity at a suitable and sustainable pace.

The result is that more hands are needed to collect the milk and harvest the crops. Previously, much of the milk was only produced on a subsistence level. Now, milk produced in Banaskantha is consumed throughout the state, and the industry has grown to keep pace. The consistently growing number of BDMSA milk cooperatives, from none in 1989, to 11 working and 16 more proposed in 1999, is testimony to the increasing opportunity for employment in the field.

Fields that previously produced one meager, withered crop, now produce an abundant harvest, sometimes even twice or thrice a year. As this increased production requires more hands to reap the crop, more hands reap the benefits as well. With an increase in employment opportunities, many other opportunities come into reach. SEWA has been instrumental in achieving this goal and has also continued to build on the progress.

2. Increased Income

The rise in demand for labor from increased employment opportunities has had a predictably positive effect on wages. In 1989, when agricultural work was scarce and only temporary when available, the normal wages were as low as Rs. 10 per day. In 1999, wages were as high as Rs. 60 per day in Banaskantha. Furthermore, those wages are possible for many more days out of the year and for many more people.

In a similar vein, employment options have also increased, with their effect on opportunity and income. For example, craft production has been shifted from a part-time leisure activity to a full-time occupation. Previously, women would usually embroider only when there was no work in the fields. Even for those who sold to the traders, the wages for agricultural work outweighed the reward for producing crafts.

Now, the situation has reversed. The women will only answer the increased demand in the fields when the wages provide sufficient incentive above and beyond the benefits of craftwork. Thus, the other employment options have themselves played a significant hand in raising the agricultural wage rate, which is, as mentioned before, the foundation of the rural labor market. It has soaked up some of the surplus labor and given the workers bargaining power.

Ownership of the means of production has also become a reality that has increased the income of these women. Salt farming, for example, had previously been an entry point to the cycle of debt and indentured servitude. With access to start-up capital that provides for ownership of the means of production, some women have been able to shift cycles. Debt has been replaced by profit and obligations replaced by further opportunity.

The sum of the increased employment opportunities can be added up in rupees. When these rupees are then put in the hands of the women, it translates more directly into health and happiness for the whole family. For the poor women of Banaskantha and Kutch, with increased income, life's necessities suddenly become affordable.

3. Improved Nutrition

The most immediate necessity for the rural poor is nutrition, and it can only be achieved on a sustainable basis once employment and income are secured. Good nutrition is crucial for good health, personal strength and the ability to work. Without food, you do not have energy. Without energy, you cannot work. Without work, you get no income. Without income, you cannot get food. This cycle of deterioration can only be overcome with a consistent income.

The government has placed much emphasis on meeting the poor halfway on this endeavor of assuring food. The fair price shops offer food at a subsidized rate that is more affordable to the poor and less susceptible to fluctuations in price. However, for the rural poor, the answer is not always so simple. The poor quality of the rationed food, the abuses of the shopkeepers responsible for distributing it, and the inaccessibility of the shops can still inhibit the rural poor from achieving good nutrition.

SEWA's answer to this, the Shakti Packet, has come a long way in filling the gap. In the most remote villages, where there are no fair price shops, the Shakti Packet is there. The quality of the food is the best available, and it is specific to the communities' tastes. The Shakti Packet compensates for the challenges of isolation and inadequate management of resources, making it possible for the women to put their hard-earned money to the best use possible.

Furthermore, the value of the Shakti Packet is underlined in a time of emergency, such as the flood in 1997. In rural areas, where the supply lines can be tenuous, nutrition is one of the points of greatest risk. The Shakti Packet addresses this risk and helps ensure that the community has the energy to survive and rebuild when the emergency subsides.

4. Improved Access to Healthcare

The first step towards better health is good nutrition. But, accidents and disease are a fact of life, and their consequences can have a negative impact in many areas. With employment as the basis for sustainable development, SEWA has given priority attention to occupational health. For example, eye clinics for the craftswomen have directly addressed the hazards of that line of work. In addition to improving the quality of life, the curative aspect of the effort improves productivity. Women who had previously had poor vision are suddenly able to see their work more clearly, work faster and at a higher level of quality.

The mobile van represents the great lengths to which SEWA can go to ensure that their members' health is looked after. The salt workers have the bad combination of an occupation conducive to poor health and isolation from conventional health facilities. Yet, even they are brought into the health fold every month.

In addition to the direct delivery of services, should the need arise, the assurance of future medical help is there. The insurance scheme is an affordable safety net that addresses one of the greatest threats to financial solvency and provides accessibility to professional health care. Moneylenders generate a large proportion of their business providing funds for health emergencies. Having insurance prevents poor health from infecting other aspects of life, such as income and assets.

5. Improved Access to Childcare

Women are the ones who assume the greatest responsibility for taking care of the children. This responsibility has its rewards, but it also has its burdens. In a poor rural household, where every income-earner counts, the constant care and supervision a child requires can be counterproductive in relation to the family's other needs, such as food, clothing and shelter.

For example, salt farming is a labor-intensive occupation that makes childcare a challenging task. Production of salt itself requires great care and attention. Furthermore, it is undertaken in conditions of extreme heat in an area where relief from the sun is not readily available. In short, it is no place for a child. SEWA's part in advocacy of childcare centers for families in this occupation has significantly improved the situation. Not only are these children supervised. Their diets are augmented and their health monitored. Meanwhile, the women are able to devote their time to making income to support their families.

6. Improved Housing, Water and Sanitation

As one of the starting points of the efforts in Banaskantha, the provision of water has greatly improved. Its availability has had an immeasurable but strong impact in many ways. Water is the basis of good sanitation, and the improved supply has undoubtedly reduced the prevalence of the factors that contribute to the spread of disease. Water is also essential for hygiene, another component of good health.

But, access to water has provided another boon that ties in to the other points in this conclusion. Easy access to water allows women more time to fulfill some of their other multitude of duties. In some cases, village ponds or recharged wells have cut by hours the time a woman has to spend fetching water. The implications of this fact are many, including the increased time available for income-generating activities.

Better housing also has an impact on the time commitments of poor women. Houses made of mud and dung require frequent repair and even complete reconstruction in the case of heavy rains. These tasks mean a great deal of time spent by the women that could be spent more gainfully. The housing loan scheme addresses this issue head on, allowing the women to build homes that are stronger, more resistant to the elements and less demanding of time.

A further advantage of a house made of better materials is the fact that it protects the woman's livelihood. Artisans, for example, need to store their tools, raw materials and finished products in a place where they are safe from rain, sun, and dirt. Otherwise, their value is lost. In addition, the women's other assets are protected and the fruits of their labor safe.

7. Increased Assets

The consolidation of all these gains, as well as the assurance that they will continue to grow, is achieved through the increase of assets in the women's names. Although they are the most effective managers of assets, women rarely have that chance. SEWA has counteracted that tradition and the members are in many ways increasing the assets in their name. Their houses are in their names. They are expanding their herds with cattle in their own names. All across the spectrum of occupations, they are building their productive assets in particular.

The capacity of poor women to manage these assets is also growing. They learn to save their money on a regular basis and pay back loans at a rate that is more reliable than that of any other sector of the human population. As their ownership of assets and ability to manage them increases, the women are preparing themselves to continue the progress at an ever-increasing rate.

Also, the women themselves become assets to their communities. They actively generate employment opportunities. They improve their environment through social forestry and erosion control. As a group, with their collective strength, they make their voices heard for better and more efficient use of resources for the development of their communities.

8. Strengthening of the Organization

With every individual success, the organization becomes stronger. The collective power of the members creates a synergy that can make an impact at the highest levels. For example, the gum collectors have struggled vigorously against one of the most notoriously difficult government agencies. The fact that the gum collectors, among the poorest of the poor rural women, have been able to make their demands heard by a seemingly indifferent bureaucracy is a victory in itself.

There have been plenty of other clear-cut victories that members have won for themselves. Each member, whose income rises, is a victory for all the members of the organization. Each woman, who builds a new and better house in her name, is a victory for all the members of the organization. Each victory gives the members and their organization leverage. The bargaining power they accumulate, through the example of their success and the freedom from debt and oppression they achieve, allows the organization to continue to grow and achieve collectively.

9. Strengthening of Women's Leadership

Likewise, with every success the organization enjoys, the individuals become stronger. What it means to be a SEWA member has continued to gain significance, and the activity in Banaskantha has made a large contribution to that effect. As the organization has become stronger, the women have had more opportunity to take leadership roles. Members from many backgrounds have shared their experiences with people from ministers of state to the district officials. In the process, these same members have made their demands known.

Most importantly, they have made these demands in the same manner as they have begun to do many other things: with confidence. Their confidence derives from their newfound knowledge of themselves, their acquired appreciation for their role in society and their profound self-respect. In short, they have become empowered.

These leadership instincts have been further developed through capacity-building. Their leadership ability begins to grow as they learn more about their trade and organize around it. Leaders arise in craft groups, among gum collectors, and salt farmers. They learn from each other and through the various training programs in which they participate. Emboldened by their experience and the interaction they share, they step further and more confidently. They also encourage their other SEWA sisters along the way.

10. Increased Self-reliance

Invigorated by good nutrition, strengthened by good health, free from the constant obligations of childcare, supported by a good home and the independence that assets afford, and encouraged by a sense of belonging and the experience of leadership behind them, these women are increasingly self-reliant. They now have alternatives in life. They have options for employment. They can choose how to spend the money they earn.

The women also choose the direction they want their organization to take. They have decided to add two more goals to the list: increase access to education for themselves and their children and increase access to energy. Many have traveled to other parts of the state, the country, and some even to other parts of the world. They have shaped greater expectations from life and are increasingly learning how to make the necessary progress. If the investment in capacity-building is the best approach toward self-reliance, then self-reliance is the best strategy toward assuring that all these points are not only achieved, but are also self-sustainable.

A collective effort, and the organized strength it engenders, enables the poor to actively implement such strategies for themselves. Because the poor are intimately aware of their position, and more determined than anybody to alleviate the condition, their voices need to be heard at every stage from planning to implementation. More so than any others, individually, the poor are weak. But, collectively, they have a wealth of experiences and abilities that increases their strength beyond their numbers.

Biography: Destined to Be Together

Mumtazben comes from the town of Radhanpur. As the commercial and political center of the western Banaskantha, Radhanpur is a relatively active town and a hub for the surrounding villages. Partly for this reason, Radhanpur has been the headquarters for SEWA's work. If SEWA had not come to Radhanpur, however, Mumtazben would have probably missed out on the active life she now pursues.

In 1989, when her cousin Sairaben took a job with SEWA, the new women's group in town, it caused quite a stir in the household. Young women taking work independently, with people who were new in the area, was not acceptable. It was not acceptable to the family, nor was it generally acceptable to the community in general. But, Sairaben is a tough-willed, independent person.

Sairaben was the first local organizer to join SEWA in Banaskantha, and immediately she acquired passion for her work: the kind of passion one tries to share with friends. Mumtazben and Sairaben were not only cousins, but also best friends. As such, Sairaben told her cousin everything about her new experiences and tried to furtively convince Mumtazben to join, too.

Mumtazben was interested but knew her own parents would oppose. Meanwhile, Sairaben told Reemaben, the coordinator of SEWA's new office in Banaskantha, all about her cousin. Sairaben praised Mumtazben's strength, intelligence and hard work and convinced Reemaben that she should meet Mumtazben. Like elopers, the two cousins stealthily sneaked out of their house one night and went where Reemaben was staying. The three of them talked for hours about SEWA and the plans for Banaskantha. Mumtazben was enthralled with the experience and that night became determined to follow in Sairaben's footsteps.

Mumtazben and Sairaben tactfully persisted with their family members to convince them to agree to let Mumtazben join SEWA. They used many angles but found the most success when they argued that, if the two of them were working together, it would be much safer and less scandalous. The team effort worked, and the family relented.

Mumtazben began as a dairy organizer. This activity underwent a period of rapid growth when SEWA began, and Mumtazben played a key role. She worked hard to help rebuild the collapsed dairy cooperative system and contributed significantly to the progress. Therefore, once craft activity began to grow, Mumtazben was shifted to help guide it successfully. Again, she proved her cousin's earlier praise well-deserved and found herself taking on more and more responsibilities.

Today, Mumtazben is the local coordinator of the BDMSA. In this position, she manages an organization of 40,000 women. She had been educated up to the seventh standard. In the face of the difficulties she overcame to get so far, this is a notable achievement. However, for some, an education limited to this level could be debilitating while trying to tackle a complex management portfolio. Mumtazben, however, has found the inner strength to rise to the challenge. Reemaben, who originally recruited Mumtazben, particularly cites her strength in crisis management. From a major relief effort after the devastating cyclone of 1999, to an early tempest within the BDMSA office itself along religious lines, Mumtazben has been the one to bring the calm after the storm. These are skills of character, not the classroom.

Now she works long hours and jokes with Sairaben about how they are always missing family functions because they have work to do. They do not mind and find that their family does not mind either. The family has a great deal of pride in and respect for their daughters. They would like to have more time with them, but what do you expect when daughters elope? Especially in this case, since they eloped with 40,000 other women!

Chapter 11

A DIFFERENT KIND OF DEREGULATION

Feeling that 'informal sector' does not adequately describe the breadth or magnitude of the 93 percent of the working population that the phrase was meant to describe, Ela Bhatt has begun to use a different nomenclature: the 'people's sector.' The people's sector encompasses the same contract, casual, and piece-rate laborers, vendors, small-scale entrepreneurs and others that the informal sector is meant to denote. However, the 'people's sector' claims more accurately the significance that the work of these individuals deserves. The people's sector, along with the public sector and private sector, is meant to be a part of the triumvirate of economic activity. Conventional thought may cast doubt on the legitimacy of the assertions of a people's sector, but a brief consideration of the actual proportions of the Indian economy indicates that it is, at the least, the third sector. Though, perhaps, it should be considered first.

As it is considered now, under the titles of 'informal' or 'unorganized,' this sector is defined in an overtly negative manner. Among the implications is the idea that the informal sector's lack of formality precludes it from being a significant contributor to the economy. As the unorganized sector, it is assumed to be inherently inefficient. The reality is that the people's sector is already a significant part of every aspect of the national economy, and the globalization process is making it even larger.

While it largely relies on the public and private sectors for marketing and infrastructure, it is feasible that the people's sector is responsible for at least a third of national production. Agriculture is the largest source of production in India. Similarly, agricultural labor, the single largest source of employment in the country, is the exclusive domain of the people's sector. The people's sector also accounts for a significant portion of the service industry, especially when one considers domestic service in all its forms.

Next, among SEWA's first members were head-loaders and cart-pullers. Add to their numbers the camel- and bullock-cart drivers, as well as the independent taxi and rickshaw drivers, and the sum is a significant portion of the transportation industry that lies within the auspices of the people's sector. Thus, while the people's sector largely relies on the public and private sectors for infrastructure and marketing, the latter two also rely heavily on the people's sector for production, services, and transportation. This interdependence should convey mutual interest in each other's welfare.

By currently accepted measures of production in terms of monetary value, the people's sector is not as large as the number of people involved would indicate. While 93 percent of the Indian population works in the people's sector, an equal percentage of the gross national product does not come from that source. However, this imbalance is not a reflection of the inactivity of the vast majority of the population. Rather, it is a reflection of the lack of infrastructure, capital, skills, information, and independence that has been afforded to the people's sector. It is an improvement on this paucity of employment related resources, and not some ill-conceived charity to compensate for the troubles of transition, that should be considered in the course of the liberalization process that India now faces.

SEWA's experience indicates that there are ways to bring increased infrastructure, capital, skills, information and independence to the people's sector in a way that is in complete harmony with the liberalization process. Through organization and capacity-building, local communities are capable of expanding and managing their own resources. There is also a wide base of traditional skills, which, if recognized and nurtured, can become competitive in the marketplace. Organized and informed, the people's sector is 'bankable.' Together, they may no longer be limited by custom and geography to the sphere of their village, where they face a monopolistic market because their options are only as great as the number of middlemen dealing with them.

Through cooperatives, mandals, unions and other forms of organization, the people's sector can keep pace with broadening markets. Organization can incorporate the people's sector into the global economy. However, the global economy has to make an effort to incorporate the people's sector. The alternative includes ever-widening societal gaps in income and information, excluding the majority of the world's population. In the long run, this would make the reach of the economy anything but global. The people's sector is not part of the problem. It is part of the solution.

As India enters an era of deregulation, much of the national and international focus is on software, information technology and other large, promising industries. Furthermore, the focus within that focus is on changes at the highest levels. The voices for change come mostly from large domestic producers and even larger multinationals. The changes they are lobbying for, if implemented judiciously, could ultimately have positive results. However, past experiences with deregulation around the world have had mixed results, and many people are justified in their doubts. The only certainty is that the poor are the most vulnerable to the negative impacts of any changes. The reasons for their vulnerability are several. But, chief among them is the fact that there has traditionally been little room for the voice of the poor in the economic liberalization dialogue. Therefore, it has often been their short- and long-term well-being that has been compromised, either knowingly or unknowingly.

Institutions such as the World Bank and various other development agencies have made an effort to reform their own historically destructive policies in order to minimize the negative impact of economic restructuring on the poor. These reforms are the brainchildren of highly trained economists and other social scientists and professionals. Indeed, their fields have become increasingly focused on protecting the interests of the vulnerable in a process dominated by the powerful, as partly evidenced by the rising stature of welfare economics. However, their voice for the poor should not be mistaken for the voice of the poor.

Though they do not have academic degrees, and more often than not, cannot even read or write, the poor have something to offer to the development debate. SEWA's experience is an illustration of the value of their potential contribution. What the SEWA members catalyzed after their interaction with the Chief Minister of Gujarat, for example, was a different kind of deregulation—different from the high-level restructuring that generally dominates both government and private sector attention.

The different kind of deregulation that SEWA achieved does not contradict the general direction of the more conventional deregulation reforms. The SEWA effort complements and deepens the other changes and brings the benefits to those who are otherwise neglected, balancing the liberalization process. While AT&T presses the Indian government to loosen its grip on telecommunications, Honda lobbies for lower import tariffs, or Tata Steel argues for decreased public sector competition, what similar abundantly resourceful salt, tree or gum mega-company can likewise press for an end to counterproductive government over-involvement in those respective sectors? Even if such unlikely entities do exist, their motivations would probably not be necessarily devoted to improving the lot of the small producer. The mega-companies will instead focus attention on unlocking the potential of the educated, English-speaking, technology-oriented Indian workforce, and gaining access to the middle-class consumers. While the size of this Indian middle-class population, at least 200 million strong, is large by most standards, it is still dwarfed by comparison with the 800 million other Indians of less interest to those looking for emerging markets.

However, issues facing the poorest of the poor in India are not entirely different from those facing the emerging corporate classes. The Permit Raj stifled entrepreneurs at all levels, as the policies of the Forestry Department made painfully apparent. Now, as the regulations begin to melt, SEWA members have weighed in for the small, self-employed producers. Considered in the context of the macro-level changes taking place globally, SEWA's achievement is not only in concert with development opinion. The voice of the SEWA members provides the missing harmony to the chorus of other powerful voices calling for deregulation.

Stability during Transition

A primary threat to Indian society in the coming years, and especially to the poorer sections of that society, will be that of transition. The transition brought about by the economic reforms will be comprehensive and not only limited to the economic sphere. Methods of production will shift as new technologies are introduced. The products produced will change as new relationships of comparative advantage are introduced. Income gaps will increase. Employment opportunities will disappear in old sectors, and hopefully reappear in new, but will certainly require different skills. Public services such as healthcare and utilities will become increasingly privatized. Even the spread of consumer products, such as television, to villages will have an impact as the values and aspirations of rural society are shaped by images of life radically different from their own.

Most changes, including those just mentioned, have already begun to take place. These changes are heavily influenced by Western society. However, Western society has experienced a much less turbulent transition period than India is likely in for. In the West, the liberalization process grew out of a natural cultural and intellectual continuum, dating back to Adam Smith and before. Over the course of centuries, Europe and North America integrated the changes now culminating under the aegis of economic liberalization, at a natural and gradual rate.

In India, the process of liberalization is being accelerated and imposed. Centuries of change are being condensed into Five-Year Plans. Industries and institutions that have long evolved along one line are suddenly being restructured along sometimes radically different lines. The impetus for these changes largely originates from the external payments crisis and subsequent conditions of the 1991 International Monetary Fund loan that obligated India to adopt an aggressive economic reform package. Thus, external rather than internal pressure initiated and continues to drive the liberalization process. All these factors should raise serious concerns over the implementation of the imminent reforms.

Though humans instinctively fear change, it is the most constant, natural and pervasive state in the world. Reform itself is not inherently bad. In fact, several reforms have been among SEWA's main objectives. It is the manner of the reforms that is important. As mentioned, liberalization is often an unbalanced affair. As in most debates at a national level, it is the most powerful, and not necessarily the most practical, who have the most influence. Under such circumstances, it is usually the government that has the responsibility of pursuing the interests of those who otherwise do not have the resources to participate in the debate.

However, the liberalization debate is unique in the sense that part of the principle is to disenfranchise the state from directly providing many of the services of vital interest to its citizenry. Though this does not limit the government in its capacity to argue on behalf of most policies aimed at protecting the poor during the restructuring, it does remove many of the safety nets that would be crucial in the event of the failure of the accepted policies to protect the vulnerable sectors of the population. Limiting the role of the government in this manner opens a void that could swallow the fates of a great many people.

Community-based organizations, like SEWA, have the potential capacity to fill the void left by the disenfranchisement of the state in the liberalization process. In a society such as India, where a tradition of social service has become part of the fabric of life, an abrupt end to such services could have a disastrous effect. The list of such services includes not only health care, but also such fundamental necessities as food for a still highly disaster-prone population, or water and electricity for communities that may not independently have the resources to acquire such things. In some cases, a culture of dependency has evolved. However, to immediately sever such relationships would now be even more dangerous than continuing them.

Community-based organizations are an alternative between dependency on the government and helplessness. Such organizations are a bridge between the state and civil society that can improve communication between the two and also fulfill more effectively many of the roles sometimes considered the exclusive domain of one or the other. As an entity representing hundreds and even thousands of people, a community-based organization can incorporate into one single voice the cacophony of voices, often calling for the same thing but in different words. The size of the organization not only brings unity in voice, but also gains the attention of the leaders in a democratic society. Beyond that, an established organization can earn the credibility needed in order to be entrusted to manage the resources and to put the words into action.

Community-based organizations also offer an alternative in that they can provide a host of services, but in a manner that avoids a dependency relationship. Or, rather, community-based organizations can provide those services in a manner that fosters self-dependency. The communities themselves choose the manner in which the services are provided and take an explicit interest in encouraging their sustainability. These roles can be particularly important at a time such as the present in India when changes of such import are on the horizon.

The SEWA experience shows that leadership for the community and by the community can be effective. The SEWA experience further points out that impoverished rural women have many significant contributions to make to the development process, as empowered participants, and as leaders. However, for this participation and leadership to be effective, the women must be given the opportunity to develop their own abilities as income-earners and as leaders.

Employment and income are the first interventions because of their centrality to all other aspects of life. An employed person can afford to send her children to school. An employed person can afford to avail herself of medical services when she is ill, or even to prevent many illnesses in the first place. Certainly, improvements need to be made with the public education system and the public health system in India. However, if children are needed to supplement the household income in order that the family can eat, they cannot go to school, no matter how good that school may be. As the needs for medical care increase with rising expectations and technological input, the expenses needed to cover those costs will also increase. Employment covers those costs on an individual and social scale, and it does so on a self-maintaining basis. The power that employment brings is the power to afford sustainable progress in the quality of life, and not just temporary improvements. Yet, why does the Human Development Index, praised for its sensitivity in ascertaining the human condition through instruments beyond GDP statistics, not have any measure for employment? Employment must be recognized for its true value.

In addition to recognizing the primacy of employment in bringing about sustainable development, the importance of time must also be more fully realized. As the current process goes, most development projects have time-frames thrust upon them that are entirely determined outside the affected community. In some cases, these time-frames are unrealistic, and this can result in retribution against the community and hypocrisy on the part of the development agency involved when the goals are not met. Instead, the process of formulating the manner of intervention and the period over which it is to be implemented should be a shared decision between the community and the other institutions involved. This role can be facilitated by community-based organizations.

SEWA members generally envision a process of deregulation that does not eliminate the role of the government, but streamlines the ways in which the state becomes involved. India is the world's biggest democracy. It has over 600 million eligible voters. But, democracy and citizenship do not rest on the vote alone. Democracy is a partnership between the government and the people. It is too easily assumed that power rests in government, but in reality that is no basis for a true democracy. For the relationship to function properly, the local communities need to be empowered, enabling them to fulfill their duties as full partners. The most successful partnerships are those that exist between equals. Those who enter into such a relationship must be equally empowered, equally capable and equally clear about their goals and respon-sibilities. SEWA's role has been to help facilitate the local communities' abilities to fulfill their duties as partners in India's development endeavor.

In the process of deregulation advocated by the IMF and others, the state transfers many responsibilities to civil society. In the process of deregulation that SEWA is trying to put forward, the civil society assumes many of those responsibilities in a manner that will not alienate or jeopardize the vulner-able sectors of the population. The IMF focuses on capital-equipped private interests assuming the role of directing the development of the industrial sector. SEWA focuses on organized private interests, in the form of community-based organizations, assuming the role of directing the development of the people's sector.

Essentially, development should become privatized in the sense that the private citizens most directly involved in the development process should be the ones who identify the needs, choose among the courses of action and implement the decisions. SEWA's first intervention along these lines is to generate awareness among the community members. Once they are consciously aware of their needs, organization enables them to articulate their demands in a clear and unified voice.

Even in 'liberalized' Western economies, the state is the single largest repository of societal resources. Such will continue to be the case in India, although the degree of direct involvement by the government will decrease over time. However, the government will still play a significant role in many ways, one of which is by deciding the allocation of the resources at its disposal. Thus, it is the responsibility of the communities, as partners, to clearly express the need and how it could best be addressed.

The SEWA experience offers many insights into how the process of sustainable development can be undertaken. The efforts must be demand-driven and need-based. To achieve this end, awareness must be generated, and the ability to effect change must be cultivated, and the change must be inclusive of the poor and women. Organization and capacity-building should be the means. The goal should be progress that is appropriate in the Indian context, driven by the values and fully realized capacities of all sectors of the Indian nation, especially the otherwise neglected sectors of the population. There were strong elements of these principles in India's struggle for independence from colonialism, and those, too, have since been developed even further. The same ideas of empowerment and self-worth should now guide India in the struggle of the whole population for its economic independence, as it struggles towards its second freedom.

Biography: Model Entrepreneur

Ramibai had a multitude of jobs before she became a SEWA member. She had participated in the government's drought-relief earth-digging program, fetched water for other people, cleaned houses and made craft products for the Gujarat State Handicraft Development Corporation. But, those days are all behind her now. Parallel to her days of multifarious employment, she now has acquired training in a whole spectrum of skills.

To begin with, as a SEWA member, Ramibai has had training in team-building. She learned how to encourage communication and trust while leading the group towards productive goals. She used this training first as a leader of Nani Nakhatrana's craft group. Since then, that group has become a primary source of income for the members.

Ramibai's leadership skills proved so effective with the craft group that she was later chosen a leader of one of the village's three savings groups. As a leader there, she has helped the savings group rapidly evolve to the point where they have become consistent savers and highly capable borrowers. Her group was one of the first ones to implement the Internal Lending System, and to meet with much success there.

Ramibai has also had training in marketing. Like many of her SEWA sisters, she has utilized this training by working at exhibitions. However, one of the more innovative ways she has put this training into action is by spreading the word about her craft group to the taxi drivers in the area. In an area frequented by tourists, this strategy has brought results on many occasions.

Ramibai has also had training in developing the characteristics of a leader. She has been able to put this training to good use as President of the Kutch Craft Association. She has learnt to gain the trust of the fellow-members and be reliable in her duties. Furthermore, she has learnt a lot about her organization through SEWA's Members' Education. Ramibai now has a much deeper understanding of the full breadth of the activities SEWA is involved in, and the Gandhian spirit behind them. Combining her leadership skills with her deep understanding of the organization she leads, she has been prepared well for her position.

Lastly, she also uses her understanding of the organization and her leadership skills as part of the savings spearhead team. Her responsibilities with this team include recruiting new groups and training and monitoring their members and leaders. It is perhaps in this position that she has to utilize her training most. To recruit new groups effectively, she does not need to generate interest. The demand for new groups is strong. But, she does have to impress upon the new members the spirit behind what they are doing. It is the clear understanding of what it is to be a leader and a SEWA member that helps her motivate the new savings groups to be strong and disciplined.

However, her responsibilities at the district level have not forced her to neglect her duties in her village. In fact, it has helped her do a better job. As a member of the savings spearhead team, Ramibai went on an exposure trip that introduced her to the concept of the Internal Lending System. She was inspired by the practicality and possibilities of the system and told fellow-members about it. Now, hers is one of three savings groups in the district that have begun to rotate their funds internally. All the members including her have taken loans, and she has purchased a ghee-making machine so that she can increase her income from her growing herd of cows and buffaloes.

However, the peak of her entrepreneurship is represented by the new tractor sitting in her front yard. In the past six years, she has been gradually building her productive assets and financial skills to the point where she is able to go to a conventional bank and take a loan. Her savings group cannot yet provide the Rs. 30,000 Ramibai needed for the down payment on the tractor, but it did give her the confidence and ability needed to get the loan from the bank. Now, she rents the tractor out to other farmers, and will soon have the loan paid back.

As a corollary to her success in grass-roots capitalism, Ramibai has discovered that good fortune follows those who take chances. She made the large investment in the tractor, planning that it would pay for itself over time. What Ramibai did not plan on was winning the raffle that was part of the sales promotion at the tractor dealership. However, the nice cold water from the new refrigerator that was the prize is a welcome sight when she and her family get home from a profitable day in the fields.

Epilogue

EARTHQUAKE RELIEF
AND RECOVERY

On the morning of 26 January 2001, as some in Gujarat were gathering for the public celebrations of Republic Day and others either enjoying their day of rest or working as usual, a violent earthquake rocked the state and brought on a minute and a half of destruction, from which many will never recover. The earthquake measured 7.9 on the Richter scale, with the epicenter 20 kilometers from the main city of Bhuj, in the district of Kutch. Shock waves leveled buildings, pipelines were broken, wells caved in, bridges collapsed and communication was severed. The terror of the cataclysmic event soon gave way to the realization that the loss of life and property represented one of the most tragic natural disasters in modern history.

The scope of the damage was so comprehensive that, even months after the earthquake, the total losses are still difficult to estimate. Some of the more widely cited estimates include 30,000 deaths and 325,000 houses collapsed. However, the grief and suffering cannot be measured, perhaps not even imagined, by those not forced to live through it. Many of the survivors had to come to terms with their losses in their villages, isolated from relief, homeless, without food or water, and living in fear of recurrent aftershocks that would not let them mourn in peace.

Progress for the BDMSA and the Kutch Craft Association had been steady in the face of the drought that had occupied the year between the occurrence of the earthquake and the period over which the preceding pages were written. Local leaders gained in experience, as even more leaders arose in the villages throughout the respective districts. With their emergence, the district associations also became increasingly capable and independent. Through diverse and intense efforts in marketing, sales in goods ranging from crafts and gum to trees and milk rose steadily. Furthermore, through the hardships of drought, these efforts were proving themselves to be sustainable. Even fodder and water supplies, through the crucial organizational efforts of the members, were holding out. The earthquake wiped out some of that progress, and put much of the rest at risk.

Kutch and Banaskantha, as well as Surendranagar, where SEWA is also active, were the most heavily affected districts from the earthquake. The 60,000 members in these districts were of immediate concern to SEWA, and the district federations throughout the state were quick to respond. While Banaskantha and Kutch were among the pioneers of the SEWA movement in rural areas, they were not alone by 2001. On 27 January, the day after the earthquake, a team of organizers from SEWA and the Disaster Mitigation Institute left Ahmedabad for areas closer to the epicenter, while another team of SEWA organizers from several districts assembled in Ahmedabad. The latter team discussed an overall strategy and returned to their own districts for a comprehensive damage assessment. As each of the team members returned from the districts other than Banaskantha, Kutch and Surendranagar, they fortunately were able to report little serious damage. At this early stage, it was only just becoming apparent what had happened in the northern districts.

Therefore, the organizers from the non-affected districts divided up and went to the three affected districts, meeting with the local teams and making the first trips to the villages. Before two weeks had passed, over 50 SEWA organizers and leaders from around the state had set up headquarters in Radhanpur and Bhuj. Their first priority was to support relief, to ascertain quickly the immediate needs of their members and the communities in which they lived as well as other villages in the area. The immediate task was to get the appropriate resources to those who needed them.

However, the first team that left Ahmedabad for Banaskantha and Kutch the day after the earthquake had a different experience. After quick preparations, this team of organizers from SEWA and a team from the DMI were dispatched from the quickly evolving earthquake response headquarters for SEWA in Ahmedabad. The damaged communication lines throughout the region in the hours after the earthquake left everyone unsure of what to expect. So, the first team was to provide a damage assessment and report back to Ahmedabad, where phone lines were restored.

The assessment team's first stop was Radhanpur at the BDMSA office. The local leaders had no way to communicate with Ahmedabad, but they had overcome their own losses and were doing what they could. The BDMSA organizers had already visited a few villages while two others from the local team were working at the local government hospital. The Radhanpur hospital was the functionally undamaged hospital nearest to the epicenter and many refugees seeking care had already come there. Over the next few days, Radhanpur became a main destination for a stream of families seeking medical attention and relief.

One member from the SEWA team and one from the DMI team remained in Banaskantha to survey villages and report back to Ahmedabad, while the rest headed for Kutch for the same purpose. As the team approached Bhuj, the magnitude of the devastation became clearer. The frequency of collapsed buildings increased with every mile. Bhuj itself was pandemonium. As those present described it, people were running around for many hours even after the earthquake, with fear and panic almost as intense as when the tremor was occurring. The Kutch Craft Association office was still standing, but damaged beyond repair and likely to collapse. Those from Ahmedabad searched out the organizers living in Bhuj to learn of their condition. Fortunately, all were alive, though they had lost homes and some had lost family members. The expanded Kutch team offered each other what support and relief they could, and those who could manage to do so began their journeys to the villages.

From the initial and sporadic reports from Banaskantha and Radhanpur, and other information reaching Ahmedabad, SEWA arranged the first shipment of relief goods to the affected areas by the morning of the 28 January. These trucks were filled with water, dry foods, and blankets for villages apparently in the greatest need. But, the need was significant and the relief effort had to be expanded in a manner that was as efficient and appropriate as possible under the circumstances.

As a labor union, why did SEWA feel compelled to plunge into the relief and rehabilitation effort? The most immediate answer is the concern of the organization about its members. Beyond the bonds of friendship and family that members from other districts had developed in their work with members from the affected areas, they had also entered together under a contract. The obligations of that contract are embodied in the Ten Points discussed before, and the earthquake adversely affected every one of those points. At the personal level, members lost their homes, tools, and other assets. Some suffered injury or worse to themselves or their families. As communities, they lost their resources for childcare, water and healthcare. The interpersonal relationships forged through SEWA compelled those members in the unaffected areas to respond to the need of their sisters.

At the organizational level, it was apparent that SEWA was in one of the strongest positions for any institution to contribute to the relief and recovery effort. Physical structures had collapsed, but the mechanisms of the organization, experience, personnel and structure, were more resilient and likely to be intact or easily repaired. The BDMSA and the Kutch Craft

Association were conceived and nurtured in an atmosphere of adversity, coping with droughts and cyclones since their adolescence. The earthquake doubtless dealt a blow to the district associations' evolving independence. However, these district associations represented one of the few, if not the only, extensively experienced, capable and community-based organizations in the area heavily affected by the earthquake. The implications of this unique position—in the face of what immediately loomed as the task of ascertaining the specific needs of the community and navigating the channels of emergency distribution of resources—meant that the BDMSA and the Kutch Craft Association had an obligation to contribute. Toward that end, SEWA's initial efforts were focused on supporting the district organizations and linking them with aid resources.

Therefore, once the general situation in the districts was understood, some organizers and leaders met in Ahmedabad to plan and take action on a larger scale. The most immediate need was that of gathering information. Those who had already visited some of the villages reported their own discussions and observations with the affected communities, and guided the formation of an emergency survey. It had to be basic, because it had to be fast. But, it also had to strike at the heart of the needs and demands of the communities. This was action research that had to provide accurate answers to questions that were understandable to the community, and information that could immediately direct an appropriate response. From this meeting, the SEWA earthquake response quickly went into action.

At an increasing pace with each passing day, over 50 organizers and grassroots researchers went from house to house in over 120 villages and 48,000 households. With their survey, they ascertained:

- the extent of damage to the houses, from habitable to heavily damaged or fully collapsed;
- the loss of household goods, with additional focus on tools, equipment and other productive assets;
- the number and type of injuries suffered; and
- the damage to community resources such as childcare centers, community halls, water supply and health facilities.

The teams did not just gather information, but disseminated it as well. In almost all these communities, the research teams were the first to arrive and inform the community members of the government response at that point, and of what to expect in the future, with relief materials immediately in their wake.

The deaths, loss of public resources, and even confusion about why the earth beneath their feet had shaken, left communities demoralized and sometimes even paralyzed. The villages were cut off from food and water, with their clothing, utensils, blankets, and other assets trapped and torn under debris. They passed the cold desert night in hunger, many suffering severely from the trauma. The researchers encountered people who suffered from serious psychosis as a result, including one woman who had not spoken or eaten since the quake. Another woman would sit in the street with a broken board from what used to be her home, and beat the ground every time an aftershock occurred. The whole community suffered both mentally and physically to a degree that is hard to imagine.

The researchers spent as much time informing and comforting the communities as conducting the survey and distributing relief materials. The information collected from the survey continued to direct the relief efforts to a greater degree as the supply process quickly gained momentum. Besides using the information from the survey to direct their own relief and rehabilitation efforts, the SEWA teams also submitted their data to the district governments.

Some villagers mentioned that a government official had walked through the main street of the town, observing the damage from a distance and not even talking with the community members. When the SEWA teams went from house to house, villagers would invite them into the homes, warning them of the instability of the structures. Collapsed roofs and interior walls, cracked support beams and other structural damage that was invisible from the street were easily apparent from this perspective, but often missed by the rushed assessment of the government officials. In many cases, these weakened structures suffered even more damage or fully collapsed in subsequent aftershocks, after the official had taken his brief tour.

As the information from the surveys flowed in, SEWA responded with truckloads of supplies that rendezvoused in Ahmedabad at the end of each day and drove overnight to the respective district headquarters. By morning, the distribution of tents, food, cooking utensils, water, blankets, medical supplies, clothing, and tarps would be organized for each village, and organizers would direct the trucks through the supply route and orchestrate the efficient distribution of resources once in the villages. This network became increasingly important as log jams of supplies piled up in Bhuj and suffered from poor coordination on the part of an overwhelmed government effort.

The survey was not only in villages with SEWA members, though these were the first to be covered. In the process, SEWA also surveyed surrounding villages, many of which they expected to be isolated. In the earthquake-affected areas, SEWA was active, particularly in the most remote villages. In Banaskantha, for example, it was the pipeline's tail-end villages where SEWA started its work. In Surendranagar, SEWA initiated its work with salt farmers, living on the fringes of the desert, isolated from larger towns. SEWA was obligated and determined to bring relief to its members but, in the process, would do the same for their neighbors.

In all, SEWA teams delivered over 850 tents, 13,000 tarpaulin sheets, 32,000 blankets, 10,000 family kits, which included cooking utensils and blankets, and 100,000 kilograms of food. Supplies donated by the UNICEF, USAID, the World Food Program and others were distributed as soon as they arrived. The choice of the resources was also sensitive to the needs of the community, one example being the procurement of supplies of cooking oil at the request of many households.

Meanwhile, other demands arose from the needs assessment. In the course of the survey, particularly among the households with SEWA members, people began requesting assistance in regenerating opportunities for employment. Supply routes for raw materials and markets had been cut off, the dairy procurement process had ceased, and the earthquake had only served to compound the difficulties of the ongoing drought on the agriculturally based economy. The availability of work was not to be put off as a rehabilitation decision. The communities saw employment opportunities as a relief issue, and often ranked it as their top priority.

Our Livelihoods Are Our Relief

In response after response, the villagers pleaded for assistance in finding work. Food and shelter were important to them, but they knew that the temporary measures would come to an end. The communities would then have only delayed their suffering. Dependence on aid meant that they continued to feel vulnerable. Work was a source of sustainable income, but it was also a source of healing. It was a way to reclaim their dignity, a way for the communities to reach more quickly the rehabilitation stage and make the subsequent decisions on their own.

Once the immediate relief supplies were flowing in efficiently, the next action undertaken by the SEWA team was to arrange for artisan production packets to be distributed among the members of the craft groups, as well as to artisans in other villages that the researchers had surveyed but did not have SEWA members. These packets included a week's worth of production supplies and coincided with an intensified role for the craft spearhead teams and organizers. Before the earthquake, all the village cooperatives had become highly self-sufficient, with the leaders undertaking the supply of raw materials and delivery of finished products to the district federation headquarters in Bhuj and Radhanpur. With roads damaged, bus routes interrupted, and lives turned upside down, however, the group leaders could not sustain the process with as much independence. Nor could the newly included artisans be expected to manage on their own. Therefore, the craft packets were refilled every week by a SEWA team that would travel by jeep from village to village along with other supplies.

After the first month, as the system was set up, a sum of Rs. 300,000 in production was facilitated for 3,000 artisans, with many more demanding work as the forced idleness only increased their suffering. By the end of March, two months after the earthquake, an amount of Rs. 6 million in production was sustained for 7,000 artisans. The craftswomen, their families and communities began to rely heavily on this income and continued to demand more. It was their only means of escaping dependency on relief and reclaiming a sense of self-worth and dignity. Therefore, in addition to facilitating production, the SEWA teams needed to increase the returns through greatly enhanced marketing.

In 1999, SEWA Gram Mahila Haat (SGMH) had been initiated as a separate SEWA institution devoted to protecting rural artisans from market exploitation. The SGMH provided a platform from which the different federations could market their products, as well as providing management and technical support and marketing capital to the federations and producer groups. By the time of the earthquake, the staff of the SGMH, which had learnt from the experiences of the Banas Craft and the Kutch Craft, had begun to establish itself in the domestic and international markets. To accommodate an expanded production plan, the SGMH arranged four exhibitions for the craftwork from the earthquake-affected artisans, and arranged a website, which all combined for Rs. 5 million in sales. Part of this strategy also focused on demand within the earthquake-affected areas to help local communities replace their unique style of clothing, much of which was lost in the rubble.

The SGMH also sought connections with other professional marketing and production agencies. Through these collaborations, the SGMH has sought to streamline and expand the systems and operational plans of the producer group federation. The consequent strategies have since begun to open up the international retail market and provide a more regularized production, as well as outlets for the products.

The decrease in dairy production was also a cause of great concern for the households that the team met with. The Kutch Dairy and the Banas Dairy trucks had ceased to come to the villages and the damage to the chilling centers left no prospect of an immediate recovery. Without this subsidiary income, in the throes of a drought, many families were forced to consider either migration or the death of their cattle as the only options. The communities demanded access to fodder and an expanded fodder security system. Utilizing contacts through its federations in the districts in southern Gujarat, which was not suffering from drought or earthquake, the SEWA relief and rehabilitation teams procured over 50,000 kilograms of fodder and distributed it to over 2,000 families with 5,000 head of cattle. This helped preserve a productive asset, as well as provide nutrition and, where milk traders were still active, a source of income.

Salt farmers also suffered from the earthquake. The timing of the event could not have been worse, as the farmers' operations were in full swing, with wells dug, pumps in place and the crystallization in process. In some cases, the earthquake collapsed the wells and destroyed the pumps. Those that continued to function found their production damaged by adulterated brine. It seems that the geological disturbance stirred up minerals, particularly calcium and magnesium, which turned the brine brown in color.

To re-initiate the time-sensitive process where the damage had halted production, SEWA distributed an emergency relief fund of Rs. 30,000 to each of the five salt-farming groups. This money was then used to reopen the wells and repair or replace the brine pumps. The Gujarat Alkalis and Chemicals Limited also responded to an overture from the SGMH and coordinated access to cleaning facilities for the salt produced from the adulterated brine, while plans were discussed for a contract for sales.

For families without craft skills or access to other sources of income, SEWA quickly expanded a new program that met a great need in the communities. A few months before the earthquake, SEWA had set up a masonry training pilot program that utilized satellite communications and the expertise of a skilled mason. As the extent of the need for housing and employment became more apparent, the research teams and other members of the relief and rehabilitation team began to organize villagers for an expanded version of the masonry training. The camera-and-relay technology was set up in one village that was in particular need of reconstruction, and trainees were gathered in district offices throughout the affected area. Prepared with the support of the Disaster Mitigation Institute and the People's Science Institute, was a basic design appropriate to the building traditions of many of the communities and resistant to earthquakes, cyclones and floods, among other circumstances the region has encountered.

The skilled mason displayed the mixture of concrete, the arrangement of materials, and techniques in reinforcing the structure, among other skills. He answered questions throughout the program, transmitted during the live broadcast from members watching in the district offices. By the summer, over 800 people had received exposure to the training, either through the live broadcast, the subsequent video, posters and other supporting materials, or a combination of resources. Many of these trainees subsequently began to contribute to the reconstruction of their own, as well as other homes throughout the earthquake-affected area.

Other institutions within the SEWA movement also became involved. The SEWA Bank's insurance program had assessors on the scene right away. Within two weeks after the earthquake took place, over 2,500 policy-holders had their claims solicited, investigated, and many of them processed in that short time. As members began to reconstruct temporary shelters until the promised government support would arrive, the SEWA Mahila Housing Trust held training sessions on appropriate housing practices. Families received advice on what building materials were salvageable and how they could be improved upon. Furthermore, many of the communities affected by the earthquake had their own unique building practices and construction designs, suited to their customs and their lifestyles. The SEWA Mahila Housing Trust, therefore, began working with the communities to develop building plans and practices that accommodated these traditions, as well as enhanced concern for structural integrity.

An ongoing water campaign, initiated to address the drought, was amplified to fit the needs of the earthquake. The drought, three years old by the time the earthquake occurred, was already leading a special effort among the SEWA leaders and members to focus their energy on improving awareness of and access to water. Over the course of a year, five additional agrifilm ponds had been constructed, as well as numerous check dams and contour bunds, in addition to the new practice of constructing rainwater-harvesting tanks at the household and community levels. By the time of the earthquake, over 100 of these tanks had been constructed in Banaskantha and Kutch.

Fortunately, the tanks had been constructed well, and none were irreparably destroyed by the earthquake. However, even the smallest of cracks would leak and expand, if left unrepaired. Monsoon rains were expected and the affected households were eager to salvage the tanks at least, even if the house these supplied had crumbled. Some tanks had also served as receptacles for emergency water tanker deliveries arranged by SEWA and the government. Thus, SEWA water campaign teams, including engineers and designers, visited each and every tank to assess the damage and facilitate whatever repairs were necessary.

In the process, an even greater demand for the tanks arose, as members contemplated rebuilding their communities and coping with the issues of living in a drought- and disaster-prone region. The water campaign team, therefore, began to incorporate their repairs and relief efforts with discussions of rehabilitation. A plan for expanding the number of rainwater harvesting tanks continues to grow and to include not only more households, but more villages as well.

Childcare centers also became a focal point for the community. As schools were closed, parents were busy with all the aspects of rebuilding, and access to nutrition had become tenuous. SEWA, therefore, made a special effort to revive childcare facilities, often having to provide a tent specifically for that purpose to replace collapsed or damaged buildings. As a result, these centers became gathering places for older and younger children, since the former could no longer go to school. At these centers, the children were given nutritious meals and lessons everyday, as would have normally been the case. The psychological effect of the earthquake was especially harsh for some of the children. So the songs, games and other learning activities helped them regain some sense of normalcy.

In terms of medical help, SEWA played the role of a communicator and a facilitator. Many in the villages did not know whom to turn to when they were injured. In all the cases, clinics and hospitals were overwhelmed with patients, and overflowing with corpses. The staff was often forced to stabilize an injury, then move on, leaving the patient alive but still in need of medical care. Thus, many returned to their villages to nurse their own wounds and warn their neighbors of the chaos at the hospital. Since most of the earthquake injuries were caused by collapsing buildings, broken bones were fairly common. Therefore, many villagers opted to remain in the villages hoping that surface wounds would heal, unsure of what problems lay beneath those wounds.

Meanwhile, a Danish medical team had contacted SEWA and told them of the mobile hospital and volunteer staff under preparation in Denmark for transport to Kutch. The Danish team had difficulties communicating with the government and looked for SEWA's advice. SEWA immediately reviewed the relief landscape and tried to identify the place in the greatest need of a hospital. The team found that the area surrounding Gandhidham had suffered damage to its medical facilities and was thus far overlooked by relief medical facilities.

The SEWA team contacted the local officials and proposed to help set up the hospital in the town of Gandhidham. To the organizers' surprise, the district government was reluctant to provide a space for the mobile hospital. Apparently, the local hospital, damaged and overwhelmed but still functioning, did not want the mobile hospital within its area. Despite the initial reaction, perhaps motivated by pride and a determination to persevere, other voices in the district government prevailed, and the hospital was ultimately given a space.

Once it arrived, the team unpacked and assembled a hospital with a fully equipped operation theater, reception center and recovery room with 14 beds. The integration of the hospital was immediate and coordinated with the on-going survey by the research teams. As they conducted the survey in the villages, the teams referred patients to the mobile hospital. Many of the referees were patients who had visited an area clinic or hospital but were given expedited treatment under the circumstances. In many cases, when the patients arrived, they required surgery to replace hastily inserted implants for shattered bones. In some cases, the surgery was performed by the rotating team of Danish physicians. However, the surgical nurse and anesthesiologists who accompanied the team from the Denmark most often worked with local doctors who had no regular access to the other operation theaters in the area and so utilized the mobile hospital.

The system devised for the mobile hospital was well-suited to the situation. The remaining medical facilities were flooded with patients, and the staff remained idle while operating rooms were preceded by an increasingly large line of patients and attending surgeons waiting for a place to operate. As the Danish medical team maintained the facilities, sterilized the instruments, monitored the convalescing patients and provided support to the local doctors, a SEWA team performed many functions. First of all, any political or bureaucratic issues were handled by the SEWA team, as was the reception, basic nursing, cooking and cleaning for the patients. When a few local physicians began to abuse the facilities, scheduling the operating room, then not showing up, or using the facilities to charge their patients as if it were a private clinic though such care was supposed to be free in a government hospital, the SEWA team tactfully managed the situation.

By the time the hospital was packed back up, it had provided health services for over 1,000 patients, many of whom required surgery. The rapid services it provided, fulfilling the exact needs of the moment, primarily orthopedics, and quickly overcoming bureaucratic difficulties, offers many useful lessons in rapid coordination between organizations in times of emergency.

The need for accurate information was also an acute challenge for the effort. To keep the communities informed of what was taking place for the relief and rehabilitation effort, SEWA also returned to their satellite technology. As with the cyclone, but on an even larger scale, the earthquake had generated administrative chaos, compounded by the degree of need in the community. Information was mixed and conflicting as rumors abounded and even the facts behind government actions were uncertain. As the days passed, the communities were more dependent on accurate information than on aid. To address this need, SEWA organized a total of seven satellite communication-facilitated conferences.

Community members from around the affected region gathered in the SEWA block and district offices to participate in conferences with people such as the state rural development commissioner, the director of the state housing department and the head of the Disaster Management Authority. Through the use of the satellite technology, the members could be active participants, asking questions of the panelists and sharing their own thoughts. The resultant dialogue helped the communities connect with government resources and even had an influence on how those resources were allocated.

The combination of work opportunities and access to information, food, shelter, health and childcare services helped the communities survive the period immediately after the earthquake. SEWA utilized its familiarity and connections with many of the affected villages, serving its members who were a part of the movement, but also others who were isolated from relief. For the next stage of rehabilitation, SEWA planned to build upon the groundwork they had laid during the relief effort. SEWA had to be realistic, and ensure that their efforts in rehabilitation were genuine. Their members in the villages of Banaskantha and Kutch had become fully capable of planning and leading their own way out of the situation. Though they had lost their homes and material assets, they still had skills, and were organized. The task was to empower the local communities so they could lead their own recovery.

Rehabilitation

For the SEWA members, the devastation of the earthquake was a frustrating setback after years of hard-won progress. For some, the homes they had built had collapsed on the tools of the trades they had developed and the other precious possessions that were gradually increasing the quality and security of their lives. But, the bitterness of the loss was mitigated by the perseverance of their less destructible assets—organization and experience. The rehabilitation effort did not have to be a new beginning. They would build upon the work they did before the earthquake, and the work they did in its immediate aftermath. Water, work, shelter and childcare would be the focus. Building upon past experience, they had the ability to turn the disaster into a development opportunity.

Once the immediate relief needs were addressed, the longer-term rehabilitation process began to emerge. Yet, the transition between the two phases was not an abrupt change, but was rather an organic extension of the integrated, community-led process that had always been maintained as both a means and an end. Furthermore, the rehabilitation process drew upon not only the needs and lessons of the relief effort, but also the experience and organization of the decade of work in the affected region, the progress and lessons the work had yielded. It was specifically with these organizational and experiential assets that the disaster had the potential to be turned into a development opportunity. The focus would be on livelihood security, shelter restoration, the rebuilding of water resources, social security and micro-finance.

The affected communities had the foresight to assess effectively their needs from the long-term perspective. Within the past few years, they had faced unrelenting droughts and cyclones. The earthquake was a unique misfortune, but with many of the same symptoms of previous hardships. Housing had been damaged and destroyed. Assets were lost or at risk of being lost. Livelihoods were jeopardized. The community's health and nutritional needs were at a maximum at a time when communal resources were at a minimum. After the situation had stabilized, it was readily apparent to most community members that the minute-and-a-half earthquake meant a trial of far greater endurance.

With their realistic assessment of the ordeal ahead, the communities' interest increased in SEWA, the BDMSA and the Kutch Craft Association, as well as the sister federation in Surendranagar district. In many villages, SEWA and the local federations were the first and most effective respondents to the disaster. Many villagers saw this as a positive indication of what could be achieved in the long-run. Perhaps more importantly, the level of confidence and trust that resulted among the membership of SEWA and the local federations was greatly enhanced.

When the organization process was initiated in the previous decade, the organizers especially sought out and embraced potential leaders among the women of the communities. Special attention was given to building the capacity of these women in the expectation that the greatest progress could only be carried forth under the direction of these local leaders. A significant membership base was built in the meantime, but practical reality dictated that many among those members were not as devoted to the process as some of their neighbors. Some members passively went along with the leadership, neither completely ignoring nor completely committing themselves to the process. The benefits of their casual involvement were enough to maintain their interest but, understandably, some felt that the magnitude of their needs left little room to invest their efforts otherwise, no matter what promise it held. Obviously, there were still others within these villages who abstained entirely from becoming even nominal members. Skepticism or general disinterest, among other things, kept many from taking part fully, or at all.

The response to the earthquake catalyzed much of the dormancy among the women in these villages into a more active confidence and trust in SEWA and the local federations. The communities increasingly turned to the community-based organizations as vehicles for community mobilization, and began to take part on a larger scale. In the months after the earthquake, membership almost tripled in Banaskantha, from 20,000 to 55,000 members. Similarly, in Kutch, the membership increased from 8,000 to 14,000 women. Furthermore, among the members, both old and new, the level of activity increased substantially.

The increased confidence, trust and investment of the community was notable in itself, but by no means conclusive. The manner in which these assets were translated into progress was to be the key. Through the mechanism of the gram sabha, or 'village meeting,' the community was mobilized in a manner that has brought inclusive and substantial results.

Guided by their own individual sense of what was needed, and reinforced by the results of the surveys, the community members, gathered in villages across the region, determined that the rehabilitation was to be focused around their livelihoods, shelter, water, and access to social security and micro-finance. Each village gathered as a group and, from among those present, they formed a rehabilitation committee. The committee was not selected, but included anyone who expressed an interest. Some recognized community leaders were proposed as logical participants, while others expressed an interest on their own behalf. The sole pre-requisite was a willingness to contribute one's time and energy to the process.

The committees so formed were products of their inclusive conception, notable in their diverse and representative composition. Perhaps most notably, the poor and the women were among the leaders on the committees. Because of the organizational structure that remained intact and was galvanized by the relief efforts, the SEWA members within the community, women largely from among the poor households, were in a position to contribute much to the process. Other members of the committees included sarpanches and panchayat members, teachers, in part by virtue of their standing in the community, as well as others emboldened and moved by the circumstances.

The commonalities shared by the efforts of the rehabilitation committees across the region stem from several factors, including their shared condition, the contributions of the local federation organizers, and the intercommunication between the members of the committees from the different villages. In particular, it was universally recognized that the rehabilitation effort should not be sectoral, but should be integrated. The value of pursuing livelihood, shelter, water, childcare and other goals in an integrated manner had the potential to reap results greater than the sum of its components. Again, with this in mind, the disaster had the potential to be converted into a development opportunity.

For example, the need for work could be linked to the need for housing through an expansion of the masonry training, mentioned before. Furthermore, the training could incorporate methods that sought to make the resultant structures more resistant to earthquakes, cyclones, or droughts. In rebuilding many of the homes, plans for a roof rainwater-harvesting structure could be incorporated from the outset. Where aid resources fell short, micro-finance could fill the gap in capitalizing the reconstruction needs. The opportunities to plan in such an integrated fashion enlivened the debate and lent momentum to the application of the process in many villages.

Within a year after the earthquake, the local federations were able to construct over 750 new houses, with an additional 1,500 houses near completion. The improved designs were 'seismic-safe' and cyclone-resistant, as well as suitable to the tastes of the occupants. Over 1,500 new savings groups were formed in the three earthquake-affected districts. Furthermore, the number of members who availed themselves of insurance coverage increased from 2,000 to over 23,000.

While the capability to reconstruct and secure their physical assets was a concern, some of the systems and processes meant to sustain them were also damaged in the rubble. Without the re-establishment of market linkages, capital resources and the other components of the production cycle and sustainable economy, whatever was reconstructed would crumble again. Maybe not in a moment of violent turmoil, but during a long and anguishing decline over years of futile struggle. Only through a balance of process and production would the rehabilitation be effective beyond the short term.

To help make the rehabilitation sustainable, the SGMH arranged for the sale of the salt produced by the women in the region's salt cooperatives to the Gujarat Alkalis and Chemicals Limited. Similar efforts continued to expand the markets for crafts and gum. In these ways, the decisions made by local leaders and their neighbors are supported by SEWA and their family of sister organizations.

SEWA's and the local federations' long-term rehabilitation effort has since gotten under way and continues to build upon the information gathered by the survey, the relief efforts undertaken, and the years of experience in the earthquake-affected areas. For the relief effort, SEWA had rushed to its members and supported its local sister organizations, but reached out to their neighbors as well. However, to achieve any genuine progress, the leaders knew, the effort would have to be comprehensive, sustainable, and based upon a realistic plan. SEWA members and their communities would be the planners and managers of the process, with the family of organizations providing whatever support was asked of them.

After the earthquake, a great many organizations converged on Bhuj, as the magnitude of the tragedy generated an outpouring of support in response. The needs of the communities were all-encompassing, but most of the organizations were new to the region, and almost all were new to disaster relief. With the increase in available funding for specific types of work, many tried to adapt to the circumstances and enter a new field. SEWA had the advantage of familiarity with the region and, during the relief effort, they accepted responsibility for a scope of action beyond their normal practice. However, in the rehabilitation effort, the district associations planned to return to integrated, demand-driven, need-based community development.

The new villages, where SEWA distributed relief materials, were interested in the organization and began to enquire further. By the time the situation had stabilized, district spearhead teams went to the villages to answer the questions in greater detail. The leaders and organizers of the teams gave villagers a general description of SEWA, and focused on the increased livelihood program, the savings and credit activity, insurance, and housing. Many in the new villages were eager to be a part of these resources and chose to become a part of SEWA. Mindful of its ability to fulfill its responsibilities to the current members, SEWA and the district federations decided on a degree of expansion that would address the demand from the community without sacrificing the needs of its current members.

As mentioned before, the expansion undertaken in the earthquake-affected districts was almost a tripling of the previous membership. However, the leaders and organizers felt capable of managing that level of growth, especially in light of the desire in the community to become a part of the organization. The primary reason for opening up to new members was that the concept of a shared relationship was the basis for what SEWA envisioned as the foundation for a comprehensive and appropriate process. The victims of the earthquake needed not only access to income from a collapsed economy, but new homes, public facilities and services, as well as the numerous components of social protection and security. SEWA had been able to achieve progress in all these areas, but had done so in partnership with the communities, with a membership base in the villages that served as the core. If the rehabilitation were to achieve substantial progress, this concrete relationship would have to be the foundation.

With the prospect of funding permeating the NGO atmosphere in Bhuj, many organizations sought to expand the purview of their activities to include a much greater number of people and new area of activity. The potential supply of funds was substantial and the demand for action even greater. The combined forces pushed SEWA to compromise some of the lessons of process orientation and community-based leadership. The pressure attached to much of the funding was to use quotas as a standard of success and promote unrealistic goals in order to keep pace with other NGOs.

The government earthquake policy that was eventually released also presented a challenge to SEWA and the district federations' ability to apply their approach. The policy applied a great deal of pressure on SEWA and the district federations to adopt villages, become an instrument for dispersing direct payments, and greatly expand the list of villages under its umbrella. For SEWA, the circumstances required a great deal of self-possession.

The government policy presented three 'packages'. The first package was for villages that suffered over 70 percent damage and wished to relocate. The second package was for villages in similar circumstances, which did not wish to relocate. The third was for villages that suffered less damage, where there was a need for only some reconstruction. The funding would be commensurate with the amount of damage and consequent action, and the non-governmental community was invited to engage in a village adoption program. The government would offer a half of the funding, and the NGO the other half, for the project if the village was adopted. If the village was not adopted, the government would provide all of the funds.

Attached to these packages were time-frames that left little room for a realistic incorporation of local planning and management. The implicit expectation with the government plan was that, if a group adopted a village, the group would assume responsibility for it and be expected to dictate the rehabilitation process in order to stay on schedule. The schedule also rested upon the expectation that direct payments to individuals, with little room for any community efforts in pooling resources, was the method of allocation. Conversely, if that schedule were not adhered to, the adopting organization would face severe consequences.

SEWA wished to participate in a government effort, since the movement was confident about its own abilities and saw a partnership with the government as a way to magnify its activity. However, the government policy did not leave much room for SEWA and the local federations to build upon experience. There was little scope in the government policy for working with women, the poorest of the poor, and taking a process-oriented rather than a target-oriented approach. There were, therefore, some differences between the SEWA movement and a state government that had decided upon a system of direct payments and centrally delineated village adoption guidelines.

Some in the government and elsewhere were critical of SEWA's resistance to the government policy. The confusion arose partly out of a misinterpretation of the SEWA movement. SEWA was not a charity organization, nor a development NGO. It was a family of organizations built around a labor union and cooperative federation, and committed to a process approach. SEWA made a special effort to include women, not to the exclusion of men, but in the belief that women's valuable contributions would otherwise be excluded. Nor did SEWA believe in distributing handouts. Sustainable community development arose out of capacity-building and accountable access to resources, not charity. Others were critical of SEWA's reluctance to try and meet goals in working with dalits. SEWA worked with the poorest of the poor, many of whom were dalits. But, SEWA did not set quotas presupposing the needs of the community.

Because the government policy took several months before being announced, SEWA had already begun its rehabilitation efforts. Adhering to the lessons of experience, SEWA initiated a significant expansion of its activities that tried to balance what was realistic with what was needed. New communities were organized, while the process even began anew for some of the old communities. In a few short months, 435 new savings groups were initiated, with almost 10,000 new members. Perhaps most significantly, almost 20,000 members initiated an insurance policy. Meanwhile, for old members, accounts were kept open throughout and accommodated the circumstances. All the insurance claims were not only submitted and processed, but the process of submitting them was smoothly facilitated for those who would not have otherwise been able to file a claim on their own.

In general, the rehabilitation plan is largely a magnification of the process described in the previous pages. A vastly enhanced effort at marketing is accompanying the expansion of productive artisan groups. Housing will consist of linkages with government programs. The process of reconstruction and rehabilitation consists of facilitating access to resources for the communities. However, every effort is made to undertake a process that is led by the communities, not for the communities.

As part of the learning process, SEWA has also invested a great deal of energy in forming a Livelihood Security Fund. The concept had already arisen before the earthquake, but has become even more imperative since. The fund is a store of resources set aside to deal with emergency needs, to which the region is prone. Through droughts, cyclones and earthquakes, each disaster has had a long-term effect on the community's ability to lead its own recovery. The primary reason for this debilitation is the loss of livelihood that each disaster has brought which, in turn, erodes the community's ability to recover. Furthermore, each disaster has generated support in the immediate wake of the tragedy. The less glamorous. though more important long-term needs, however, have drawn less attention and support. A result has been that resources are dispersed but through a process that is not sustainable.

The fund is intended to prepare for the long-term needs of the victimized communities by devoting resources specifically to the regeneration of employment opportunities. The belief is that this is the most effective method for empowering the local communities to lead their own recovery, regain their dignity and maintain their progress. The Livelihood Security Fund, still in the process of formation as these words are written, will set aside resources and establish a distribution system that is specific to the needs of the recovering employment economy as well as flexible in relation to the needs of the moment. In an effort to establish this unique community-level insurance policy, SEWA has utilized the advice of a wide range of people, from government officials to academics and activists, on a task force that is forming the fund's guidelines. This process has been informed by the earthquake experience and will hopefully be in place, in the event of another emergency.

Meanwhile, the rehabilitation process carries on. The rehabilitation was not a phase separate from the relief, but rather an organic extension of a process, of which the community has been able to claim ownership. The community has been able to illustrate its ability to plan and act from a long-term perspective, recognizing linkages and integrating ideas and resources to lead an efficient and sustainable process. Community-based organizations have been strengthened by the trust and commitment the communities have invested in them. And, through these community-based organizations, women, the poor, and other traditionally marginalized components of civil society have found a place in the process.

SEWA has ultimately decided to participate in the government policy by 'adopting' a total of 39 villages. The effort to balance the imposed deadlines with a genuine process will be a considerable challenge. However, as the process pursued by SEWA and the district federations continues to evolve, it will continue to be informed by the experiences described in the preceding pages. The process will be a new beginning for the members, old and new. The SEWA family has also grown over the years, and has an increasing capacity to support fellow-members in the BDMSA and the Kutch Craft Association. The disaster is among the worst that could be imagined, but it has also brought out the best in many people, and in none more than the community members themselves. The primary challenge will be to empower them to continue to do their best to lead the process of recovery for themselves, and SEWA's experience shows that this can be done.

Works Cited

Agarwal, Bina, *A Field of One's Own: Gender and Land Rights in South Asia*, Cambridge University Press (Cambridge: 1994).

Bhat, Vighnesh N., *Public Health in India*, Amar Prakashan (New Delhi: 1990).

Chen, Martha Alter, 'Women and Watershed Development in India,' in *Women and Wasteland Development in India*, ed. Andrea Sing and Neera Burra, Sage Publications (New Delhi: 1993).

———, *Coping with Seasonality and Drought*, Sage Publications (New Delhi: 1991).

Dhagamwar, Vasudha and Enakshi Thukral, 'Legal, Illegal and Socio-legal Problems of Women in Wasteland Development,' in *Women and Wasteland Development in India*, ed. Andrea Sing and Neera Burra, Sage Publications (New Delhi: 1993).

Drèze, Jean and Amartya Sen, *Hunger and Public Action*, Oxford University Press (New Delhi: 1989).

The Economic Times, 'Panel on Power, Water for North Gujarat Farms,' 19 February 1999, Ahmedabad.

Jhabvala, R. and R. Subrahmanya, *The Unorganized Sector: Work, Security and Social Protection*, Sage Publications (New Delhi: 2000).

Deb, Kalipada, *The Challenge of Rural Development: Five Decades of Indian Experience*, MD Publications (New Delhi: 1997).

Kamalamma, G., *Health and Nutritional Status in India*, APH Publishing Corporation (New Delhi: 1996).

Murthy, Sharmila, 'A Survey of Rural Micro-Finance Activity in Gujarat,' unpublished.

Rose, Kalima, *Where Women are Leaders: The SEWA Movement in India*, Vistaar Publications (New Delhi: 1992).

Sainath, P., *Everybody Loves a Good Drought*, Penguin Books (New Delhi: 1996).

Schulpen, Lau, 'The Same Difference: A Comparative Analysis of Dutch Aid Channels to India,' *Nijmegen Studies in Development and Cultural Change*, vol. 26. Saarbrucken Verl. fur Entwicklungspoltik (Saarbucken, Germany: 1997).

SEWA, *Self-Employed Women's Association, Half Yearly Report: July–December 1993*, unpublished.

Singh, Katar and Saumindra Bhattacharya, 'The Salt Miner's Cooperatives in the
   Little Rann of Kachchh in Gujarat', in *Cooperative Management of Natural Resources*,
   ed. K. Singh and V. Ballabh, Sage Publications (New Delhi 1996).

The Times of India, 'Gum Prices Rise,' 11 October 1997, Ahmedabad.

United Nations Development Program (UNDP), *Human Development Report
   1999*, Oxford University Press (New Delhi: 1999).

United Nations Fund for Population Activities (UNFPA), *India: Towards
   Population and Development Goals*, Oxford University Press (New Delhi: 1997).

Index

About the Author

Daniel W. Crowell is currently a postgraduate student in Economics at the London School of Economics. He came to India on a Fulbright Fellowship over 1999–2000, which is when he researched and wrote this book.

Mr. Crowell has been associated with several different facets of community development, including serving as the Program Coordinator at the Center for Public Services' Migrant Farmworker Program while an undergraduate at Gettysburg College, Pennsylvannia, and being a primary school teacher with Unidas Para Vivir Mejor (UPAVIM) in Guatemala.